Platonism *and* Anti-Platonism
in Mathematics

Platonism *and* Anti-Platonism *in* Mathematics

MARK BALAGUER

OXFORD
UNIVERSITY PRESS

OXFORD
UNIVERSITY PRESS

Oxford   New York
Athens   Auckland   Bangkok   Bogotá   Buenos Aires   Cape Town
Chennai   Dar es Salaam   Delhi   Florence   Hong Kong   Istanbul   Karachi
Kolkata   Kuala Lumpur   Madrid   Melbourne   Mexico City   Mumbai   Nairobi
Paris   São Paulo   Singapore   Taipei   Tokyo   Toronto   Warsaw

and associated companies in
Berlin   Ibadan

First published in 1998 by Oxford University Press, Inc.
198 Madison Avenue, New York, New York 10016

First issued as an Oxford University Press paperback, 2001

Oxford is a registered trademark of Oxford University Press, Inc.

Library of Congress Cataloging-in-Publication Data
Balaguer, Mark.
Platonism and anti-Platonism in mathematics / Mark Balaguer.
p.   cm.
Includes bibliographical references and index.
Includes index.
ISBN 0-19-505154-8; 0-19-514398-1 (pbk.)
1. Mathematics—Philosophy.   2. Platonists.   I. Title.
QA8.4.B345   1998
510'.1—dc21   97-33108

9 8 7 6 5 4 3 2 1

Printed in the United States of America
on acid-free paper

This book is dedicated to two women who have given
me undying love and support—my mother, Marcella Balaguer,
and my wife, Reina Roberts.

Acknowledgments

Several people have read portions of this book and offered helpful comments, and I would like to express my appreciation to all of them. They include Jody Azzouni, Melchor Balaguer, Daniel Bonevac, Stuart Cornwell, Seth Crook, Russell Dale, Anthony Everett, Hartry Field, Ricardo Gomez, Bob Hanna, Jerry Katz, Arnold Koslow, Charles Landesman, Maureen Linker, Michael Liston, David MacCallum, Penelope Maddy, Colin McLarty, Henry Mendell, Elliott Mendelson, Yiannis Moschovakis, Tom Oberdan, David Pitt, Michael Resnik, Stephen Schiffer, Barbara Scholz, Stewart Shapiro, Tom Slaughter, Adam Vinueza, and Edward Zalta. Chapter 3 was read at the University of Colorado, Boulder, where I received some very helpful comments from several people in the audience, especially George Bealer. Chapter 4 was read at a meeting of the Association of Symbolic Logic at the University of Wisconsin, Madison, and I received useful feedback there from a number of people, including Geoffrey Hellman and Charles Parsons. Chapters 3 and 4 were read at UCLA, where I received helpful comments from Joseph Almog, Paul Hovda, Tony Martin, and Yiannis Moschovakis, among others. Chapters 6 and 7 were read at the University of California, Irvine, where I received useful comments from Pen Maddy, Jeff Barrett, and Peter Woodruff. Chapter 8 was read at Cal State, Los Angeles, where I received helpful comments from several people, including Jenny Faust, Danny Herwitz, Kayley Vernalis, and Henry Mendell.

Among these people, four deserve to be singled out. From Jerry Katz and Mike Resnik, I have learned a lot about how to be a platonist; and the position developed in Part I of this book is influenced by the works of these two philosophers. From Hartry Field, I have learned a lot about how to be an anti-platonist; and the position developed in Part II owes quite a bit to his work. And from my father, Melchor Balaguer, I have learned a lot about how to be a thinker; and the position developed in Part III owes something, I think, to a desire to synthesize that I acquired from him.

Much of the research for this book was funded by a dissertation fellowship from the City University of New York, two fellowships from the National Endowment for the Humanities—one a summer fellowship and the other a yearlong fellowship—and a Creative Leave grant from California State University, Los Angeles. I would like to express my gratitude to all three of these institutions. Finally, I would like to thank all of my colleagues in the philosophy department at Cal State, Los Angeles, for providing such a wonderful environment in which to write philosophy.

Los Angeles, California
September 1997   M.B.

Contents

Platonism *and* Anti-Platonism
in Mathematics

Introduction

1. The Project of this Book

This book is a work in the philosophy of mathematics. But what does that mean? Well, it might mean either of two different things, for there seem to be two strands in this area of philosophy, two projects that people have taken to be the central project of the philosophy of mathematics. One is the *hermeneutical project* of providing an adequate interpretation and account of mathematical theory and practice; the other is the *metaphysical project* of answering the question of whether or not there exist abstract objects.

First, some terminology. An *abstract object* is an object that exists outside of spacetime or, being more careful, a *non-spatiotemporal* object, that is, an object that exists but not in spacetime.[1] In any event, such objects are non-physical, non-mental, and acausal. The belief in such objects is called *platonism*, and the disbelief, *anti-platonism*. A *mathematical object* is just an abstract object that would ordinarily be thought of as falling in the domain of mathematics, for example, a number, function, or set. Finally, *mathematical platonism* is the view that there exist mathematical objects, and *mathematical anti-platonism* is the view that there do not exist such objects. For the sake of rhetorical elegance, I will often use 'platonism' and 'anti-platonism' to refer to these two views.[2]

The hermeneutical and metaphysical projects are, of course, not entirely separate. Philosophers primarily interested in the former almost invariably advance views regarding the latter, that is, they adopt either platonism or anti-platonism. And philosophers primarily concerned with the latter almost invariably (indeed, in this case, we can probably drop the 'almost') advance views regarding the former, that is, they adopt some interpretation of mathematical theory and practice. The difference between the two is a difference in attitude about what is important. For instance, upon noticing that mathematicians are somewhat cavalier about ontology, philosophers of the hermeneutical bent might themselves be inclined to become cavalier about ontology, whereas philosophers of the metaphysical bent would never do this; they would ask what, if anything, this attitude of mathematicians tells us about the ontology of mathematics.

A wonderful example of a philosopher primarily interested in the metaphysical project is Hartry Field; almost all of his work in the philosophy of mathematics is aimed at showing that we do not need to believe in mathematical objects. A good example of a philosopher primarily interested in the hermeneutical project is David Hilbert. A more contemporary example is Penelope Maddy, although she is not a great example because at times she seems very concerned with the metaphysical project. A much better, but lesser known, example of a contemporary philosopher primarily interested in the hermeneutical project is Jody Azzouni.[3]

I will be primarily concerned with the metaphysical project in this book. Of course, that is not to say that I am going to *ignore* the hermeneutical project. I will present an interpretation or "picture" of mathematics that (not surprisingly) I think is exactly true to mathematical practice.[4] Moreover, I think that any philosophy of mathematics that *didn't* satisfy this constraint (regardless of whether it was primarily concerned with hermeneutics or metaphysics) would be unacceptable for that very reason. Thus, all I mean to point out by placing myself in the metaphysical tradition is that the ultimate goal of my study is metaphysical; I want to look at mathematical theory and practice in order to see if it tells us anything about the *world*, in particular, to see if it tells us whether or not there exist abstract objects.

And here's what I am going to argue about the metaphysical project: it doesn't work. That is, I want to argue that we cannot discover a rational reason for believing or disbelieving in abstract objects by studying mathematical theory and practice, that is, that there are no good arguments for or against platonism in the philosophy of mathematics.

Now, this might seem like a purely negative result, but there is a sense in which the findings of this book are not just positive but doubly positive. The reason is that I argue for the above negative conclusion about the metaphysical project by showing that *platonism and anti-platonism are both perfectly workable philosophies of mathematics*. This is what the bulk of the book is about. In part I, I develop a novel version of platonism and show how it survives all the traditional arguments against platonism, most notably Benacerraf's two arguments; and in part II, I develop a novel version of anti-platonism (or more precisely, a novel way of defending a recently developed version of anti-platonism) and show how it survives all the traditional arguments against anti-platonism, most notably the Quine-Putnam indispensability argument.

In the last chapter of the book, I try to strengthen my conclusion. I argue, first of all, that it's not just that we *currently* lack an argument for or against mathematical platonism; rather, it's that we could *never* discover such an argument. But this is still an epistemological thesis, for the claim here is that *we* could never discover whether or not there exist mathematical objects. In the second half of the last chapter, I try to motivate a metaphysical conclusion, namely, that there is, after all, *no fact of the matter* as to whether there exist abstract objects.

(I said above that the bulk of the book will be dedicated to showing that platonism and anti-platonism are both defensible views. But I am now saying that in the final chapter, I will argue that there is no fact of the matter as to whether or not platonism or anti-platonism is correct. Thus, there is a sense in which my argument in the last chapter contradicts my claim that platonism and anti-platonism are defensible. For to argue that there is no fact of the matter as to whether platonism or anti-platonism is correct is surely to provide some sort of criticism of those two views and, hence, to argue that they are not entirely defensible. This, I think, is correct. But for the sake of rhetorical elegance, I will ignore this pont until the last chapter. During the first seven chapters, I will defend platonism and anti-platonism against the most important traditional objections to these views, and I will write as if I think platonism and anti-platonism are completely defensible. But the last chapter does undermine them.)

2. Mathematical Platonism and Anti-Platonism

Before giving a more detailed outline of this book, I want to say a bit more about the two central views that I will be concerned with — that is, mathematical platonism and mathematical anti-platonism. In broad outline, the former is the view that (a) there exist mathematical objects such as numbers (which are non-spatiotemporal and exist independently of us and our mathematical theorizing) and (b) our mathematical theories describe such objects. And anti-platonism is (in broad outline) the view that (a) there do *not* exist abstract objects such as numbers and, hence, (b) our mathematical theories have to be interpreted in some other way. But there are various versions of both of these schools of thought, and that's what I want to discuss now. In subsection 2.1, I will provide an initial sketch of the version of platonism that I am going to defend in this book and describe how it relates to other versions of platonism; and in subsection 2.2, I will sketch the version of anti-platonism that I will defend and explain where it stands with respect to other versions of anti-platonism.

2.1 *The Various Versions of Platonism*

The version of platonism that I am going to develop in this book — I will call it *plenitudinous platonism*, or alternatively, *full-blooded platonism* (FBP[5] for short) — differs from traditional versions of platonism in several ways, but all of the differences arise out of one bottom-level difference concerning the question of *how many* mathematical objects there are. FBP can be expressed very intuitively, but also rather sloppily, as the view that *all possible mathematical objects exist*. The first bit of sloppiness can be eliminated from this definition by noting that I am using 'possible' in its broadest sense here; in other words, FBP is the view that all *logically possible* mathematical objects exist. This guarantees that FBP is incompatible with non-plenitudinous versions of platonism that deny the existence of certain sorts of mathematical objects but assert that these objects are, in some sense, "metaphysically impossible". (More needs to be said about what exactly is meant by 'logically possible'. I will address this in chapter 3, section 5, but for now, it is sufficient to note that the sort of possibility at work here is a very broad, logical possibility.)

But there is still more sloppiness in the above definition of FBP that needs to be addressed. This can be appreciated by noticing that if we formalized this definition, it would read:

($\forall$x)[(x is a mathematical object & x is logically possible) →x exists].

Putting the definition in this form brings to light two related problems. First, the definition seems to suggest that existence is a predicate, to be applied to some objects in the domain but not others. And second, it seems to make use of a *de re* sort of possibility; that is, it seems to suggest that there are possible objects that may or may not be actual objects. I want to distance myself from all of this. I do not think there are any such things as objects that "don't exist" or that are "possible but not actual". On my view, all objects are ordinary, actually existing objects.[6] The idea behind FBP is that the ordinary, actually existing mathematical objects exhaust all of the logical possibilities for such objects; that is, that there actually exist mathematical objects of all logically possible kinds; that is, that all the mathematical objects that logically possibly *could* exist actually *do* exist; that is, that the mathematical realm is plenitudinous.

Now, I do not think that any of the four formulations of FBP given in the previous sentence avoids all the difficulties with the original formulation, but it seems to me that, between them, they make tolerably clear what FBP says— especially given my caveats about what FBP *doesn't* commit to. Indeed, it seems to me that the only real unclarity that remains is what exactly is meant by 'logically possible'; but, again, I will discuss this in chapter 3, section 5. (I should also say here that in chapters 3 and 4, I will discuss some of the important consequences of FBP; thus, at that point, the "overall FBP-ist picture" will become much more clear.)

Now, it might seem that if we want a really precise statement of FBP, we ought simply to state the thesis in a formal language. I am hesitant to do this for two different reasons. First, I'm inclined to doubt that there is any really adequate way to formalize FBP, and second, I think that, in any event, it is a mistake to think of FBP as a formal theory. FBP is, first and foremost, an informal philosophy of mathematics, and that is how I will develop and motivate the view in this book. Nevertheless, I do think it might help clarify FBP to say a few words about how one might go about trying to state it in a formal language. Before I do this, however, I want to emphasize that my sole aim here is to help the reader get clear about what FBP says; nothing important depends on finding an adequate formalization of FBP.

This caveat noted, let me say that I think we can come *close* to capturing FBP in a second-order modal language. To see this, let 'x' be a first-order variable, let 'Y' be a second-order variable, let 'Mx' mean 'x is a mathematical object', and consider, as a first shot, the formula

$$(Y)[\Diamond (\exists x)(Mx \ \& \ Yx) \rightarrow (\exists x)(Mx \ \& \ Yx)].$$

The reason this only comes *close* to capturing FBP is that whereas FBP commits to the existence of all the mathematical objects that possibly could exist, the above formula doesn't entail that there exist *any* mathematical objects, because it is silent on the question of whether it is *possible* that there exist mathematical objects; that is, because nothing is said here to guarantee that the antecedent of the conditional will ever be true, in any of the substitution instances of the formula. Now, this might seem like a rather large problem—so large that we ought not to claim that this formula even approximates FBP. But I think this overstates the problem; for the sort of possibility in question here is logical possibility—that is, the '◇' here is being read as logical possibility—and it is entirely trivial that the existence of mathematical objects is logically possible. In other words, it seems to me that the above formula does come close to capturing FBP, because if we combine it with the trivial thesis that the existence of mathematical objects is logically possible, then intuitively, we do seem to come close to capturing FBP. (Of course, there is still an unclarity here about what exactly is meant by 'logically possible', but again, I will address this later.)

I suppose that we might come closer to capturing FBP by using the formula

$$(\exists x)(Mx) \ \& \ (Y)[\ \Diamond\ (\exists x)(Mx \ \& \ Yx) \rightarrow (\exists x) \ (Mx \ \& \ Yx)],$$

since it does involve an existential commitment to mathematical objects. But the improvement here is limited, because while this formula certainly lessens (in a certain sense) the difficulty encountered by the original formula, it doesn't entirely eliminate it.

In any event, it should be pretty clear at this point what FBP says. And it should also be clear, I think, that FBP is a non-standard version of platonism. This is simply because traditional versions of platonism are non-plenitudinous, or non-full-blooded; that is, they admit some kinds of mathematical objects but not others. Now, this issue of the number of mathematical objects that platonists commit to has been almost completely ignored in the literature, but I am going to argue in part I that it is crucially important; in particular, I will argue that (a) FBP is a defensible view, and (b) all non-plenitudinous versions of platonism are indefensible.

(I don't mean to suggest that I am the first to defend a view like FBP. Edward Zalta and Bernard Linsky have defended a similar view; they claim that "there are as many abstract objects of a certain sort as there possibly could be." But their conception of abstract objects is rather unorthodox, and for this reason, their view is quite different, in several respects, from FBP.[7] I do not know of anyone else who has claimed that the mathematical realm is plenitudinous, in the manner of FBP, but there are a few philosophers who have made claims that bring this picture to mind. Hilbert, for instance, once wrote in a letter to Frege:

> if the arbitrarily given axioms do not contradict one another with all their consequences, then they are true and the things defined by the axioms exist. This is for me the criterion of truth and existence.[8]

Likewise, Poincaré says that "in mathematics the word exist . . . means free from contradiction".[9] And finally, Michael Resnik says that "a pure [mathematical] theory can be falsified by showing that it fails to characterize any pattern at all, that is, that it is inconsistent",[10] and in making this claim, he seems to be saying that such theories can be falsified *only* in this way. But while these passages bring to mind the FBP-ist picture of a plenitudinous mathematical realm, I do not think that any of these philosophers would endorse FBP. First of all, it is clear that neither Hilbert nor Poincaré meant to endorse any sort of platonism at all, let alone FBP. In other words, neither meant to say that there are mathematical objects that exist independently of us and our mathematical theories. As for Resnik, if he were to endorse an FBP-ist view at all, it would be a structuralist version of FBP, a view holding that all the mathematical structures that possibly could exist actually do exist. But I do not think that Resnik would endorse this view, because (a) he doesn't think of structures as entities at all, and (b) he seems to want to avoid the use of modalities like 'possible' in characterizing his view.[11] Indeed, it seems to me that if anyone endorses a structuralist version of FBP, it is probably Stewart Shapiro.[12,13] But whatever we end up saying about whether these various philosophers endorse views like FBP, the important point to note here is that— to the best of my knowledge, anyway—no one has used FBP to fend off the traditional objections to platonism in the way that I will in the first half of this book.[14])

A second divide in the platonist camp that needs to be discussed here—the first being the one between FBP and non-plenitudinous versions of platonism— is the divide between *object-platonism* and *structuralism*. I have presented platonism as the view that there exist abstract mathematical objects. But this is not exactly correct. The real core of the view is the belief in the abstract, that is, the belief that there is something real and objective that exists outside of spacetime and that our mathematical theories characterize. The claim that this abstract something is a collection of *objects* can be jettisoned without abandoning platonism. Thus, we can say that, strictly speaking, mathematical platonism is the view that our mathematical theories are descriptions of an abstract *mathematical realm*, that is, a non-physical, non-mental, non-spatiotemporal aspect of reality.

Now, the most traditional version of platonism—the one defended by, for example, Frege and Gödel—is a version of object-platonism. Object-platonism is the view that the mathematical realm is a system of abstract mathematical objects, such as numbers and sets, and that our mathematical theories, such as number theory and set theory, describe these objects. Thus, on this view, the sentence '3 is prime' says that the abstract object that is the number 3 has the property of primeness. But there is a very popular alternative to object-platonism, namely, structuralism. According to this view, our mathematical theories are not descriptions of particular systems of abstract objects; they are descriptions of abstract *structures*, where a structure is something like a *pattern*, or an "objectless template"— that is, a system of *positions* that can be "filled" by any system of objects that exhibit the given structure.[15] One of the central motivations for structuralism is that the "internal properties" of mathematical objects seem to be mathematically unimportant. What is mathematically important is structure—that is, the relations that hold between mathematical objects. To take the example of arithmetic, the claim is that any sequence of objects with the right structure (that is, any *ω-sequence*) would suit the needs of arithmetic as well as any other. What structuralists maintain is that arithmetic is concerned not with some particular one of these ω-sequences but, rather, with the structure or pattern that they all have in common. Thus, according to structuralists, there is no *object* that is the number 3; there is only the fourth position in the natural-number pattern. (The reason this view is still a version of platonism is that structures and positions are being taken here to be real, objective, and most important, abstract.[16])

The dispute between object-platonists and structuralists will not play an important role in this book, because I do not think that platonists need to take a stand on the matter. Now, structuralists would certainly question this; they think that by adopting structuralism, platonists improve their standing with respect to both of the great objections to platonism, that is, the epistemological objection and the multiple-reductions objection.[17] But during the course of this book, I will show that this attitude is wrong. First of all, I will argue that structuralism doesn't do any work in connection with these problems after all. (I will be very brief in this connection; I will make this point in relation to the epistemological problem in chapter 2, subsection 6.5, and in relation to the multiple-reductions problem in chapter 4, section 3.) But the really important thing I will do here is provide solutions to these two problems that work for both structuralism and object-platonism. What I will contend is that platonists can solve the problems with their view by adopting FBP (and that they can solve them *only* in this way) and that FBP is consistent with both object-platonism and structuralism.[18]

The last paragraph suggests that there is no reason to favor structuralism over object-platonism. But the problem here is even deeper: it is not clear that structuralism is even *distinct* from object-platonism in an important way. I say this not because structures can be taken to be mathematical objects — although I think they should be taken as such — but rather because *positions* in structures can be taken as mathematical objects. Now, to argue this point properly, I would have to give a very clear account of what an *object* is, and I am not going to do this here, because the present question is really an aside — whether positions count as objects is wholly irrelevant to the arguments that I will develop in this book. But, prima facie, it's not clear why positions *shouldn't* be considered objects. We can refer to them with singular terms, quantify over them in first-order languages, ascribe properties to them, and so on. What else is needed? Perhaps the claim is that positions aren't objects because they don't have any internal properties, that is, because there is no more to them than the relations that they bear to other positions. We'll see in a moment that there's reason to doubt the suggestion that there is no more to a position than the relations it bears to other positions. But even if this were right, it's hard to see why it would entail that positions aren't objects. There may be some intuitive connection between objecthood and the possession of internal properties among *concrete* objects, but I don't see why anyone would think that there is such a connection among abstract objects.

In light of these remarks, one might suggest that the structuralists' "objects-versus-positions" rhetoric is just a distraction and that structuralism should be defined in some other way. One suggestion along these lines, advanced by Charles Parsons,[19] is that structuralism should be defined as the view that mathematical objects have no internal properties, that is, that there is no more to them than the relations they bear to other mathematical objects. But it seems doubtful that any mathematical objects satisfy this constraint; after all, mathematical objects have properties like being non-spatiotemporal and being non-red, and these don't seem to have anything to do with any structural relations that they bear to other mathematical objects. Indeed, it seems to me that the property of having only structural properties is *itself* a non-structural property, and thus that this definition of structuralism is simply incoherent. A second suggestion here is that structuralism should be defined as the view that the internal properties of mathematical objects are not mathematically *important*, that is, that structure is what is important in mathematics. But whereas the last definition was too strong, this one is too weak. For as we'll see in chapter 4, traditional object-platonism is perfectly consistent with the idea that the internal properties of mathematical objects are not mathematically important; indeed, it seems to me that just about everyone who claims to be an object-platonist would *endorse* this idea. Therefore, this cannot be what separates structuralism from traditional object-platonism.

I don't think that structuralists would dispute this last point. That is, I don't think they want to define their view in terms of a mere claim about what's mathematically interesting, or important. They seem to want to go beyond this and make an ontological or metaphysical claim that clearly distinguishes their view from traditional versions of platonism. But the problem is that it's simply not clear what claim they could make here. We've already seen that two likely suggestions here fail, namely, the suggestion that mathematics is about positions in structures, as opposed to objects, and the suggestion that mathematical objects have only structural properties. I don't want to pursue this any further, but for whatever it's worth, I doubt that structuralists can meet the challenge I'm presenting here. That is, I doubt that there is any important difference between the structuralist conception of mathematical objects as "positions" and the traditional conception of mathematical objects.[20]

I want to reiterate here that I agree with the structuralist observation that all mathematically important facts are structural facts, as opposed to facts about the internal properties of mathematical objects. (Indeed, I think this is an important point, and in chapter 4, I will use it as a premise in one of my arguments.) Moreover, to grant another structuralist point, I admit that it's often convenient for platonists to speak of mathematical theories as describing structures, and indeed, I will sometimes speak that way in this book. My point here has simply been that in speaking of structures (and "positions in structures"), we are not speaking of "non-objects", or of objects that "lack internal properties"; we're speaking of ordinary mathematical objects. Moreover, as I pointed out a few paragraphs back, I do not think that we can solve any philosophical problems with platonism by claiming that mathematical objects can be thought of as "positions in structures".

Before going on, I would like to make a side point. I said a few paragraphs back that I do not intend to discuss the question of what an object is. This might seem like an oversight; for since this book is primarily concerned with the question of whether there exist any abstract objects, it might seem very important that we get clear about the meanings of words like 'object', 'abstract', and 'exist'. But the point of the above remarks is that talk of objects here is irrelevant. If one wishes to adopt a narrow notion of object, then this book is concerned not with the question of whether there are abstract *objects*, but with the question of whether there is abstract *stuff*, of some sort or other. But in any event, I will not adopt a narrow notion of object; I will adopt a broad notion, so that anything we can speak of—for example, a position in a structure—is an object, and the question of whether there is any abstract stuff *reduces* to the question of whether there are any abstract objects. Finally, what about the terms 'abstract' and 'exist'? Well, I said above that 'abstract' means 'non-spatiotemporal', but I do not want to say anything more than this right now. I want to rest content, for most of the book, with a "naive" understanding of the terms 'exist' and 'non-spatiotemporal'. But in the final chapter, the question of what the sentence 'there exist abstract objects' could really *mean* will take center stage.

2.2 The Various Versions of Anti-Platonism

The main divide in the anti-platonist camp is between the *realists* and the *anti-realists*. The former hold that although our mathematical theories do not describe abstract objects, they do describe concrete (i.e., spatiotemporal) objects. And the latter hold that our mathematical theories are not about any objects at all, that is, that these theories are factually empty. (One way of formulating realistic anti-platonism is as the view that mathematical objects are concrete objects. This, however, can be confusing, because the term 'mathematical object' is ordinarily used in a way that implies that the objects in question are abstract.)

Prima facie, there seem to be two kinds of realistic anti-platonism, one holding that mathematics is about physical objects and one holding that it's about mental objects. The most prominent advocate of the former view is John Stuart Mill,[21] who believes that mathematics is the most general of the natural sciences. Just as botany gives us laws about plants, mathematics, according to Mill, gives us laws about all objects. For instance, the sentence '2 + 1 = 3' tells us that whenever we add one object to a pile of two objects, we will end up with three objects. It does not tell us anything about any abstract objects, like the numbers 1, 2, and 3, because, on this view, there are simply no such things as abstract objects. The view that mathematics is about *mental* objects, on the other hand, is known as *psychologism*;[22] to use the same example, the view here is that '2 + 1 = 3' is about certain ideas in our heads, namely, the ideas of 1, 2, and 3. In chapter 5, we will see that psychologism is actually better interpreted as a version of anti-realism, because the objects that it takes mathematics to be about do not exist independently of us. In other words, whereas platonists and Millian empiricists claim that mathematicians discover facts about objective entities, advocates of psychologism make the anti-realistic claim that mathematicians construct their objects and are, therefore, primarily inventors.

Not counting psychologism, there are still several different versions of anti-realistic anti-platonism. One such view is *conventionalism*, which holds that mathematical sentences are analytically true. On this view, '2 + 1 = 3' is like 'All bachelors are unmarried': it is true solely in virtue of the meanings of the words appearing in it. A second view here is *deductivism*, or *if-thenism*, which holds that mathematics gives us truths of the form 'if A then T' (or 'it is necessary that if A then T') where A is an axiom, or a conjunction of several axioms, and T is a theorem that is provable from these axioms. In connection with our example, then, deductivists claim that '2 + 1 = 3' is, strictly speaking, false, but that it can be taken as shorthand for a longer sentence that is true, namely, '(it is necessary that) if the axioms of arithmetic are true, then 2 + 1 = 3'. A related view is *formalism*, which holds that mathematics gives us truths about what holds in various formal systems; for instance, one truth of mathematics is that the sentence '2 + 1 = 3' is a theorem of the formal system PA (i.e., Peano Arithmetic). Another version of formalism — *game formalism* — holds that mathematics is a game of symbol manipulation; on this view, '2 + 1 = 3' would be one of the "legal results" of the "game" specified by the axioms of PA. Two other versions of anti-realism worth mentioning are Wittgenstein's (which is related in certain ways to game formalism and conventionalism, but distinct from both) and Chihara's (which seeks to replace the existence claims of mathematics with assertions about what open-sentence tokens it is possible to construct). But I do not want to try to give quick, one-sentence definitions of these two views, as I did for the above views, because I do not think it is possible to do this. To capture the central ideas behind the views of Wittgenstein and Chihara would take a bit more space, but there is really no reason to go into this here.[23]

I will argue in chapter 5 that the best version of anti-realistic anti-platonism — and indeed, the best version of anti-platonism — is *fictionalism*.[24] This view differs from other versions of anti-realistic anti-platonism in that it takes mathematical sentences and theories at *face value*, in the way that platonism does. Fictionalists agree with platonists that the sentence '3 is prime' is about the number 3[25] — in particular, they think it says that this number has the property of primeness — and they also agree that if there is any such thing as 3, then it is an abstract object. But they disagree with platonists in that they do not think that there is any such thing as the number 3 and, hence, do not think that sentences like '3 is prime' are true. According to fictionalists, mathematical sentences and theories are fictions; they are comparable to sentences like 'Santa Claus lives at the North Pole'. This sentence is not true, because 'Santa Claus' is a vacuous term, that is, it fails to refer. Likewise, '3 is prime' is not true, because '3' is a vacuous term — because just as there is no such person as Santa Claus, so there is no such thing as the number 3. Now, on the version of fictionalism that I will defend, this means that '3 is prime' is simply false. But it should be noted that this is not essential to the view. What is essential to mathematical fictionalism is that (a) there are no such things as mathematical objects, and hence, (b) mathematical singular terms are vacuous. Whether this means that sentences like '3 is prime' are false, or that they lack truth value, or something else, depends upon our theory of vacuity. I will adopt the view that such sentences are false, but nothing important will turn on this.[26]

It might seem odd that I would claim that fictionalism is the best version of anti-platonism, for on its face, the claim that '2 + 1 = 3' is false seems almost ludicrous. But there is a sense in which fictionalism is the obvious view for anti-platonists to endorse. Since anti-platonists do not believe in abstract objects, and since, prima facie, mathematics is about abstract objects, it would seem that anti-platonists ought to say that mathematics is fictional. Moreover, I will argue in chapter 5, section 4, that anti-platonists do not secure any advantage by reinterpreting mathematics in a non-face-value way that makes it come out true. One might think that they could, in this way, make it easier to account for the applicability of mathematics, but I will argue that this is an illusion.

One obvious question that arises for fictionalists is this: "Given that '2 + 1 = 3' is false, what is the difference between this sentence and, say, '2 + 1 = 4'?" The difference is analogous to the difference between 'Santa Claus lives at the North Pole' and 'Santa Claus lives in Tel Aviv'. In other words, the difference is that '2 + 1 = 3' is part of a certain well-known mathematical story, whereas '2 + 1 = 4' is not. We might also express this idea by saying that while neither '2 + 1 = 3' nor '2 + 1 = 4' is true *simpliciter*, there is another truth predicate — namely, 'is true in the story of mathematics' — that applies to '2 + 1 = 3' but not to '2 + 1 = 4'. This seems to be the view that Field endorses;[27] but there is a bit more that needs to be said on this topic.

First of all, it is important to realize that the above remarks do not lend any metaphysical or ontological distinction to sentences like '2 + 1 = 3'. For according to fictionalism, the story of mathematics is itself fictional. More to the point, there are *alternative* mathematical "stories" consisting of sentences that are not part of standard mathematics. Thus, the real difference between sentences like '2 + 1 = 3' and sentences like '2 + 1 = 4' is that the former are part of *our* story of mathematics, whereas the latter are not. Now, of course, fictionalists will need to explain why we "use" or "endorse" this particular mathematical story, as opposed to some alternative story, but this is not hard to do. The reasons are that this story is pragmatically useful, that it's aesthetically pleasing, and most important, that it dovetails with our "way of thinking". This last point might be a bit obscure, but it will become clearer during the course of the book. For now, I will just try to clarify the point by giving an example of what I have in mind: the theories of arithmetic that we "endorse" dovetail with (and, indeed, are tailor-made to dovetail with) our concept of number.

Second, one might worry here that when fictionalists endorse the sentence

(A) '3 is prime' is true-in-the-story-of-mathematics,

they commit to abstract objects. For, prima facie, it seems that the best and most straightforward interpretation of (A) is that it says that a certain sentence type (namely, '3 is prime') is a member of a certain set of sentence types (namely, the "story of mathematics"). I do not think that fictionalists should try to deny this; they should admit that this is the best way to read (A). Thus, since fictionalists do not think there are any such things as sentence types or sets of sentence types, they should say that sentences like (A) are fictional, that is, strictly speaking, false.

Now, one might object that if fictionalists endorse this stance, then the appeal to the predicate 'is-true-in-the-story-of-mathematics' does not provide them with a way of distinguishing '3 is prime' from '4 is prime' after all. For fictionalists will have to say the same thing about sentences like

(B) '4 is prime' is true-in-the-story-of-mathematics

that they say about sentences like (A) — namely, that they're fictional. We can see how fictionalists can respond to this objection by turning our attention to concrete *tokens* of '3 is prime' and '4 is prime', which fictionalists do believe in. What fictionalists should say in this connection is that concrete '3-is-prime' tokens have a certain property that concrete '4-is-prime' tokens do not have. Now, if we help ourselves to platonistic jargon, we can capture this fact very easily by saying

(C) Concrete '3-is-prime' tokens are tokens of a type that is true-in-the-story-of-mathematics.

But fictionalists cannot claim that (C) is true, because it commits to abstract objects. Thus, it appears that they need to find a nominalistic way of describing the fact in question here.

It seems to me that the problem of finding an appropriate nominalistic description here is a special case of a much more general problem with fictionalism, namely, the problem of applicability and indispensability. The problem of applicability is that there are facts about the physical world that, apparently, can be expressed only by using sentences that refer to abstract objects, for example, the mathematically formulated sentences of empirical science. (This is a problem because if there really are facts of this sort, then we would *seem* to be committed to the existence of abstract objects.) In any event, the present problem is that there is a fact about the physical world (namely, the above-mentioned fact about concrete '3-is-prime' tokens) that, apparently, can be expressed only by using a sentence that refers to abstract objects, for instance, a sentence like (C). Therefore, this problem is clearly a special case of the general problem of applicability.

This is a very important point to note. For as we will see very shortly, the problem of applicability is the central problem with fictionalism. I dedicate all of chapter 7 to solving it. Moreover, the solution I provide will be very general: it will apply to all cases in which we use abstract-object talk to describe facts about the physical world, and in particular, it will apply very straightforwardly to the special case that I've been discussing in the last couple of paragraphs.[28] For this reason, I do not want to say anything more on this topic now.

3. Synopsis of the Book

I have said that the central project of this book is to show that there are no good arguments for platonism or anti-platonism by showing that both of these views are defensible, that is, that there are no good arguments *against* either of them. In part I, I argue that platonists can solve all the problems with their view by adopting FBP, and in part II, I argue that anti-platonists can solve the problems with their view by adopting fictionalism. Now, the conclusion that I want to defend in the last chapter of the book relies upon the claim that FBP and fictionalism are the *only* tenable versions of platonism and anti-platonism, respectively. Thus, for this reason, the first half of the book contains not just a defense of FBP but also a (brief and sketchy) attack on all non-full-blooded, or non-plenitudinous, versions of platonism; and the second half of the book contains not just a defense of fictionalism but also a (brief and sketchy) attack on all other versions of anti-platonism. What I want to do now is give a brief summary of all of this.

In chapter 2, I present the epistemological argument against platonism, due originally to Benacerraf,[29] in what I think is its strongest form. In a nutshell, the argument is that platonism could not be correct, because it is incompatible with the fact that human beings have mathematical knowledge. Thus, the challenge to platonists is to explain how human beings could acquire knowledge of abstract mathematical objects. After laying out the argument, I carve up the logical space of possible responses to the argument and systematically consider them. I begin by arguing that platonists cannot solve the epistemological problem by claiming that human beings are capable of coming into some sort of information-gathering *contact* with mathematical objects. (There are two different versions of this strategy, one associated with Gödel and the other with Maddy;[30] I argue that neither can succeed.) I then consider various ways of explaining how human beings could acquire knowledge of mathematical objects, despite the fact that they cannot come into any sort of contact with such objects. I argue that some of these explanations (namely, those due to Quine, Steiner, Parsons, Hale, and Wright[31]) fail outright, whereas others (namely, those due to Resnik, Shapiro, Katz, and Lewis[32]) can be made to work, but only if they are employed in connection with FBP. (I also argue, however, that since these philosophers don't acknowledge that they need to rely upon FBP—or provide any defense for this reliance or, for that matter, even broach the *topic* of FBP—their solutions to the epistemological problem are flawed and unacceptable.)

In chapter 3, I bring FBP to the fore. I argue that if we accept this view, then the epistemological problem can be solved very easily. I do this not by simply finding a hole in Benacerraf's argument, but by actually providing a *recipe* for acquiring knowledge of abstract objects. That is, I explain very clearly how human beings can acquire knowledge of abstract mathematical objects without the aid of any contact with such objects. And it seems to me that unlike the platonist epistemologies discussed in chapter 2, my epistemology totally eliminates the feeling of *mystery* surrounding the question of how spatiotemporal creatures like ourselves could acquire knowledge of non-spatiotemporal mathematical objects. The reason I am able to do this is very simple: I abandon traditional platonism in favor of FBP and make full use of this shift in constructing my epistemology. Now, one might worry that the move from traditional platonism to FBP creates as many problems as it solves. But I argue in chapter 3 that this is wrong, that there is no reason why platonists cannot adopt FBP and, indeed, that there are independent reasons for thinking that FBP is the best version of platonism there is.

In chapter 4, I argue that by adopting FBP we can also solve the other great problem with platonism, that is, the multiple-reductions or non-uniqueness problem.[33] Moreover, scattered throughout the book, I also provide solutions to a few other worries that one might have about platonism.[34] And so, at this point, I conclude that FBP is a defensible view, that is, that it survives *all* attacks. Thus, I turn to part II and the attacks on *anti*-platonism.

In chapter 5, I use essentially Fregean arguments to dispense with all non-fictionalistic versions of anti-platonism, and I argue that the only really important problem with fictionalism is the Quine–Putnam problem of accounting for the indispensable applications of mathematics to empirical science.[35] There are two strategies that fictionalists can use in responding to this problem. They can either (a) deny that there are any indispensable applications of mathematics to physics, or else (b) admit that there *are* some applications of this sort and simply account for them from a fictionalist point of view. I discuss these two strategies in chapters 6 and 7, respectively.

The first strategy is Field's.[36] He argues that mathematics is, in fact, not indispensable to empirical science and that the mere fact that it's *applicable* — that is, applicable in a dispensable way — can be accounted for without abandoning fictionalism. The first claim — that mathematics is dispensable from physical theory, that is, that physical theory can be *nominalized* — is the controversial part of the program, and there have been a number of different objections to Field's proposed method of nominalization. The most pressing of these objections, in my mind, is Malament's claim that Field's method cannot be extended to cover quantum mechanics (QM).[37] In chapter 6, I respond to this objection. And I don't just show that Malament's argument is misguided; I actually sketch a strategy for nominalizing QM and do much of the work toward filling in the details. Now, I do not *completely* nominalize QM, and moreover, I do not attempt to respond to any of the other objections that have been raised against Field's program. Thus, chapter 6 does not provide a complete response to the Quine–Putnam argument. The point here is simply to argue that this general strategy of response is more plausible than many people have supposed.

In chapter 7, I pursue the second fictionalist strategy for responding to the Quine–Putnam argument. In other words, I assume, for the sake of argument, that there do exist indispensable applications of mathematics to empirical science, and I simply account for these applications from a fictionalist point of view. I do not think that anyone has attempted this strategy before, so to the best of my knowledge, the explanation I offer is original. One of the main virtues of my explanation is that it does not collapse into an instrumentalism about empirical science. It explains how we can simultaneously endorse realism about empirical science, fictionalism about mathematics, and the thesis that mathematics is indispensable to empirical science. Chapter 7 does what chapter 6 fails to do: it provides a complete refutation of the Quine–Putnam argument against fictionalism. Thus, my position with respect to this argument is that I suspect it can be solved via Field's program of nominalization, but that it doesn't matter, because even if mathematics is indispensable to empirical science, fictionalists have another solution available to them. Moreover, as we will see, there are a variety of reasons for thinking that this other solution is superior to Field's.

So it follows from the arguments of part II that fictionalism, like FBP, is a tenable philosophy of mathematics. Thus, we are left with two views — one claiming that all the mathematical objects that logically possibly *could* exist actually *do* exist, and the other claiming that *no* mathematical objects exist — but no way of deciding which is right. This gives us the first conclusion of the book, what I call the *weak epistemic conclusion*. The conclusion here is that we do not have any good arguments for or against mathematical platonism, that is, for or against the existence of abstract mathematical objects. (One might think that the very fact that there are no good arguments here lends support—via Ockham's razor—to anti-platonism, that is, to fictionalism. But I argue at the end of part 2 that this argument also fails.)

Finally, in chapter 8, I try to strengthen my conclusion in two ways. I argue in section 2 for what I call the *strong epistemic conclusion* and in section 3 for what I call the *metaphysical conclusion*. These two conclusions can be formulated as follows:

> *Strong epistemic conclusion*: It's not just that we *currently* lack a cogent argument that settles the dispute over mathematical objects—it's that we could *never* have such an argument.

> *Metaphysical conclusion*: It's not just that *we* could never discover whether platonism or anti-platonism is true—it's that there is *no fact of the matter* as to which of them is true. In other words, there is no fact of the matter as to whether there exist any abstract objects.

One point worth emphasizing here is that the metaphysical conclusion applies to *all* abstract objects, as opposed to just *mathematical* objects, which is what the two epistemic conclusions apply to. Now, I do think that the epistemic conclusions can be generalized; in other words, I think that generalized versions of these conclusions, which apply to all abstract objects, are true; but the arguments I give in this book apply only to the special case of mathematical objects. My argument for the metaphysical conclusion, on the other hand, applies to all abstract objects.

PART I

PLATONISM

Some place where there isn't any trouble. Do you suppose there *is* such a place, Toto? There *must* be. It's not a place you can get to by a boat or a train. . . . Somewhere, over the rainbow, way up high, there's a land that I heard of once in a lullaby.

—Dorothy Gale (early)

The Epistemological Argument Against Platonism

1. Introduction

In this chapter, I will discuss Benacerraf's epistemological argument against platonism, which holds, in a nutshell, that platonism cannot be right because it precludes the possibility of mathematical knowledge. I will begin by formulating the argument in what I think is the best possible way. I will then move on to a discussion of some possible solutions to the problem. This discussion will serve simultaneously as a historical survey of the answers that platonists have actually given to the epistemological problem and as a search of the logical space of possible solutions that might be given. I will concern myself with seven different proposed solutions to the problem: one developed by Gödel; another by Maddy; a third by a host of contemporary platonists, most notably Parsons; a fourth by Wright and Hale; a fifth hinted at by Quine and developed by Steiner and Resnik; a sixth by Katz and Lewis; and finally, a seventh by Resnik and Shapiro. I will argue that the first five suggestions fail outright. What I say about the last two will not really amount to a refutation, but I will make it clear that (a) they can work only if a certain other epistemology (that is, response to Benacerraf) works, and (b) they are inferior to this other epistemology.

This "other epistemology" that I speak of here is my own epistemology. In chapter 3, I will argue at length that it provides an acceptable explanation of how human beings could acquire knowledge of abstract mathematical objects and, hence, that it provides an acceptable response to the Benacerrafian challenge. The point of chapters 3 and 4 is to show that the version of platonism I develop there — namely, FBP — is a tenable version of platonism. The point of the present chapter is to show that FBP is the *only* tenable version of platonism. Thus, part of what I will argue in connection with Katz, Lewis, Resnik, and Shapiro is that their epistemologies can work only if FBP is assumed. And again, I will argue that all other platonist epistemologies fail outright.

2. Formulating the Epistemological Argument

I begin by stating a classical version of the epistemological argument against platonism, a version inspired by Paul Benacerraf's seminal paper, "Mathematical Truth". After that, I will explain how we can improve upon this version of the argument.

I say that the classical version of the argument is *inspired* by Benacerraf's paper, because it really isn't explicitly stated there. It is buried in Benacerraf's argument for the claim that the standard Tarskian semantics for mathematics is incompatible with our best epistemology — or rather, what Benacerraf thinks is our best epistemology, namely, the causal theory of knowledge (CTK). In its broadest formulation, CTK holds that in order for a person S to know that p, it is necessary that S be causally related to the fact that p in an appropriate way. But, of course, there are many different ways of spelling out this "appropriate" causal relation, and so there are many different versions of CTK. In any event, what Benacerraf argues, more or less, is that CTK is incompatible with a Tarskian semantics for mathematics because it is incompatible with platonism.[1] Thus, while Benacerraf didn't put it this way, his paper contains an argument against platonism that takes CTK as a premise. That argument proceeds roughly as follows.

(1) Human beings exist entirely within spacetime.[2]

(2) If there exist any abstract mathematical objects, then they exist outside of spacetime.

Therefore, by CTK,

(3) If there exist any abstract mathematical objects, then human beings could not attain knowledge of them.

Therefore,

(4) If mathematical platonism is correct, then human beings could not attain mathematical knowledge.

(5) Human beings have mathematical knowledge.

Therefore,

(6) Mathematical platonism is not correct.

The argument for (3) is everything here. If it can be established, then so can (6), because (3) trivially entails (4), (5) is beyond doubt,[3] and (4) and (5) trivially entail (6). Now, in connection with the argument for (3), the first thing to notice is that (1) and (2) entail that human beings could not be causally related to any mathematical objects. (Indeed, this seems to follow from (2) alone: if mathematical objects exist outside of spacetime, then they are *causally inert* and, hence, couldn't be causally related to us, because they couldn't be causally related to anything.)

But if we add CTK to the claim that human beings could not be causally related to mathematical objects, we seem to be led to (3).

The most popular response to Benacerraf's argument has been to reject CTK. Platonists admit that their view is incompatible with CTK, but they claim that the problem lies with the latter rather than the former. Now, some platonists have allowed that *some* versions of CTK are true, but they maintain that those that are true are compatible with platonism. In other words, they admit that there are causal constraints on knowledge but argue that these constraints are so loose that they allow for knowledge of mathematical objects. But regardless of the details of the argument, the general strategy of responding to Benacerraf by rejecting CTK has been almost universally accepted by platonists.[4] Moreover, I think this strategy is acceptable; that is, I think there are good arguments against CTK, or at least the versions of CTK that threaten platonism. (My argument for this can be found in chapter 3. I explain there how human beings can acquire knowledge of mathematical objects without satisfying any non-trivial causal constraint. Thus, I simply provide a counterexample to CTK.)

But it turns out that the whole topic of CTK is a red herring, because the epistemological argument can be reformulated so that it doesn't rely upon that theory. Anti-platonists can argue as follows: "(1) and (2) imply that mathematical objects (if there are such things) are totally inaccessible to us, that is, that information cannot pass from mathematical objects to human beings. But this gives rise to a prima facie worry (which may or may not be answerable) about whether human beings could acquire knowledge of mathematical objects. In other words, it gives rise to a prima facie reason to believe (3), that is, to believe that human beings could not acquire knowledge of mathematical objects.[5] Thus, since (3) trivially entails (6), it also gives rise to a prima facie reason to believe (6), that is, to believe that platonism is false."[6]

So my suggestion here is that instead of adding CTK to (1) and (2) in an effort to *establish* (3), we should let (1) and (2) stand alone, because they already give rise to a prima facie reason to believe (3).[7] Now, if we proceed in this manner, then the epistemological argument won't establish that platonism is false, but it will generate a prima facie reason to suspect that platonism is false, and this, I think, is all that anti-platonists need. After all, if there is a prima facie reason to suspect that platonism is false, then presumably, we won't be comfortable endorsing platonism unless we can find a way of answering this prima facie suspicion. But in any event, I don't think anti-platonists can do any better here; I don't think they can *establish* (3) because, as I will explain in chapter 3, I think (3) is false. In other words, I think that human beings *can* acquire knowledge of abstract mathematical objects, and so I do not think it is possible to establish the falsity of platonism with an epistemological argument of the above sort.

Here's another way to think of my version of the epistemological argument. What I am doing is using (1) and (2) to motivate a prima facie suspicion about the platonist's ability to account for the fact that human beings have mathematical knowledge and then simply issuing a challenge to platonists to account for this fact. Seen in this light, my version of the argument is virtually identical to Field's.[8] He, too, refrains from trying to establish the falsity of platonism with the epistemological argument. What he argues is that (1) and (2) generate a prima facie reason to doubt that platonists can account for the reliability of our mathematical beliefs. Now, this might sound a bit different from what I have argued, but I do not think there is any important difference between challenging platonists to account for the reliability of our mathematical beliefs and challenging them to account for our ability to acquire mathematical knowledge.[9] Thus, in what follows, I will speak of both challenges, and I will assume that they can be answered together, with a single explanation.

3. A Taxonomy of Platonist Responses

We've seen that the only way to block my version of the epistemological argument against platonism is to undercut the prima facie reason to believe (3). There are three ways to do this. First, we can argue that (1) is false and that the human mind is capable of, somehow, forging contact with the mathematical realm and thereby acquiring information about that realm; this is Gödel's strategy, or so I will argue. Second, we can argue that (2) is false and that human beings can acquire information about mathematical objects via normal perceptual means; this is Maddy's strategy. Third, we can accept (1) and (2) and explain why (3) doesn't follow — or more to the point, why (3) is nonetheless false. This is the most popular strategy among contemporary platonists. Its advocates include Quine, Steiner, Parsons, Hale, Wright, Resnik, Shapiro, Lewis, and Katz.

That these are the only three plausible avenues of response is a virtue of my version of the epistemological argument, because all three of these responses are *positive* responses in the sense that they involve the construction of an epistemology. One of the main drawbacks of Benacerraf's version of the argument is that it allows platonists to respond in a purely negative way, namely, by refuting CTK. What anti-platonists really want from platonists is an epistemology, that is, an explanation of how human beings could acquire knowledge of abstract mathematical objects. The nice thing about my version of the epistemological argument is that it more or less forces platonists to respond in this way, because all three of the plausible strategies of response involve the construction of an explanation of how we could acquire knowledge of mathematical objects.[10]

It is worth noting in this connection that the third strategy is quite different from the first two, because it involves the construction of what might be called a *no-contact* epistemology. The first two strategies involve the claim that human beings are capable of coming into some sort of *contact* with mathematical objects, or of achieving some sort of *access* to them. In other words, the claim here is that information can pass from mathematical objects to human beings and that this is why we are capable of acquiring knowledge of such objects. In contrast, platonists who use the third strategy admit that we are *not* capable of any sort of contact with mathematical objects, and they try to explain why we are nonetheless capable of acquiring knowledge of such objects.

In any event, we now have a taxonomy of platonist responses to the epistemological argument. In section 4, I will consider and reject the Gödelian strategy.

In section 5, I will consider and reject the Maddian strategy. In section 6, I will consider various versions of the third strategy, finding problems with them all. Then in chapter 3, I will develop a new version of the third strategy, and I will argue that this version works, that is, that it successfully explains how spatiotemporal creatures like ourselves could acquire knowledge of abstract mathematical objects.

4. Contact with Other Worlds: Gödel

In subsection 4.1, I will describe and refute the first strategy of responding to the Benacerrafian challenge, that is, the strategy of rejecting (1). I will be very brief, because I think that the view under consideration here is extremely implausible on its face and that the arguments against it are very obvious and decisive. Indeed, the view is so untenable that one might wonder why I am bothering to discuss it at all. The reason is that I think the view in question is *Gödel's* view, and so I think it is worth taking the time to refute it. Now, the claim that Gödel really did have this implausible view in mind is controversial; thus, in sub-section 4.2, I will briefly digress from the main line of argument and offer a bit of textual evidence for this interpretation.

4.1 *Refutation of the Strategy of Rejecting (1)*

If the strategy of rejecting (1) can be motivated at all, it is in the following way. One might think that the best way to answer the Benacerrafian challenge is to maintain that we acquire knowledge of abstract mathematical objects in much the same way that we acquire knowledge of concrete physical objects. Platonists with this attitude might claim that just as we acquire information about physical objects via the faculty of sense perception, so we acquire information about mathematical objects by means of a faculty of *mathematical intuition*. The problem with this suggestion is that it seems impossible for us to receive information from mathematical objects: since they are abstract and causally inert, mathematical objects could not generate information-carrying signals, and in any event, the suggestion that such a signal could somehow "pass" from a non-spatiotemporal mathematical realm to our heads seems unintelligible.[11] But platonists can respond to this objection by claiming that the view is unintelligible only if we take mathematical intuition to involve a sort of *cross-realm* contact, that is, a flow of information from non-spatiotemporal things to things existing in spacetime. Platonists who take this line will maintain that the unintelligibility here can be eliminated by rejecting (1). The idea here is that if we maintain that human minds are *themselves* immaterial and non-spatiotemporal — that they are not dependent upon brains — then we might be able to construct a view according to which we acquire information from mathematical objects even thought there are no signals that pass from the mathematical realm into spacetime.

This view can be quickly dispensed with. First of all, the claim that we can avoid the unintelligibility in the cross-realm view by rejecting (1) just seems false.

For even if minds are immaterial, it is not as if that puts them into informational contact with mathematical objects. The idea of information passing from one non-spatiotemporal object to another is no more intelligible than the idea of infor-mation passing from a non-spatiotemporal object to a physical object. The notion of an information transfer is a causal, spatiotemporal one; it makes sense only when the sender and receiver are both physical objects.[12]

So the first difficulty with the rejection of (1) is that it is unhelpful — it just doesn't solve the epistemological problem with platonism, that is, the lack-of-access problem. The second difficulty is just as obvious: (1) is, in fact, true. Now, of course, I am not going to develop an argument for this claim here, because it would be entirely inappropriate to break out into an argument against Cartesian dualism in the middle of a book on the philosophy of mathematics. But it is worth emphasizing that what is required here is a very strong (and hence, implausible) version of dualism. One cannot motivate a rejection of (1) by merely arguing that there are real mental states, like beliefs and desires and pains, or by arguing that our mentalistic idioms cannot be reduced to physicalistic idioms. One has to argue for the *ontological* thesis that there exists immaterial human mind-stuff.

Now, the obvious response that an advocate of mathematical intuition would make to all of this is that while the above arguments are correct, they are totally irrelevant, because they are directed against an implausible version of the theory of mathematical intuition. The proper way to develop that theory is either (a) to follow Maddy and claim that mathematical objects are spatiotemporal and that mathematical intuition is based upon ordinary sense perception, or (b) to follow people like Parsons, Steiner, and Katz in denying that the faculty of mathematical intuition involves any sort of information-gathering contact with mathematical ob-jects. Moreover, the sheer implausibility of the view based on the rejection of (1), and the obviousness of the arguments against it, suggest that no one could seriously believe it, least of all someone as brilliant as Gödel. Surely we ought to interpret his remarks on mathematical intuition along the lines of the no-contact theory; we should think of them as providing a vague suggestion that has been made more precise (in various different ways) by people like Parsons, Steiner, and Katz.

I agree that the strategy of rejecting (1) is the most implausible way of devel-oping a theory of mathematical intuition. But I cannot be accused of a straw man fallacy here, because I am going to discuss the other two ways of developing the theory: in section 5, I will dispose of the Maddian theory, and in subsection 6.2, I will dispose of the no-contact theory. Before I do this, however, I want to digress for a moment and argue that Gödel did *not* have the no-contact theory (or the Maddian theory) in mind, that he really was thinking of the strategy of rejecting (1). The reader should keep in mind, however, that these exegetical remarks really do constitute a digression. My main concern in this chapter is to consider all of the plausible strategies in the logical space of responses to the epistemological argument. It really doesn't matter which of these strategies Gödel had in mind. Thus, even if my interpretation of Gödel is wrong, no harm will be done, because I am not going to ignore the other view that one might attribute to him, that is, the no-contact view.

4.2 Interpreting Gödel

I do not think it is obvious that Gödel held a nonspatiotemporal-contact theory of mathematical intuition, as opposed to a no-contact theory. After all, he made only a few scattered remarks in this connection, and they were all rather cryptic and metaphorical. Moreover, I admit that the idea that Gödel could have held such an implausible view is rather puzzling.[13] Nonetheless, I think that the textual evidence suggests he did. The three central claims of the non-spatiotemporal-contact view — the claims that distinguish it from the no-contact view — are (i) that mathematical intuition is analogous to sense perception, (ii) that mathematical intuition involves a sort of information transfer between abstract mathematical objects and human beings, and (iii) that (1) is false. Here is some evidence for thinking that Gödel believed all three of these claims.

As for (i), I think it is fair to say that the central theme running through *all* of Gödel's remarks on mathematical intuition is the analogy to sense perception. Indeed, the most commonly cited remark of Gödel's on this topic involves a direct claim that intuition is "something like a perception" of mathematical objects.[14] Now, I do not think that, by itself, this motivates the claim that Gödel endorsed a non-spatiotemporal-contact view of mathematical intuition. After all, Frege spoke of a "non-sensible perception" of abstract objects,[15] but I do not think that he meant to commit to the sort of view under consideration here. But Gödel is different, because it seems that he endorsed theses (ii) and (iii) in conjunction with thesis (i).

In connection with (iii), that is, the claim that (1) is false, the important point to note is that Gödel believed not just that human minds are immaterial — by itself, that would show nothing — but that we are led to this conclusion by reflecting on mathematics. He says, for instance, that we are "driven to take some vitalistic viewpoint" and that there is no "possibility of a purely mechanistic explanation of psychical and nervous processes".[16] Now, the problem here is that Gödel did not make these remarks in connection with a discussion of mathematical *intuition*. If he had, then I think it would be clear that my interpretation of him is correct. What Gödel thought is that immaterialism about the mind follows from his incompleteness theorem. This theorem tells us that for any consistent axiom system, there are propositions that are undecidable in that system. Gödel claims, however, that, despite this, there are no mathematical propositions that are *absolutely undecidable*, that is, "undecidable, not just within some particular axiomatic system, but by *any* mathematical proof the human mind can conceive".[17] From this, together with the incompleteness theorem, it follows that the set of humanly provable mathematical propositions cannot be recursively axiomatized and, hence, that the human mind cannot be reduced to a Turing Machine. And Gödel concludes from this that the human mind cannot be reduced to any sort of machine at all.

Now, I do not think that this is a good argument for immaterialism about the mind, but that's another story. Our question here is whether Gödel wanted to use this immaterialism in his theory of mathematical intuition. The answer, I think, turns on whether Gödel endorsed thesis (ii), whether he thought that mathematical intuition involves an *information transfer* between mathematical objects and human minds. Now, again, I am not convinced that Gödel really did endorse this thesis, but I suspect that he did. Consider, for instance, the following passage:

> It should be noted that mathematical intuition need not be conceived of as a faculty giving an *immediate* knowledge of the objects concerned. Rather it seems that, as in the case of physical experience, we *form* our ideas also of those objects on the basis of something else which *is* immediately given.[18]

And later in the same paragraph, he says that while data about physical objects arise from sense perception, the "presence in us [of mathematical data] may be due to another kind of relationship between ourselves and reality". All of this seems very suggestive to me of a contact-based, information-transfer view of mathematical intuition. The suggestion seems to be that something is *given to the mind* in mathematical intuition. What's given is, of course, not mathematical objects *themselves* — that would be inconsistent with the platonistic view that mathematical objects exist outside of our minds — but rather, the *mathematical analog of sense data*, that is, something like *intuition data*. Gödel seems to think that the mind proceeds from these data to a belief in the existence of objective entities that, in some sense, give *rise* to the data via some kind of "relationship between ourselves and reality". In short, he seems to think that mathematical intuition is really *just like* sense perception.

That, anyway, is how it seems to me. I acknowledge that Gödel's remarks can be interpreted in other ways. But since all of this is irrelevant to what I am doing in this book, I will move on.

5. Contact in This World: Maddy

I now move on to the attempt to solve the epistemological problem with platonism by rejecting (2). The view here is still that human beings are capable of acquiring knowledge of mathematical objects by coming into contact with them, that is, receiving information from them, but the strategy now is not to bring human beings up to platonic heaven but, rather, to bring the inhabitants of platonic heaven down to earth. Less metaphorically, the idea is to adopt a naturalistic conception of mathematical objects and argue that human beings can acquire knowledge of these objects via *sense perception*. The most important advocate of this view is Penelope Maddy (or rather, the *early* Maddy, for she has since abandoned the view).[19] She writes:

> I intend to reject the traditional platonist's characterization of mathematical objects ... [and] bring them into the world we know and into contact with our familiar cognitive faculties.[20]

Maddy is thinking mainly of *sets* here.[21] Thus, her two central claims are that sets are spatiotemporally located — a set of eggs, for instance, is located right where the eggs are — and that sets are perceptible, that is, that they can be seen, heard, smelled, felt, and tasted in the usual ways.

I will argue here that this view, which we can call *naturalized platonism*, doesn't work. I will argue not just that *Maddy's* view doesn't work, but that no version of naturalized platonism works. In particular, I will argue that even if we grant that (2) is false and that sets exist in spacetime, so long as we hang onto some version of *platonism* — and we'll see in subsection 5.1 that naturalized platonists *have* to do this — we cannot maintain that human beings receive any relevant perceptual information about sets, and so we cannot solve the epistemological problem with platonism by rejecting (2).

Before beginning my argument, I should note that Maddy does not rest content with the bare claim that sets are perceptible. She spends a great deal of time explaining how we proceed from perceptions of sets to knowledge of the axioms of set theory. In particular, she explains how our perceptions of sets lead to mathematical intuitions about sets and how these intuitions combine with pragmatic considerations in a way that leads us to adopt the axioms of Zermelo-Fraenkel set theory (ZF). I want to point out, however, that *in the context of Benacerraf's problem*, all of this is irrelevant, because that problem is already solved by the bare claim that mathematical objects are perceptible. Now, of course, this bare claim doesn't constitute a *complete epistemology* of mathematical objects, but what it does do is erase any worry about the *possibility* of our acquiring knowledge of mathematical objects. Thus, since Benacerraf's argument is supposed to raise just such a worry, it seems to me that the bare claim of perceptibility completely undermines that argument.[22]

For this reason, I will entirely ignore Maddy's theory of mathematical intuition. That is, I concede that if she is right about the perceptibility of sets, then even if her entire theory of intuition is wrong, she has succeeded in explaining how we can acquire knowledge of sets: we can know about sets because we can see them. What I am going to do is attack the initial claim of perceptibility. (I should note, however, that while I will ignore the topic of intuition, I will, at the end of my argument, say a few words about why Maddy's appeal to pragmatic considerations cannot solve the problems that I raise for her view.)

5.1 Why Naturalized Platonists Have to Hang onto Platonism

One might be inclined to think that Maddy is not really a platonist at all. For since platonism is usually defined as a belief in abstract objects, and since, in this context, 'abstract' is ordinarily taken to be synonymous with 'non-spatiotemporal', there is a prima facie reason to categorize Maddy's view as a version of anti-platonism. The idea here, I suppose, is that to naturalize platonism by bringing abstract objects into spacetime is like naturalizing theism by taking God to be the Lincoln Tunnel. Thus, on this view, Maddy hasn't naturalized platonism at all — she's *abandoned* it.

At times, Maddy seems willing to go along with this. Thus, she writes: "On some terminological conventions, this means that sets no longer count as 'abstract'. So be it; I attach no importance to the term."[23] Now, of course, this sort of attitude is often acceptable. Questions about whether a view gets counted as xism or yism are usually not important; all that matters is whether the view in question is correct. But in this particular case, the question of whether Maddy's view is platonistic *is* important. There are two reasons for this. The first is operative only relative to our current project of seeking an answer to Benacerraf's challenge; that is, it's not important to Maddy's view, considered in itself. The reason is just this: what we are doing right now is looking for a solution to the epistemological problem with *platonism*; thus, if Maddy's view is a thoroughgoing anti-platonism (i.e., if there's no interesting sense of 'abstract' that applies to Maddian sets), then her view is of no interest to us at all. What we are currently trying to determine is whether there's any way that platonists can solve Benacerraf's problem by rejecting (2). Thus, if by rejecting (2) we ipso facto abandon platonism, then the answer to our question is "No", and we can move on.

Now, of course, this point is not relevant to the question of whether Maddy's view — considered in itself — is *correct*. But there is also a second reason why it matters whether Maddy's view is platonistic, and this reason *is* relevant to the question of whether her view is correct. The reason is simple. If Maddy were to endorse a thoroughgoing anti-platonism, that is, if she were to claim that sets are ordinary concrete objects, then her view would be essentially equivalent to the Millian view that sets are *aggregates of physical matter*.[24] But this aggregate theory of sets (ATS) is untenable, and what's more, Maddy knows it's untenable. She argues, following Frege, that sets could not be mere physical aggregates, because while a set has a determinate number of members, an aggregate of physical matter does not. For instance, if we have three eggs in a carton, then 3 is the only number that applies to the set of eggs, but the aggregate of egg-stuff consists of "three eggs, . . . many more molecules, [and] even more atoms".[25] Another problem with ATS (which Maddy doesn't mention) is that it is incapable of distinguishing the set containing the three eggs from the set containing this set. According to ATS, these two sets are identical with the same aggregate of egg-stuff, and so they are identical with each other. More generally, advocates of ATS — or at least the purely anti-platonistic version of ATS that maintains that *all* sets are physical aggregates — cannot countenance the existence of higher-rank sets, and so they cannot salvage the truth of hierarchical set theories like ZF.

The only way for naturalized platonists to avoid ATS is to maintain that while sets are not abstract in the *traditional* sense, that is, do not exist outside of space-time, they are nonetheless abstract in some non-traditional sense. Naturalized platonists need to maintain that each physical aggregate is associated with infinitely many sets. Our aggregate of egg-stuff, for instance, is associated with a set of atoms, a set of eggs, a set containing the set of eggs, a set containing the set containing the set of eggs, a pair containing these two singletons, and so on. But all of these sets are made of the exact same matter and have the exact same spatiotemporal location. Thus, in order to maintain that these sets really do differ from one another — and from the original physical aggregate — naturalized platonists have to claim that they differ from one another in *non-physical* ways and, hence, that there is something non-physical or abstract about them.[26]

Another way to appreciate this is to remember that the point of Maddy's naturalization program is to avoid the epistemic horn of Benacerraf's dilemma.

But if in the process of naturalizing, Maddy collapses into a thoroughgoing anti-platonism, that is, into ATS, then she has merely traded camps and thrown herself headlong toward the *semantic* horn of the dilemma. For as we have seen, if she takes this view, she will not be able to get off the ground floor of the set-theoretic hierarchy and, hence, will not be able to salvage the truth of hierarchical set theories like ZF. Thus, if Maddy's naturalization program is to have any hope of generating a tenable philosophy of mathematics, it has to be thought of as an attempt to locate a position *between* traditional platonism and ATS-anti-platonism. In other words, Maddy has to maintain that sets are neither traditional abstract objects (that is, non-spatiotemporal objects) nor ordinary concrete objects. That is, she has to maintain that while sets exist in spacetime, they are nonetheless abstract in some non-traditional sense.

I think that Maddy does do this. She claims that a singleton containing an egg is identical with the *egg-as-individuated-thing*.[27] Now, she doesn't say how this view is to be extended to pairs, triples, and so on, but presumably a pair of eggs would be identical with the *two-eggs-as-individuated-things-taken-together*, or something like that. Maddy's view, then, is that sets are distinct from their corresponding physical aggregates because they are *structured* differently. But since sets are made of the same matter as their aggregates, and since they share their locations with these aggregates, this structural difference must be a non-physical or abstract difference, and so it seems fair to conclude that Maddian sets are abstract in a certain non-traditional way. (Or to put the point in Maddy's own terms, while there are *some* terminological conventions on which Maddian sets aren't abstract, there are *other* terminological conventions on which they *are* abstract.)

But the particular sort of non-traditional abstractness that applies to *Maddian* sets is irrelevant here. For I am going to argue that human beings could not receive any relevant perceptual information from *any* kind of naturalized-platonist set. In other words, I will argue that as long as sets are abstract in *some* sense of the term — or, to be more precise, as long as they are abstract in a way that enables naturalized platonists to avoid ATS — human beings could not receive any relevant perceptual data from them.

5.2 *Problems for Naturalized Platonism*

Before giving the main argument of this subsection, it is worth noting that there are actually two views contained in Maddy's (early) writings on mathematics between which she remains neutral. The first, which Maddy calls *physicalistic platonism*, is the view that *all* sets are naturalized-platonist sets. The second, which we can call *hybrid platonism*, is the view that in addition to naturalized-platonist sets, there are also sets that are abstract in the traditional sense, that is, sets that exist outside of spacetime. Now, the non-spatiotemporal sets that are most important to hybrid platonism are the *pure* sets, that is, the sets built up from the null set.[28] For the idea behind hybrid platonism is to salvage the traditional platonist claim that set theories like ZF are about pure sets while still using an appeal to sense perception to solve the epistemological problem. The solution to the epistemological problem would, I think, go something like this: we acquire perceptual knowledge of naturalized-platonist sets, and then we proceed to knowledge of non-spatiotemporal sets—in particular, pure sets—via some sort of theoretical inference.

The distinction between hybrid platonism and physicalistic platonism will not really matter here. For if I can show that human beings cannot receive any relevant perceptual information from naturalized-platonist sets, then *both* of these views will be refuted. Nonetheless, I would like to point out here that hybrid platonists are worse off, epistemologically speaking, than physicalistic platonists are. For even if human beings could acquire perceptual knowledge of naturalized-platonist sets, it's hard to see how this could lead to knowledge of non-spatiotemporal sets. The whole point of Benacerraf's argument is that it's hard to see how knowledge of things in spacetime could lead to knowledge of things outside of spacetime. Thus, it seems that in claiming we can acquire perceptual knowledge of naturalized-platonist sets, hybrid platonists make no progress whatsoever in explaining how we could acquire knowledge of non-spatiotemporal sets. Indeed, they seem to be in no better shape than a traditional platonist who claims (misguidedly, I think) that we can acquire knowledge of sets via "some sort of theoretical inference" from perceptual knowledge of physical aggregates. Now, I suppose that hybrid platonists might claim that their inference is justified, while the inference of this misguided traditional platonist is not, because, unlike physical aggregates, their naturalized-platonist sets are *of the same kind* as non-spatiotemporal sets, or some such thing. But, of course, the Benacerrafian reply to this would be that unless we have some independent way of acquiring knowledge of non-spatiotemporal sets, we could not have any good reason to suppose that they are "of the same kind" as naturalized-platonist sets. We would have to allow that it *may* be that non-spatiotemporal sets are totally *different* in kind from naturalized-platonist sets.

In short, then, it seems to me that if the appeal to perceptibility is going to be of any help in connection with the epistemological argument, naturalized platonists are going to have to maintain that the sets we perceive are the very sets that set theory is about. Thus, from this epistemological point of view, it seems that naturalized platonists ought to favor physicalistic platonism over hybrid platonism. (Unfortunately for naturalized platonists, this creates something of a dilemma for their view, because there are other considerations that suggest hybrid platonism is superior to physicalistic platonism. For instance, once we bring the objects of mathematics into spacetime, we seem forced to make the counterintuitive claim that the truths of mathematics are subject to empirical falsification and, moreover, we seem to be left without a natural account of what certain mathematical objects are supposed to *be*—for instance, the null set, negative numbers, and real numbers.[29])

In any event, I now proceed to argue for the central thesis of this section, that is, the thesis that human beings cannot receive any relevant perceptual data from naturalized-platonist sets (i.e., sets that exist in spacetime but are nonetheless abstract in some non-traditional sense that makes them distinct from their corresponding physical aggregates). Now, it is pretty obvious that I can acquire perceptual knowledge of physical aggregates, but as we have seen, there is more to a naturalized-platonist set than there is to the aggregate with which it shares its location. There is something *abstract* about the set, over and above the aggregate, that distinguishes it not just from the aggregate but from the infinitely many other sets that share the same matter and location. Can I perceive this abstract component of the set? It seems that I cannot. For since the set and the aggregate are made of the same matter, both lead to the same retinal stimulation. Maddy herself admits this.[30] But if I receive only one retinal stimulation, then the perceptual data that I receive about the set are identical to the perceptual data that I receive about the aggregate. More generally, when I perceive an aggregate, I do not receive *any* data about *any* of the infinitely many corresponding naturalized-platonist sets that go beyond the data I receive about the aggregate. This means that naturalized platonists are no better off than traditional platonists, because we receive no more perceptual information about naturalized-platonist sets than we do about traditional non-spatiotemporal sets. Thus, the Benacerrafian worry still remains; there is still an unexplained epistemic gap between the information we receive in sense perception and the relevant facts about sets.[31]

How might Maddy respond to this argument? Well, there are two different responses suggested in her writings. The first is that the set/aggregate case is analogous to the psychologist's case in which we see one and the same picture first as a young woman and then, suddenly, as an old woman.[32] Maddy tries to back this up with a bit of neurophysiology, giving a scientific explanation for why we can, with the same retinal stimulation, sometimes see a set and sometimes see an aggregate. The explanation relies upon the notion of a *cell-assembly*. A cell-assembly is, basically, a neural recognizer: every time I recognize an object as a type-X object, it is because my X-cell-assembly is activated. (Thus, cell-assemblies correspond to concepts: I have one for horses, one for cars, one for circles, and so on. Moreover, the formation of a cell-assembly corresponds to the acquisition of a concept; after a lot of perceptual experience with objects of a given kind, a cell-assembly is formed in my brain and I acquire the corresponding concept.) In any event, Maddy's claim is that whether we see a set or an aggregate on a given occasion depends upon whether a set cell-assembly or an aggregate cell-assembly is activated.

To begin with, the set/aggregate case is simply not analogous to the case of the psychologist's picture, for in the former case, there are *two different objects*, whereas in the latter case, there are not. The picture of the old woman and the picture of the young woman are one and the same thing. What we're doing here is seeing one object in two different ways. Moreover, I do not think that the appeal to cell-assemblies is relevant to my objection. My claim is that we never receive any perceptual data from naturalized-platonist sets that go beyond the data we receive from aggregates. But this would still be true even if we *grant* that in response to these data, my brain has gone ahead and developed two different cell-assemblies, one for sets and one for aggregates, and that sometimes when I point my eyes at an aggregate, my set cell-assembly is activated.

The second response to my argument that's suggested in Maddy's writings is this: the fact that we can see a set, even when we only receive data from the corresponding aggregate, is analogous to the fact that we can see a physical object, even when we only receive data from the front side of a time slice of the object.[33]

One might try to respond here by arguing that this is simply a bad analogy; in particular, one might claim that since the front side of an egg is a *part of* that egg, it follows that seeing the front side of an egg involves seeing that egg, whereas this is not true in the set/aggregate case, because aggregates are not parts of sets in anything like the same way.[34] But it seems to me that this dispute is a terminological one: whether physical aggregates are *parts of* naturalized-platonist sets and whether we *see* such sets depends on how we define 'part of' and 'see'. The important point to note here is that even if we decide to say that we "see" naturalized-platonist sets, the fact remains that when we "see" them, we receive no more information about them than we receive about traditional-platonist sets when we see physical aggregates. Thus, all of this is irrelevant to my argument.

I conclude, then, that Maddy does not have a response to my argument. Moreover, I do not see any way for naturalized platonists to respond. The reason, in a nutshell, is that there seems to be an incompatibility between abstractness and perceptibility. Naturalized platonists need some sort of abstractness to account for the truth of theories like ZF and, hence, to avoid the semantic horn of Benacerraf's dilemma. But as soon as they let in any sort of abstractness, it becomes impossible for them to use an appeal to sense perception to avoid the epistemic horn of the dilemma. Thus, while Maddy's (early) view is in many ways ingenious, it is, I think, untenable.

5.3 *Extrinsic Modes of Justification*

In this sub-section, I would like to consider whether the naturalized platonist's situation is improved by Maddy's claim that mathematical axioms can be justified not only intrinsically (that is, via perception-based intuition) but also *extrinsically* (that is, via pragmatic considerations). Now, this is not the Quinean claim that mathematical theories can be justified by their usefulness in empirical science.[35] For Maddy, pragmatic reasons for accepting an axiom candidate can arise *within mathematics*. For instance, we might be inclined to accept a certain axiom candidate if it provided a solution to an open mathematical question.[36]

I do not wish to deny that axioms can be justified pragmatically. I merely want to point out that platonists cannot use this fact to respond to Benacerraf. I have two arguments here. The first is identical to the argument against using *proof* to respond to Benacerraf. Benacerraf's point is that if platonism were true, then we couldn't *get started* mathematically. Neither the method of proof nor that of (intra-mathematical) pragmatic justification is relevant to this point, because both of these modes of justification rely upon previous mathematical knowledge. (This is why Maddy also wants a faculty of intuition; but as we've seen, her appeal to such a faculty fails.) The second argument is that Maddy has said nothing to explain *why* pragmatic modes of justification are legitimate in mathematics (that is, why pragmatic considerations lead us to true rather than false mathematical beliefs). That such an explanation is needed is obvious: Benacerraf's argument can no more be answered by merely *asserting* that we can attain mathematical knowledge via pragmatic considerations than by asserting that we can attain mathematical knowledge via intuition. In both cases, the platonist has to say *how* we are led to mathematical truth.

This last point suggests a final argument against naturalized platonism: pragmatic modes of justification are legitimate in mathematics; naturalized platonists cannot account for this fact; therefore, their view is false. Now, in fairness to Maddy, I should note that she is quite aware that she needs an explanation here. But she claims that this problem is equally pressing for all philosophies of mathematics. Whether or not this is true, it is clearly a problem for all versions of *platonism*. For since platonists think that we should accept a mathematical sentence only if it corresponds to the objective mathematical facts, they have to explain how it could be legitimate to accept a sentence merely because it entailed a solution to some open problem. That is, they have to explain why pragmatic value is evidence for truth. (One might think that since pragmatic considerations are relevant to the construction of empirical as well as mathematical theories, this problem is no worse for mathematical platonists than it is for scientific realists. But the two cases are radically different: if an empirical hypothesis is pragmatically useful, we seek independent, *non-pragmatic* confirmation for it, and until such confirmation is obtained, the hypothesis is considered suspicious and ad hoc; but in mathematics, non-pragmatic support is not required.)

But while I agree with Maddy that this is a problem for all versions of platonism, I will argue in chapter 3, section 4, that *plenitudinous* platonists, that is, FBP-ists, can *solve* the problem. Thus, we really do have another argument against naturalized platonism here. In any event, I now conclude that naturalized platonism is an untenable view and, hence, that platonists cannot adequately respond to Benacerraf's challenge by rejecting (2).

6. Knowledge Without Contact

We have seen that mathematical platonists cannot solve the epistemological problem with their view by claiming that human beings are capable of coming into some sort of contact with (i.e., receiving information from) mathematical objects. Therefore, if platonists are to solve the epistemological problem, they must explain how human beings could acquire knowledge of mathematical objects without the aid of any contact with them. In other words, they have to explain how (3) could be false while (1) and (2) are true. In sub-sections 6.2–6.5, I will argue against four different explanations that platonists have offered here. (As far as I know, these four explanations are the only ones that have been suggested.) Then in chapter 3, I will develop my own explanation and argue that it is correct.[37]

Before I turn to all of this, however, I want to say a few words about the epistemological views of two no-contact platonists—Crispin Wright and Bob Hale[38]—who try to solve the epistemological problem with platonism *without* providing an explanation of how we could acquire knowledge of non-spatiotemporal objects. I do not think this can be done, and I think it is worth taking the time to undermine these two views.

6.1 Platonism for Cheap?: Wright and Hale

Wright begins by asking us to consider the following flawed platonist stance: "We can acquire knowledge of sentences about abstract objects by finding sentences that have the same truth conditions but which *aren't* about abstract objects. For instance, we can acquire knowledge of

(D) The direction of line a is identical to the direction of line b

by noticing that it has the same truth conditions as

(L) Line a is parallel to line b,

which is not about abstract objects and, hence, epistemically unproblematic." The problem with this explanation, according to Wright, is that if (D) and (L) really have the same truth conditions, and if (D) is really about abstract objects, then (L) must also be about abstract objects. Nonetheless, Wright thinks that platonists have here the basis of an adequate response to the Benacerrafian challenge. For he argues that even if we admit that (L) is about abstract objects, we do not have to admit that it is epistemically problematic. His attitude seems to be that knowledge of (L) seems unproblematic *in advance* and that the discovery that (L) is tacitly about abstract objects ought to be taken as showing not that knowledge of (L) is really problematic after all, but that knowledge of abstract objects is sometimes unproblematic.

Wright's position here can be quickly refuted. The fact that knowledge of (L) seems unproblematic is entirely irrelevant in the present context. Indeed, while we're at it, we might as well point out that knowledge of (D) seems unproblematic as well and, for that matter, that most mathematical knowledge — for instance, knowledge that 3 is prime — seems unproblematic. Anti-platonists do not want to claim that there is a problem with our mathematical knowledge. Their point is, rather, that *if* such knowledge were about abstract objects, then it *would* be problematic. Thus, what platonists need to do, in order to respond to this, is explain why our mathematical knowledge *wouldn't* be problematic, even if it *were* about abstract objects. That is, they need to explain how our unproblematic mathematical knowledge could be knowledge of abstract objects. For the Benacerrafian point is that without such an explanation, we have reason to suspect that this unproblematic knowledge really *isn't* knowledge of abstract objects. It seems to me, then, that Wright has said absolutely nothing to answer the Benacerrafian challenge: he has merely asserted the truism that knowledge of lines is unproblematic, whereas what he needs to do is explain *how it could be* that the unproblematic knowledge that we have here could be knowledge of non-spatiotemporal objects.

Wright seems to allow for the possibility of a response along these lines, but his rhetoric makes the response seem extremely implausible, as if it were the last desperate attempt to salvage an uncompromising and, in his words, "obdurate" nominalism.[39] In fact, however, the response is nothing but a reiteration of the original epistemological argument against platonism, together with the observation that Wright has said nothing to answer that argument. (Wright responds to this "obdurate nominalism" by attacking CTK; but we've already seen that this is unhelpful, that platonists need to address *CTK-free* versions of the epistemological argument.)

Hale's epistemological stance is very similar to Wright's. Like Wright, he places a good deal of significance upon his ability to perform the negative task of refuting CTK and shirks the responsibility of performing the positive task of explaining how we could acquire knowledge of abstract mathematical objects. Moreover, Hale tries to motivate this stance in a similar way: whereas Wright motivates it by appealing to the initial plausibility of the claim that we have knowledge of things like lines, Hale motivates it by appealing to the initial plausibility of the claim that mathematical knowledge is a priori knowledge, that is, knowledge of conceptual linkages. He says that this conception of mathematical knowledge "has considerable initial plausibility, quite independently of any prior attachment to any platonistic interpretation of" what this knowledge is about and, indeed, that this conception of mathematical knowledge is "sufficiently plausible for positive supporting argument to be unnecessary".[40]

The problem with Hale's view is similar to the problem with Wright's view. The problem is that anti-platonists can *admit* that mathematical knowledge is a priori and simply maintain that we cannot take this knowledge to be knowledge of abstract mathematical objects unless platonists can provide an explanation of how we could acquire knowledge of such objects despite our lack of contact with them. And it is worth noting that when Hale points out that the a priorist conception of mathematical knowledge is independent of platonism — that is, that it's consistent with anti-platonism — he already admits that anti-platonists can make this move.[41]

6.2 No-Contact Mathematical Intuition: Parsons, Katz, Steiner, and Others

Several contemporary platonists seem to think that progress can be made toward explaining how we could acquire knowledge of mathematical objects by adopting what might be called the *no-contact theory of intuition* (NCTI). The view here is that we possess a psychological apparatus whose only ultimate sources of information are the naturalistic sources of perception and introspection, but that nevertheless generates intuitive beliefs and thoughts about mathematical objects (or structures or patterns). Since this faculty of mind is not based upon any sort of informational access to mathematical objects, we can call it a faculty of no-contact mathematical intuition. Advocates of NCTI include Charles Parsons, Jerrold Katz, and Mark Steiner, among others.[42] Moreover, there are a number of platonists, such as Michael Resnik and Stewart Shapiro,[43] who seem to dislike the *word* 'intuition' but endorse views that are more or less equivalent to what I am calling NCTI.[44]

Now, depending on which of these philosophers we read, we will get a different version of NCTI, that is, a different theory of the "inner workings" of the faculty of no-contact intuition. Parsons's theory, for instance, plays off the type-token distinction: he claims that in perceiving concrete tokens, we sometimes have intuitions of the corresponding types, which of course, are abstract objects. A related view—developed by Steiner and, in a slightly different lingo, by Resnik and Shapiro—is that intuition is based upon *abstraction*: we see a collection of physical objects, and we abstract away from their physical properties until we arrive at a mathematical intuition or belief about, for instance, the set or pattern that the objects exemplify. Another popular move is to model the theory of no-contact intuition after Kant's theory of a priori knowledge and pure intuition. This line has been pursued by Parsons and developed very thoroughly by Katz, who thinks of intuition as a process of constructing internal representations of objective abstract entities.[45]

I am not going to describe any of these versions of NCTI in detail, because the details of these views are irrelevant to what I want to say about NCTI. What I want to argue is that NCTI does no epistemological work for platonists, that is, does nothing to explain how human beings could acquire knowledge of mathematical objects despite their lack of contact with such objects. The first thing to note in this connection is that platonists cannot solve the epistemological problem with their view by merely asserting that we acquire knowledge of mathematical objects via the faculty of no-contact intuition. Before this stance could be acceptable, platonists would have to explain how this faculty of intuition could be *reliable*, given that it's a *no-contact* faculty. After all, without such an explanation, we would have no reason to think that no-contact intuitions could lead to *knowledge*. But to explain how the faculty that generates our mathematical intuitions and beliefs could be reliable, despite the fact that it's a no-contact faculty, is not significantly different from explaining how we could acquire knowledge of mathematical objects, despite the fact that we do not have any contact with such objects. Thus, by appealing to NCTI, platonists make no progress whatsoever toward solving the epistemological problem with their view.

Now, in defense of NCTI-platonists, I should note that almost all of them *admit* that they owe an explanation of how our no-contact mathematical intuitions and beliefs could be reliable (and as we will see in the next few sections, they go on to attempt such explanations).[46] But nevertheless, I think they would all dispute my claim that the appeal to NCTI is epistemologically unhelpful, that it merely puts the problem into different words. But if they would dispute this claim, then the question arises: "How, exactly, is NCTI supposed to help?" I can think of two different ways in which one might respond to this question. First, one might maintain that NCTI is important, because platonists have been challenged to explain not just how human beings could acquire *knowledge* of mathematical objects, but also how they could acquire *beliefs* about such objects. The idea here is that NCTI can be used to account for the latter, but that, in order to account for the former, platonists need to supplement NCTI with an explanation of reliability. Second, one might claim that by spelling out the details of the faculty of no-contact intuition, we can actually make some progress toward explaining why this faculty is *reliable*, because we can show that it operates in an epistemically praiseworthy way.

This second suggestion can be dispensed with very quickly. Once we acknowledge that the faculty of intuition is a no-contact faculty, that is, that it generates intuitions "blindly", so to speak (i.e., without "checking its work against the math-ematical facts"), it seems pretty clear that from an epistemological point of view, it doesn't matter *how* the faculty of intuition operates. It may as well be a process of *creative writing* or *dreaming up*, instead of anything so respectable-sounding as abstraction. Indeed, we will see in chapter 3 that knowledge of mathematical objects *could* be based upon a process of dreaming up.

As for the first suggestion, I submit that platonists *cannot* use an appeal to NCTI to solve the worry that people have had about the possibility of our having beliefs about mathematical objects. The reason can be appreciated by noticing that there are multiple senses of the term 'about'. In some senses of the term, a belief state can only be about an object to which it is "connected" in an appro-priate sort of way, whereas according to other senses of the term, there is no such requirement. Indeed, according to some senses of the term, a belief state can be said to be "about" something that doesn't even exist; for example, a little girl's belief that Santa Claus is fat can be said to be "about Santa Claus" even though, in point of actual fact, there is no such person as Santa Claus. We might say that the girl's belief is *thinly about* Santa Claus to emphasize that we are using the term in a metaphysically thin sense.[47]

Now, no one doubts that human beings could have beliefs that are thinly about mathematical objects. Indeed, the existence of a single mathematical pla-tonist establishes this, for in such a person, we have someone who wholeheartedly believes that there are abstract mathematical objects (e.g., the number 3) and that these objects have certain properties (e.g., primeness). Now, of course, it may be that there are no such things as mathematical objects and, hence, that there is nothing "out there in the world" corresponding to our platonist's beliefs, but this does not change the fact human beings are capable of arriving at beliefs that are thinly about mathematical objects. It seems, then, that when people express doubts about the possibility of our acquiring beliefs about mathematical objects, they are clearly thinking of a metaphysically *thick* sort of aboutness: the worry is that there is no way for our beliefs to be "connected" to abstract objects in an appropriate sort of way. And, of course, the driving force behind this worry is precisely that our mathematical beliefs are *no-contact* beliefs. It therefore seems that no amount of elaboration on the faculty of no-contact intuition could help to ease this worry. By merely giving the psychological and/or neurological details of how we manage to generate no-contact mathematical intuitions and beliefs, we do nothing to ease the worry that because these intuitions and beliefs are no-contact intuitions and beliefs, they could not be *about* anything outside of spacetime.

Now, I suppose that NCTI-platonists might respond here by claiming that, on their view, the faculty of no-contact intuition provides us with beliefs and intuitions that are about mathematical objects in an appropriately thick sense of the term. But in order to motivate this claim, NCTI-platonists would have to explain *how this is possible*, given that we are talking here about a faculty of *no-contact* intuition. But this is not significantly different from what platonists need to do to solve the original problem of belief; that is, it's not significantly different from explaining how our mathematical beliefs could be appropriately about ab-stract mathematical objects, given that we do not have any contact with such objects. Therefore, NCTI is no more helpful with the problem of belief than it is with the problem of knowledge.[48]

Now, I would like to emphasize here that to argue that NCTI is epistemologically unhelpful is not to argue that it's false. Indeed, it seems to me that if we understand NCTI as the view that human beings are capable of arriving at no-contact-intuitions and beliefs that are *thinly* about mathematical objects, then the view is not only true but trivially true. For we've already seen that the existence of a single mathematical platonist establishes that human beings are capable of arriving at beliefs that are thinly about mathematical objects, and there doesn't seem to be any reason why we can't say that some of these beliefs are intuitions. Thus, as long as we reject the idea that human beings are capable of coming into contact with mathematical objects, it seems that NCTI, understood in this weak way, is clearly true.[49] Therefore, I think it's fair to say that there is nothing *problematic* about the appeal to NCTI. Indeed, one might consider it somewhat illuminating, since it provides an alternative way of formulating the epistemological challenge to platonism. But in any event, let us move on now and consider some more attempts to answer this challenge.

6.3 Holism and Empirical Confirmation: Quine, Steiner, and Resnik

A second attempt to explain how we can acquire knowledge of mathematical objects despite our lack of contact with them is hinted at by Quine and developed by Steiner and Resnik.[50] The claim here is that we have good reason to believe that our mathematical theories are true, because (a) these theories are central to our overall worldview, and (b) this worldview has been repeatedly confirmed. In other words, we don't need contact with mathematical objects in order to know that our theories of these objects are true, because *confirmation is holistic,* and so these theories are confirmed every day, along with the rest of our overall worldview.

The problem with this view is that confirmation holism is, in fact, false. Confirmation may well be holistic with respect to the *nominalistic* parts of our empirical theories, but the mathematical parts of our empirical theories are *not* confirmed by empirical findings. Indeed, empirical findings provide no reason whatsoever for supposing that the mathematical parts of our empirical theories are true. I will argue this point in chapter 7 by arguing that the nominalistic contents of our empirical theories could be true even if their platonistic contents are fictional.

But even without an argument for the claim that mathematical theories cannot be empirically confirmed, it is easy to see that platonists cannot solve the epistemological problem in the above Quinean manner. The reason is that mathematicians know that their theories are true *when they first construct them,* that is, before they're used in applications, and platonists need to provide an explanation of this fact. The point, of course, is that what's needed here is an explanation of the sort that we needed to begin with, that is, an explanation of how human beings could acquire knowledge of abstract mathematical objects despite their lack of contact with such objects. Thus, the Quinean appeal to applications hasn't helped at all — platonists are right back where they started.

That mathematicians really do know that their theories are true before they're used in applications is so obvious that it hardly requires argument.[51] But for whatever it's worth, here is an argument for that claim. If we didn't have knowledge of unapplied mathematical theories, then the process of constructing a mathematical theory would be a process of making a *stab in the dark*. That is, it would be a process of elimination: mathematicians would have to construct their theories and then wait and see which ones got applied and confirmed. (This is simply because working mathematicians wouldn't have any other way of proceeding; they wouldn't have any way of knowing whether their theories were true *while they were working*.) But it is obvious that mathematical theory construction is *not* a process of elimination, because mathematical theories almost always turn out true. In short, if we didn't have knowledge of unapplied mathematics, we would expect almost all mathematical theories that get applied to prove false; but in fact, the opposite is true.[52]

(In defense of Resnik, I should say that he seems to acknowledge the point I am making here, and as we will see in sub-section 6.5, he goes on to try to provide an explanation of how we might acquire knowledge of unapplied mathematical theories. As for Steiner, though, he seems to think that the *only* justification we have for our mathematical theories is an after-the-fact empirical justification. Now, we saw in sub-section 6.2 that he appeals to mathematical intuition, in addition to confirmation holism, but his purpose in doing this is to account for the *genesis* of our mathematical beliefs, not their justification.)

6.4 Necessity: Katz and Lewis

We now come to an explanation of why knowledge of abstract objects doesn't require contact with such objects that is, initially, more promising. Katz claims that a faculty of no-contact intuition can engender knowledge of mathematical objects, because the beliefs produced by this faculty are *necessarily* true. The reason we need contact with (i.e., perception of) the objects of our empirical knowledge is that these objects could have been different. Thus, for instance, we have to look at a fire engine in order to know that it is red, because it could have been blue, that is, it is only contingently red. The situation with respect to mathematical knowledge, however, is not the same. We don't need any contact with the number 4, for instance, in order to know that it is the sum of two primes, because it is necessarily the sum of two primes, that is, it could not have been otherwise. As Katz puts it:

> if we construct a sufficiently articulated concept of the number four in intuition,
> we will be able to see that the concept is a concept of an object that is the sum
> of two primes.[53]

David Lewis has given a very similar argument. He claims that in order for our beliefs about contingent matters to be of any epistemic worth, they must depend counterfactually upon the facts that they correspond to. This is why we demand that such beliefs be based, epistemically, upon some sort of contact with the objects that they are about. But Lewis claims that we cannot demand such contact in the case of beliefs concerning necessities, because we cannot demand that such beliefs depend counterfactually upon the facts that they correspond to. The reason is that the counterfactuals in these cases simply don't make any sense. Lewis puts it like this:

> nothing can depend counterfactually on non-contingent matters. For instance nothing can depend counterfactually on what mathematical objects there are. . . . Nothing sensible can be said about how our opinions would be different if there were no number seventeen.[54]

Field has offered several objections to this appeal to necessity. The most important of these objections, in my view, is this: even if we cannot demand that platonists explain how our mathematical beliefs would be different if the mathematical facts were different, "there is still a problem of explaining the *actual* correlation between our" mathematical beliefs and the mathematical facts.[55] In other words, even if mathematical truths are necessarily true, Katz and Lewis need to explain *how we know* that they're true. And this is no trivial matter: if S is some conjecture about the natural numbers that's undecidable in our best axiomatic theories, then I might know that either S or $\sim$S is necessarily true, but this doesn't help me decide which is true and which is false.

The same basic objection can be formulated a bit differently, and a bit more graphically, in Katzian terms. Katz claims that once we've constructed our concept of 4 in intuition, we can see that 4 *must* be the sum of two primes. But there is an obvious problem with this: Katz needs to explain how we could know how to construct the concept of 4 in the first place. Anti-platonists can admit that *if* we have some initial knowledge of 4, then we can know that it is the sum of two primes; but they will demand that platonists explain how we get this initial knowledge of the number 4. This, I believe, is what Field is getting at when he asks for an account of the *actual* correlation between our mathematical beliefs and the mathematical facts. In Katz's terms, what we need is an account of the actual correlation between the number 4 and our representation of the number 4, that is, an account of how human beings could know what to do when they construct their representations of mathematical objects. And this problem ought to seem ominous; it ought to seem that human beings could no more know how to proceed in constructing their representations of mathematical objects than a sculptor could know how to proceed in constructing a statue of a man whom she had never seen nor felt nor heard about.

Katz–Lewis platonists might try to respond here as follows: "The information contained in our representation of the number 4 is merely that 4 is the successor of 3. Thus, in asking how we know how to construct our representation of 4, what is really being asked is how we know that 4 is the successor of 3. But the answer to *this* question is obvious: this is simply the *definition* of the term '4'."

The point of such a response, I suppose, would be to suggest that the construction of representations of mathematical objects is actually a very trivial thing, that is, that it is not at all problematic. But nothing of the sort has been established. Platonists can claim that the term '4' is just an abbreviation for the term 'successor of 3', but what anti-platonists will demand is an explanation of how we could know that there is an object in the mathematical realm that *answers* to this description. In other words: it's very easy to give definitions of mathematical singular terms like '4', but it's not so easy to see how we could know which terms and definitions actually refer to something.

It is important that this response not be misunderstood. Anti-platonists are not demanding here an account of how human beings could know that there exist any mathematical objects at all. That, I think, would be an illegitimate skeptical demand. (I will explain why this is so in chapter 3, in connection with my own platonist epistemology.) All we can demand from platonists is an account of how human beings could know the *nature* of mathematical objects, *given* that such objects exist. But when anti-platonists demand an account of how we could know that there are objects answering to our mathematical definitions, they mean to be making a demand of this latter sort. The point might be put as follows: "Even if we assume that there *are* mathematical objects, we cannot assume that *any* definite description we come up with—for instance, 'the successor of 3'—will actually pick out an object. Thus, platonists have to explain how we could know *which* of the infinitely many possible descriptions and singular terms actually refer."

The anti-platonist who makes this last remark has overlooked a move that Katz–Lewis platonists can make: they can say that, in fact, we *can* assume that any mathematical definite description we come up with will actually pick out an object (or more precisely, that all mathematical descriptions that are *internally consistent* actually refer). Platonists can motivate this claim by adopting FBP. For if all the mathematical objects that possibly *could* exist actually *do* exist, as FBP dictates, then all (consistent) mathematical descriptions and singular terms will refer, and any (consistent) representation of a mathematical object that someone could construct will be an *accurate* representation of an actually existing mathematical object. Thus, it looks like the objection to the Katz–Lewis view has been answered.

Now, at this point, a number of objections might be raised, for instance, objections having to do with the tenability of FBP and the legitimacy of platonists adopting it here, that is, assuming that it is true. But I want to put these objections on hold for now. I will return to them in chapter 3, where I argue that FBP is the best version of platonism there is—that, in fact, there are *no* good objections to it—and that once we adopt this view, it becomes very easy to solve the epistemological problem, that is, to explain how human beings could acquire knowledge of mathematical objects without any contact with them. What I want to do now is say a few more words about the Katz–Lewis necessity-based epistemology.

The main thing I want to point out here is that we should not think of the appeal to FBP as showing that the necessity-based epistemology can be made to work. It would be more accurate to say that what is going on in the paragraph before last is that we are *replacing* the necessity-based epistemology with an FBP-based epistemology. More precisely, the point is that once platonists appeal to FBP, there is no more reason to appeal to necessity at all. (This point is already implicit in the above remarks, but it will become very clear in chapter 3 when I develop an FBP-based epistemology that doesn't depend upon any claims about the necessity of mathematical truths.) The upshot of this is that the appeal to necessity isn't doing any epistemological work at all; FBP is doing all the work. Moreover, for the reasons already given, the necessity-based epistemology cannot be made to work *without* falling back on the appeal to FBP. Thus, the appeal to necessity seems to be simply out of place when it is used for epistemological reasons, that is, when it is used as a means of responding to Benacerraf and explaining how human beings could acquire knowledge of mathematical objects.

Now, in fairness to Katz and Lewis, I should point out that, unlike most platonists (e.g., Quine, Steiner, Maddy, and Gödel), it seems likely that both Katz and Lewis *are* FBP-ists. Neither of them ever explicitly admits this, nor even raises the question, but it seems to me that the writings of these two philosophers suggest they both believe that all the mathematical objects that possibly could exist actually do exist. Thus, in contrast to the views of people like Quine, Steiner, Maddy, and Gödel, there's a sense in which the views of Katz and Lewis *work*. But, nevertheless, it's clear that the epistemological remarks of Katz and Lewis are unsatisfactory and that they do not have an adequate response to the Benacerrafian challenge. For they both need to rely upon FBP, but neither acknowledges this and, more important, neither deals with the *objections* that a reliance upon FBP naturally leads to.

Before going on, I would like to point out that there is another problem with the Katz–Lewis view, a problem that I have not yet remarked upon. We saw above that the appeal to necessity is of no epistemological help to platonists. But I now want to argue that this appeal is actually *harmful*. The reason is that it is doubtful that our mathematical theories are necessary in any interesting sense. To begin with, it is pretty obvious that they aren't logically or conceptually necessary, because the existence claims of mathematics—for example, 'There exists a number between 5 and 7' and the null set axiom—are neither logically nor conceptually true.[56] Now, Katz–Lewis platonists might respond here by granting this point and claiming that our mathematical theories are *metaphysically* necessary. But it's hard to see how they could justify this stance. They might claim that sentences like '2 + 2 = 4' and '7 > 5' are metaphysically necessary for the same reason that, say, 'Cicero is Tully' is metaphysically necessary—because they are true in all worlds in which their singular terms denote, or something like that—but this doesn't help at all in connection with existence claims like the null set axiom. We can't claim that the null set axiom is metaphysically necessary for anything *like* the reason that 'Cicero is Tully' is metaphysically necessary. If we tried to do this, we would end up saying that 'There exists an empty set' is metaphysically necessary, because it is true in all worlds in which there exists an empty set. But of course, this is completely unacceptable, because it suggests that *all* existence claims—for instance, 'There exists a purple hula hoop'—are metaphysically necessary.

The problem here is that we just don't have any well-motivated account of what metaphysical necessity consists in. Now, I suppose that Katz–Lewis platonists *might* be able to cook up an intuitively pleasing definition that clearly entails that the existence claims of mathematics—and, indeed, all purely mathematical truths—are metaphysically necessary. If they could do this, then their claim that mathematical truths are necessary would be innocuous after all. But (a) for the reasons given above, the claim would still be epistemologically useless, and (b) it seems highly unlikely (to me, anyway) that Katz–Lewis platonists could really produce an adequate definition of metaphysical necessity. It just doesn't seem to me that there is any interesting sense in which 'There exists an empty set' is necessary but 'There exists a purple hula hoop' is not.

6.5 Structuralism: Resnik and Shapiro

Finally, we come to the structuralists, Resnik and Shapiro. Both of these philosophers make a number of different points in response to the epistemological problem. For instance, they both appeal to our capacities for abstraction and pattern recognition in an effort to develop a theory of how we arrive at no-contact mathematical beliefs and intuitions. And Resnik, if not Shapiro, appeals to confirmation holism in an effort to provide some justification for our mathematical theories. But these remarks can be handled along the lines of sub-sections 6.2 and 6.3, respectively. The strategy of response that I want to discuss here is, initially, more promising.

In recent books, Resnik and Shapiro both claim that we can acquire knowledge of mathematical structures by constructing axiom systems, because such systems provide *implicit definitions* of structures.[57] I want to respond to this suggestion in the same way that I responded to the Katz–Lewis appeal to necessity. We saw in sub-section 6.4 that in order to make their view work, Katz and Lewis would have to claim that our initial, bottom-level mathematical knowledge is knowledge of simple definitions. The example I used was that we can know that 4 is the successor of 3, because 'successor of 3' is just the definition of '4'. Thus, it seems to me that the Katz–Lewis strategy collapses into the Resnik-Shapiro strategy, and what's more important in the present context, the response I gave to Katz and Lewis can be given again to Resnik and Shapiro. Putting this response into the lingo that Resnik and Shapiro use, the problem is that prima facie, it seems that platonists cannot claim that we can acquire knowledge of abstract mathematical structures by merely formulating axiom systems that implicitly define such structures, because in making this claim, nothing is said about how we can know which of the various axiom systems that we might formulate actually pick out structures that exist in the mathematical realm.

Now, as was the case with Katz and Lewis, if Resnik and Shapiro adopt FBP, or rather, a structuralist version of FBP, then this problem can be solved. For it follows from (structuralist versions of) FBP that *any* consistent purely mathematical axiom system we formulate will pick out a structure in the mathematical realm. Now, in discussing Katz and Lewis, I remarked in this connection that their responses to the epistemological problem are unacceptable, because — or partly because — they fail to acknowledge that they need to appeal to FBP here. The same thing is true of Resnik and Shapiro, although I should say that there is something more satisfying about their discussions of the epistemological problem; for while neither of them notices the above problem or appeals to FBP to solve it, they both come close to committing to the thesis that every consistent (or in Shapiro's terms, *coherent* — more on this in a moment) purely mathematical axiom system implicitly defines an actually existing structure. (Neither of them explicitly endorses this thesis, but they both seem to flirt with it.[58]) But in any event, even if Resnik and Shapiro do endorse this thesis, neither of them ever says why he is *entitled* to it. Moreover, it seems to me that the only way to motivate this thesis is to endorse FBP, or rather, a structuralist version of FBP. Thus, Resnik and Shapiro do need to rely upon some version of FBP, but neither of them acknowledges this. And since they fail to recognize that they need to rely upon FBP, they fail to *defend* the reliance upon FBP and, hence, leave large holes in their arguments. Moreover, the clarity of their epistemological remarks is significantly reduced by the inability to recognize and lay bare the ontological commitments of those remarks. We will see in chapter 3 that by bringing FBP into the open and making full use of its explanatory resources, platonists can give a much clearer and stronger and more plausible response to the epistemological argument.

In addition to all of this, I think there is also a problem with the notion of consistency in Resnik's argument and the corresponding notion of coherence in Shapiro's argument. As Shapiro sets things up, the notion of coherence is essentially equivalent to the notion of satisfiability. This means that coherence is a model-theoretic and, hence, *platonistic* notion. Thus, knowledge of coherence is just as problematic for Shapiro as knowledge of truth is. Therefore, since Shapiro's account of how we can know that our mathematical theories are true rests upon the assumption that we can know that these theories are coherent, no real progress has been made. The same problem arises in connection with Resnik's notion of consistency. When he says (or seems to say) that all consistent purely mathematical theories characterize some structure, he seems to have in mind syntactic, or deductive, consistency. (Actually, Resnik seems to want to concentrate on first-order theories, so for him, deductive consistency and satisfiability will be coextensive.) But insofar as derivations are abstract objects (in particular, ordered sets of sentence types), deductive consistency is, like satisfiability, a platonistic notion. Thus, Resnik is going to encounter the same problem that Shapiro encounters.

I end with a digression on structuralism. I said above that neither Resnik nor Shapiro says why he is entitled to the thesis that every consistent purely mathematical theory characterizes a structure. But I think it is clear that if we asked them, they would both say that this thesis is *built into structuralism*. This, I think, is false: one could endorse a non-plenitudinous or non-full-blooded version of structuralism that contradicted this thesis. Thus, it is FBP and not structuralism that delivers the result that Resnik and Shapiro need. I think this is a pretty general phenomenon: Resnik and Shapiro seem to think that structuralism does a lot more work for them than it really does. The present discussion provides one example of this: structuralism is irrelevant to the implicit-definition strategy of responding to the epistemological problem, because one can claim that axiom systems provide implicit definitions of collections of mathematical objects as easily as one can claim that they provide implicit definitions of structures. What one needs, in order to make this strategy work, is FBP, not structuralism. The same goes for the Resnik-Shapiro appeal to pattern recognition: one can claim that the psychological mechanisms responsible for the genesis of our mathematical beliefs and intuitions are related in various ways to pattern recognition without endorsing structuralism, that is, while hanging onto object-platonism.[59] Indeed, I think similar remarks can be made about everything Resnik and Shapiro say about the epistemology of mathematics: despite their rhetoric, structuralism just doesn't play an essential role in any of their arguments. Thus, I think it is fair to conclude that by adopting structuralism, platonists cannot gain any ground with respect to the epistemological problem. Moreover, we will see in chapter 4 that the same thing is true of the other important traditional problem with platonism, that is, the multiple-reductions problem.

A New Platonist Epistemology

1. Introduction

In chapter 2, I argued that in order to salvage their view, mathematical platonists have to explain how human beings can acquire knowledge of abstract mathematical objects, given that they are not capable of coming into any sort of *contact* with such objects, that is, receiving any *information* from such objects. In this chapter, I will explain how platonists can do this. In effect, I will be providing an epistemology of abstract objects, although I should say that it will not be a *complete* epistemology. I will only say enough to (a) motivate the claim that spatiotemporal creatures like ourselves *can* acquire knowledge of non-spatiotemporal mathematical objects and (b) provide a rough sketch of how this works. In short, I will provide enough of an epistemology to block the Benacerrafian epistemological objection to platonism, but I will not do any more than this; I will not go into any of the details of the epistemology that are irrelevant to the question of whether Benacerraf's objection can be answered.

2. Skeleton of the Refutation of the Epistemological Argument

What I want to argue is that if we adopt plenitudinous platonism — that is, the view I have been calling FBP[1] — we can very easily explain how human beings could acquire knowledge of abstract mathematical objects. My argument here is going to be rather long and complicated, but the intuitive line of thought is quite simple. If FBP is correct, then all consistent purely mathematical theories truly describe some collection of abstract mathematical objects. Thus, to acquire knowledge of mathematical objects, all we need to do is acquire knowledge that some purely mathematical theory is *consistent*. (It doesn't matter how we come up with the theory; some creative mathematician might simply "dream it up".) But knowledge of the consistency of a mathematical theory — or any *other* kind of theory, for that matter—does not require any sort of contact with, or access to, the objects that the theory is about. Thus, the Benacerrafian objection has been answered: we can acquire knowledge of abstract mathematical objects *without* the aid of any sort of contact with such objects.

I can formulate this as a direct response to an argument of Field's. He once wrote as follows:

> But special 'reliability relations' between the mathematical realm and the belief states of mathematicians seem altogether too much to swallow. It is rather as if someone claimed that his or her belief states about the daily happenings in a remote village in Nepal were nearly all disquotationally true, despite the absence of any mechanism to explain the correlation between those belief states and the happenings in the village.[2]

Now, I admit that I could not have knowledge of a Nepalese village without any access to it. But if all possible Nepalese villages existed, then I *could* have knowledge of these villages, even without any access to them. To attain such knowledge, I would merely have to dream up a possible Nepalese village. For on the assumption that all possible Nepalese villages exist, it would follow that the village I have imagined exists and that my beliefs about this village correspond to the facts about it. Now, of course, it is not the case that all possible Nepalese villages exist, and so we cannot attain knowledge of them in this way. But according to FBP, all possible mathematical objects do exist. Therefore, if we adopt FBP, we can also adopt this sort of epistemology for mathematical objects.

Now, of course, in order to motivate this line of thought, I'm going to have to provide a good deal of supporting argument and also clarify a few key terms, most notably, 'consistent' and 'logically possible'. But before I do any of this, I want to address an objection that may have already occurred to the reader. One might put the worry like this. "Your account of how we could acquire knowledge of mathematical objects seems to assume that we are capable of *thinking about* mathematical objects, or *dreaming up stories about* such objects, or *formulating theories about* them. But it is simply not clear how we could do these things. After all, platonists need to explain not just how we could acquire *knowledge* of mathematical objects, but also how we could do things like have *beliefs* about mathematical objects and *refer* to mathematical objects."

To appreciate my response to this worry, we need to recall the distinction I made in chapter 2 between metaphysically *thin* senses of 'about' and metaphysically *thick* senses of that term. To have a belief that is *thickly* about an object x, one must be "connected" to x in some appropriate way, whereas to have a belief that is *thinly* about x, one needn't be "connected" to it in any non-trivial way. Indeed, on the thin sense of 'about', there needn't even be any such thing as x; for instance, we can say that a little girl's belief that Santa Claus is fat is (thinly) about Santa Claus, despite the fact that there is really no such person as Santa Claus. Now, if there are any worries about how human beings could have beliefs about mathematical objects, or how they could dream up stories about such objects, then these worries are surely based upon the thick sense of 'about'. No one doubts that we could formulate beliefs and theories that are thinly about mathematical objects. But my account of knowledge of mathematical objects is going to be based solely upon the claim that we can formulate beliefs and theories that are thinly about mathematical objects. I am going to argue that if FBP is true, then we can acquire knowledge of mathematical objects by merely formulating consistent beliefs and theories that are thinly about such objects, because, according to FBP, *all* consistent purely mathematical theories truly describe some collection of mathematical objects.

One might object as follows. "You may be right that if FBP is true, then all consistent purely mathematical theories truly describe *some* collection of mathematical objects, or *some* part of the mathematical realm. But *which* part? How do we know that it will be true of the part of the mathematical realm that its authors intended to characterize? Indeed, it seems mistaken to think that such theories will characterize *unique* parts of the mathematical realm at all. This, of course, is just the point of Benacerraf's other important paper, 'What Numbers Could Not Be'[3]: since all consistent purely mathematical theories (including those that are categorical[4]) have multiple models, it seems that platonists are committed to the thesis that such theories fail to pick out unique collections of mathematical objects."

I am going to discuss this non-uniqueness objection at length in chapter 4. But I want to say just a few words about this here in order to ease the worry that considerations of this sort can be used to block the response that I want to give to the epistemological argument. What I am going to argue in chapter 4 is that non-uniqueness is simply not a problem for platonists; that is, I am going to *embrace* non-uniqueness. Thus, in connection with the epistemological problem, the point is this: if I know that some theory truly describes part of the mathematical realm, then I have knowledge of that realm, regardless of whether it describes a unique part of that realm, and regardless of whether it is "about" some collection of mathematical objects in a metaphysically thick sense of the term. And as for the intentions of the authors, there are two things I want to say. First of all, they too are irrelevant: if a mathematical theory truly describes part of the mathematical realm, then I can attain knowledge of the mathematical realm by studying that theory, regardless of what its authors had in mind. Second of all, I simply deny that the "intentions" that we have in mathematical contexts are anything like the intentions that we have in empirical contexts. In particular, I do not think there are any *unique* collections of objects that correspond to what we have in mind when we formulate our mathematical beliefs and theories; in other words, I do not think that any of our beliefs or theories are "about" any mathematical objects in any metaphysically thick sense of the term.[5] And I should say here that I do not endorse this view merely because it provides a way of avoiding various objections to platonism; on the contrary, I think this view dovetails with the actual facts about mathematical belief and mathematical knowledge. All of this will be discussed in more detail — and motivated — in chapter 4, where I discuss the non-uniqueness objection to platonism.

In any event, let me now provide a clear and precise statement of the central argument of this chapter. I will do this in Fieldian terms. He writes that the challenge to platonists is to account for the fact that *if mathematicians accept p, then p.*[6] I think this is right: what is at issue is not whether we *have* mathematical knowledge, but whether FBP-ists can *account* for this knowledge, that is, whether they can account for how the mathematical knowledge that we *do* have could be knowledge of an inaccessible mathematical realm. Now, of course, platonists do not have to account for there being a *perfect* correlation between our mathematical beliefs and the mathematical facts; this is simply because there isn't any such correlation to account for, because we're human, that is, we make mistakes. What needs to be explained is the fact that our mathematical beliefs are *reliable*, that is, the fact that *usually* (i.e., as a general rule) if mathematicians accept a purely mathematical sentence p, then p truly describes part of the mathematical realm. Thus, I will simply try to show that FBP-ists *can* account for this fact.

(Actually, I'm going to speak in terms of *theories* rather than sentences. That is, I'm going to argue that FBP-ists can account for the fact that, as a general rule, if mathematicians accept a purely mathematical theory T, then T truly describes part of the mathematical realm. This just makes the argument more general, because on my usage, a theory is just a collection of sentences, and so a sentence is really just a very simple theory. In addition to saying what a theory is, I should probably also say what a *purely mathematical* theory is. This is just a theory that speaks of nothing but the mathematical realm, that is, does nothing but predicate mathematical properties and mathematical relations of mathematical objects. In contrast to pure mathematical theories, there are also *impure* theories and *mixed* theories, which speak of both mathematical and physical objects.[7] Now, I am going to concentrate here on pure theories, but of course, to give a *complete* platonist epistemology, one would have to account for our knowledge of impure and mixed theories as well. But in order to solve the Benacerrafian epistemological problem with platonism, we needn't give a complete epistemology; we need only explain how human beings could acquire *some* knowledge of the mathematical realm, and so we can concentrate on pure theories. It is worth noting, however, that my epistemology *can* be generalized to cover impure and mixed theories.[8])

In any event, my argument proceeds as follows:

(i) FBP-ists can account for the fact that human beings can — without coming into contact with the mathematical realm — formulate purely mathematical theories.

(ii) FBP-ists can account for the fact that human beings can — without coming into contact with the mathematical realm — know of many of these purely mathematical theories that they are consistent.[9]

(iii) If (ii) is true, then FBP-ists can account for the fact that (as a general rule) if mathematicians accept a purely mathematical theory T, then T is consistent.

Therefore,

(iv) FBP-ists can account for the fact that (as a general rule) if mathematicians accept a purely mathematical theory T, then T is consistent.

(v) If FBP is true, then every consistent purely mathematical theory truly describes part of the mathematical realm, that is, truly describes some collection of mathematical objects.

Therefore,

(vi) FBP-ists can account for the fact that (as a general rule) if mathematicians accept a purely mathematical theory T, then T truly describes part of the mathematical realm.

The argument for (i) has already been given: this premise is trivial, because it is not making any strong claim to the effect that our purely mathematical theories have unique domains of mathematical objects that they are "about" in some metaphysically thick sense of the term.

The argument for (ii) will be given in section 5.

Premise (iii) is entirely trivial: (ii) tells us that FBP-ists can account for the fact that we have some skill at distinguishing consistent theories from inconsistent ones; all we have to add to this in order to get (iii) is that mathematicians use this skill in deciding what pure mathematical theories to accept — that is, that mathematicians will accept a theory only if they believe it is consistent — and that FBP-ists can account for this fact. I do not think anyone would question this. (I should note here that I am *not* saying that if mathematicians believe a theory is consistent, then they will automatically accept it. This is certainly not true: mathematicians generally require more than mere consistency before they will accept a theory. All I'm saying is that if mathematicians accept a theory, then it's (probably) consistent; in other words, the skill alluded to in (ii) makes our acceptance of a theory a somewhat reliable indicator of the consistency of the theory.)

Premise (iv) follows from (ii) and (iii) by *modus ponens*.

Premise (v) is just as trivial as (i) and (iii). FBP says that all the mathematical objects that logically possibly could exist actually do exist. But this means that every consistent purely mathematical theory truly describes some collection of mathematical objects. For if there were some such theory that *didn't* do this — that is, that spoke of a collection of objects that do *not* exist — we would have a violation of the assumption that all the mathematical objects that logically possibly could exist actually do exist. Now, of course, this argument relies upon the assumption that the notion of *logical possibility* that appears in the definition of FBP is at least as broad as the notion of *consistency* that appears in (v). But FBP-ists can obtain this result by stipulation. After all, FBP is *their* theory, and they can define it however they like. In section 5, I will reveal the exact line I want to take on the terms 'consistent' and 'logically possible', but for now, let me just say that I am going to take them to be *synonyms*, for this is already enough to deliver the result I need here.[10]

Finally, (vi) follows trivially from (iv) and (v). In the present context — that is, in the context of accounting for mathematical knowledge — FBP-ists are allowed to assume that FBP is true. But this, together with (v), gives us that all consistent purely mathematical theories truly describe part of the mathematical realm; but combining this with (iv) gives us (vi). Now, one might wonder *why* FBP-ists are allowed to assume here that FBP is true. There are at least two reasons why this assumption is legitimate. The first is this: in the present context, FBP-ists are not trying to establish their theory; they are merely trying to account for a certain fact (namely, the fact that we have mathematical knowledge) from *within* their theory; but in general, when one is trying to show that a theory T can account for a fact F, one can assume that T is true and make use of all of its resources.[11] The second reason is that (a) in the present context, FBP-ists are merely trying to respond to the epistemological argument against their view, and (b) that argument assumes FBP.[12]

As I have set things up, (vi) is precisely what I need. The Benacerrafian worry is that platonists cannot account for the reliability of our mathematical beliefs, and (vi) simply asserts that FBP-ists *can* account for it. Now, the only real gap I have left in the argument for (vi) is (ii). I will close this gap in section 5. But before I do that, I would like to address two sorts of worries. In section 3, I will address the worry that I haven't done enough, that is, that (vi) does not really eliminate the epistemological problem with platonism. And in section 4, I will respond to some objections to FBP (and I will argue that there are independent reasons for thinking that FBP is the best version of platonism there is). Now, we have just seen that this is not really necessary, that in the present context, I can legitimately *assume* FBP. But I want to quell the worry that I have solved the epistemological problem with platonism only by adopting an untenable version of platonism.

3. Internalist vs. Externalist Explanations

Consider the following objection to my line of argument. "All you've really explained is how it is that human beings could *stumble onto* theories that truly describe the mathematical realm. On the picture you've given us, the mathematical community accepts a mathematical theory T for a list of reasons, one of them being that T is consistent (or more precisely, that mathematicians believe that T is consistent). Then, since FBP is true, it turns out that T truly describes part of the mathematical realm. But since mathematicians have no conception of FBP, they do not know *why* T truly describes part of the mathematical realm, and so the fact that it does is, in some sense, *lucky*. This point can also be put as follows. Let T be a purely mathematical theory that we know (or reliably believe) is consistent. (That there *are* such theories is established by (ii).) Then the objection to your epistemology is that you have only an FBP-ist account of

(M₁) our ability to know that *if* FBP is true, *then* T truly describes part of the mathematical realm.[13]

You do not have an FBP-ist account of

(M₂) our ability to know that T truly describes part of the mathematical realm,

because you have said nothing to account for

(M3) our ability to know that FBP is true."

The problem with this objection to my epistemology is that (a) it demands an *internalist* account of the reliability of our mathematical beliefs, but (b) in order to meet the Benacerrafian epistemological challenge, platonists need only provide an *externalist* account of the reliability of our mathematical beliefs. To give an externalist account of the reliability of S's beliefs, one merely has to explain why S's methods of belief acquisition are, *in fact*, reliable; but to give an internalist account of the reliability of S's beliefs, one must do more: one must also explain how S knows (or reliably believes) that her methods of belief acquisition are reliable.

My FBP-ist account of the reliability of our mathematical beliefs is externalist: I explain this reliability by pointing out that (a) we use our knowledge of the consistency of purely mathematical theories in fixing our purely mathematical beliefs, and (b) on the assumption that FBP is true, any method of fixing purely mathematical belief that is so constrained by knowledge of consistency is, *in fact*, reliable (that is, any system of purely mathematical beliefs that is consistent will, in fact, truly describe part of the mathematical realm). I do not claim that actual mathematical knowers can justify FBP or even that they have any conception of FBP. Thus, what I need to argue, in order to block the above objection, is that I don't *need* mathematical knowers to have any conception of FBP, that is, that I don't need an internalist account of mathematical knowledge in order to refute the Benacerrafian objection to platonism.

It seems obvious to me that platonists need only an externalist account of mathematical knowledge. We can appreciate this by reflecting on the sort of epistemological challenge that Benacerraf is trying to present and by locating the empirical analog of Benacerraf's challenge, that is, the analogous challenge to our ability to acquire empirical knowledge about ordinary physical objects. According to both Field and Benacerraf—and I think they are right about this—it is *easy* to solve the empirical analog of Benacerraf's challenge: we can do so by merely appealing to sense perception. But this means that Field and Benacerraf are merely demanding an externalist account of mathematical knowledge. For an appeal to sense perception can provide only an externalist account of our empirical knowledge; it cannot provide an internalist account. To see this, let R be some simple theory about the physical world that we could verify via sense perception (e.g., the theory that snow is white). In internalist terms, all we can account for by appealing to sense perception is

(E1) our ability to know that *if* there is an external world of the sort that gives rise to accurate sense perceptions, *then* R is true.

An appeal to sense perception does *not* yield an internalist account of

(E2) our ability to know that R is true of the physical world,

because it does nothing to explain

(E3) our ability to know that there is an external world of the sort referred to in (E1).

On the other hand, an appeal to sense perception *is* sufficient for an *externalist* account of (E2). EWA-ists — that is, those who believe there is an external world of the sort referred to in (E1) — can give an externalist account of our empirical knowledge of physical objects by merely pointing out that (a) we use sense perception as a means of fixing our beliefs about the physical world, and (b) on the assumption that EWA is true, any method of fixing empirical belief that is so constrained by sense perception is, in fact, reliable. Since this is an externalist account, EWA-ists do not need to claim that actual empirical knowers can justify EWA or even that such knowers have any conception of EWA.

So the FBP-ist's situation with respect to knowledge of mathematical objects seems to be exactly analogous to the EWA-ist's situation with respect to empirical knowledge of physical objects. The FBP-ist can provide an externalist account of our mathematical knowledge that is exactly analogous to the EWA-ist's externalist account of our empirical knowledge: where the EWA-ist appeals to sense perception, the FBP-ist appeals to our ability to separate consistent theories from inconsistent theories; and where the EWA-ist appeals to EWA, the FBP-ist appeals to FBP. Moreover, the FBP-ist's attempt to provide an internalist account of mathematical knowledge and the EWA-ist's attempt to provide an internalist account of empirical knowledge break down at exactly analogous points: the former breaks down in the attempt to account for knowledge that FBP is true, and the latter breaks down in the attempt to account for knowledge that EWA is true.

It seems to me that anti-platonists can block my argument only by finding some sort of relevant disanalogy between the FBP-ist's epistemological situation and the EWA-ist's epistemological situation. They cannot allow the two situations to be analogous, because the whole point of the Benacerrafian objection is to raise a *special* problem for abstract objects, that is, a problem that is easily solvable for physical objects. Now, it *may* be that there is some *other* epistemological problem — for example, one motivated by Cartesian-style skeptical arguments — that applies to both EWA and FBP; but I am not concerned with any such problem here; I am concerned only with the Benacerrafian worry that there is a special epistemological problem with abstract objects.[14]

The upshot of all this is that Benacerraf's argument has to be interpreted as demanding an externalist account of our knowledge of mathematical objects. The anti-platonist's claim has to be that while such an account cannot be given, an externalist account of our knowledge of *physical* objects *can* be given. We cannot interpret Benacerraf as demanding an internalist account of our knowledge of mathematical objects, because this is no easier to provide for our knowledge of physical objects. (I take it that this is all entirely obvious and precisely why Benacerraf and Field formulate the demand as a demand for an externalist account of mathematical knowledge.)

The question we need to consider, then, is whether there is any relevant disanalogy between the FBP-ist's externalist account of mathematical knowledge and the EWA-ist's externalist account of empirical knowledge. I will consider two ways in which anti-platonists might try to establish such a disanalogy. The first proceeds as follows. "While it is true that most people who know things about the physical world never cognize EWA, and while it is true that even if they did, they could not justify their assumption that EWA is true, it seems that, at *some* level, people do accept EWA. But the situation with respect to FBP is entirely different: people just do not assume—at *any* level—that FBP is true."

First of all, I am not sure that either of the two central claims here is right. I am not sure that people assume—at some level—that EWA is true; and if we decide to say that they do, then I do not see why we shouldn't *also* say that they assume—at some level—that FBP is true. To assume (at some level) that FBP is true is just to assume that our mathematical singular terms refer; but it seems fairly plausible to claim that this assumption is inherent (in some sense and at some level) in mathematical practice. If a mathematician comes up with a radically new pure mathematical theory, she can be criticized on the grounds that the theory is inconsistent or uninteresting or useless, but she cannot be criticized—legitimately, anyway—on the grounds that the objects of the theory do not exist. Now, criticisms of this sort *have* emerged in the history of mathematics—for instance, in connection with imaginary numbers—but, ultimately, they have never had any real effect; that is, they have never blocked the acceptance of an otherwise acceptable theory. I think it is fair to say that at this point in time, it is not a legitimate or interesting mathematical criticism to claim that the objects of a consistent purely mathematical theory do not exist.

But the real problem with the first attempt to establish a disanalogy between FBP and EWA is that it is irrelevant. Given that we need only an externalist account of our knowledge of mathematical objects, it simply doesn't matter whether anyone assumes (at *any* level) that FBP is true.[15] My claim is that people can acquire knowledge of the mathematical realm—even if they do not assume (at any level) that FBP is true—by simply having a method of mathematical belief acquisition that (as a general rule) leads them to believe purely mathematical sentences and theories only if they are consistent. This is exactly analogous to the claim that people can acquire knowledge of the physical world—even if they do not assume (at any level) that EWA is true—simply by looking at it with a visual apparatus that (as a general rule) depicts the world accurately. And, of course, the *reason* we can acquire knowledge in these ways is that these methods of belief acquisition are, in fact, reliable.

A second way in which anti-platonists might try to establish a disanalogy between the externalist epistemologies of FBP-ists and EWA-ists proceeds as follows. "The FBP-ist is not on all fours with the EWA-ist, because FBP is not analogous to the bare claim that there exists an external physical world. FBP states not just that there *is* an external mathematical world, but that there is a very particular *kind* of mathematical world, namely, a *plenitudinous* one. Because of this, your explanation of knowledge of the mathematical realm is trivial. To see why, consider an analogous explanation. Let ZFP be a version of platonism that takes Zermelo-Fraenkel set theory to be true of part of the mathematical realm. Then ZFP-ists can give an externalist explanation of our knowledge that ZF is true because, on their view, any method of belief acquisition that leads to the acceptance of ZF will be, in fact, reliable."

The problem with this argument is that it does not establish a disanalogy between FBP and EWA, because EWA is *not* the bare claim that there exists an external world. It is the claim that there exists an external world *of the sort referred to in (E1)*, that is, the sort that gives rise to accurate sense perceptions, for instance, one containing photons, photon-reflecting objects, eyes, and so on. It seems to me that if anything, this is *farther* from the bare claim that there exists an external world than FBP is from the bare claim that there exists a mathematical realm. Moreover, there is also an empirical analog to the bit about ZFP. Let QMR be a version of realism that takes quantum mechanics to be true. Then QMR-ists can give an externalist explanation of our knowledge that QM is true because, on their view, any method of belief acquisition that leads to the acceptance of QM will be, in fact, reliable.

The externalist epistemologies of the EWA-ist and the FBP-ist are not trivial in the way that the externalist epistemologies of the ZFP-ist and the QMR-ist are. There are at least two reasons for this. I will state these reasons in terms of ZFP and FBP, but exactly analogous points could be made in terms of QMR and EWA. The first reason that the above ZFP-ist epistemology is trivial is that it does not describe a method of mathematical belief acquisition that both leads us to believe ZF *and* is reliable in general. My FBP-ist epistemology, on the other hand, does describe a method of mathematical belief acquisition that is reliable in general. Indeed, it describes a *class* of such methods, namely, the class of methods that forbid the acceptance of inconsistent purely mathematical theories.[16] The second reason that the above ZFP-ist epistemology is trivial, while my FBP-ist epistemology is not, is that ZFP is a mathematical theory, whereas FBP is an ontological theory. (Unlike ZFP, which is essentially equivalent to ZF, FBP makes no claims about any *particular* mathematical objects; it merely asserts a *general* criterion for when we ought to countenance mathematical objects.) The upshot of this is that by adopting FBP, we *explain* our ability to acquire mathematical knowledge, whereas by adopting ZFP, we do no such thing, because here, mathematical knowledge is smuggled in from the start.

I can think of no other way of trying to draw a disanalogy between the epistemologies for FBP and EWA. Thus, I conclude that the two epistemologies are on all fours and, therefore, that my externalist FBP-ist epistemology is sufficient to refute Benacerraf's argument.

Before going on, I want to guard against a possible misunderstanding. My intention in this section is *not* to provide a self-contained refutation of Benacerraf's argument; that is, my point is not that platonists do not need an epistemology for mathematical objects, because we do not have an epistemology for physical objects. On the contrary, I think we do have an epistemology for physical objects, namely, a perception-based externalist epistemology. This epistemology might not do everything we would like it to do, but it surely does a lot. My purpose in this section has, rather, been to argue that the FBP-based externalist epistemology I sketched in section 2 is on equal footing with this perception-based epistemology. It doesn't do everything we would like an epistemology of mathematics to do, but it does do a lot. Indeed, it does just as much as the perception-based epistemology does in the empirical case.

If you doubt that my explanation does a lot, consider that the Benacerrafian argument is supposed to inspire an absolute befuddlement about our ability to acquire knowledge of the mathematical realm. We find ourselves asking, "How in the world could we have *any clue* about the nature of such an inaccessible realm? How could we even begin to make a *guess* in this connection?" This is decidedly different from what skeptical arguments do to us. It is entirely obvious how people could make correct guesses about the physical world, that is, how they could stumble onto true hypotheses about it: they could do this by merely *looking* at it. All that one might wonder about is our ability to *know* things (in the skeptic's sense) about the physical world. But look what FBP does for us. It explains how rational people can formulate hypotheses that, in fact, truly describe parts of the mathematical realm: they can do this by merely constructing consistent purely mathematical theories. Of course, one might still wonder about our ability to *know* things (in the skeptic's sense) about the mathematical realm, but in the present context, this is irrelevant. For (a) all I am trying to establish here is that my FBP-based epistemology does everything in the mathematical case that the perception-based epistemology does in the empirical case, and (b) the latter does no better against skepticism than the former does.

I began this section with the worry that FBP *only* explains how our mathematical beliefs could turn out to be, in fact, reliable. The response, in a nutshell, is that this is exactly what *needs* to be explained, because the whole force of Benacerraf's argument lies in the fact that it makes us wonder how, if platonism were true, our mathematical beliefs could even be, in fact, reliable.

The only remaining hole in my argument is (ii). I will motivate this premise in section 5. But before I do that, I would like to provide a (partial) defense of FBP. Now, we have already seen that I don't *need* to do this, but I want to say a few words in this connection in order to block the objection that I have solved the epistemological problem with platonism only by adopting an untenable version of platonism.

4. Defending and Motivating FBP

I begin by fending off several different objections to FBP. Then at the end of this section, I argue briefly that FBP is actually the best version of platonism there is, that is, that non-full-blooded (or non-plenitudinous) versions of platonism are untenable.

Objection 1: FBP seems to lead to a *contradiction*. It entails that all consistent purely mathematical theories truly describe part of the mathematical realm, but there are numerous cases in which consistent purely mathematical theories contradict one another. An example is ZFC and ZF+~C (that is, Zermelo-Fraenkel set theory with and without the axiom of choice). These theories are both consistent (assuming that ZF is consistent), and so FBP entails that they both truly describe part of the mathematical realm. Thus, FBP seems to lead to the contradictory result that C and ~C are both true.

Reply: This is not a genuine contradiction. According to FBP, both ZFC and ZF+~C truly describe parts of the mathematical realm, but there is nothing wrong with this, because they describe *different* parts of that realm. In other words, they describe different *kinds* of sets, or different *universes* of sets. Thus, while it does follow from FBP that both C and not-C truly describe parts of the mathematical realm, we can obtain this result only by interpreting C in two different ways in the two different cases, that is, by assigning different sorts of entities to the expressions of C in the two different cases. Therefore, insofar as 'C and not-C' truly describes the mathematical realm, it is no more a genuine contradiction than is the sentence 'Aristotle married Jackie Kennedy and Aristotle did not marry Jackie Kennedy'. (And note that since, in mathematics, we never allow a term to shift meaning within a theory, 'C and not-C' will not be a theorem of any of our mathematical theories, except for those that contain an unrelated contradiction.[17])

We might express the idea that ZFC and ZF+~C describe different universes of sets by saying that ZFC describes universes of sets$_c$, whereas ZF+~C describes universes of sets$_{-c}$. Now, it is important to note that according to FBP-ists, ZFC does not describe a *unique* universe of sets$_c$; it describes many different universes of sets$_c$. For example, it describes some universes in which the continuum hypothesis (CH) is true and others in which it is not true. This is simply because ZFC+CH and ZFC+~CH are both consistent and, hence, both truly describe parts of the mathematical realm. In general, the point here is that if FBP is true, then there are as many different kinds of sets as there are consistent set theories.

I should note, however, that the phrase 'different kinds of sets' can be a bit misleading. One way to generate a set theory and a corresponding universe of sets is to relativize the quantifiers of another set theory. In such cases, we will have two different set theories describing different universes of sets, but it seems a bit misleading to suggest that we have two different *kinds* of sets here, because there will be entities that are members of both universes. But I think we can say that we do have two different kinds of sets here and then merely note that one of the kinds is *nested* in the other, or *less inclusive* than the other.

In contrast to the picture of nested universes of sets, there is also a picture of, so to speak, *side-by-side* universes of sets. This might be the best way to visualize the situation with respect to CH. Technically speaking, there are ZF+CH universes nested within ZF+~CH universes *and* ZF+~CH universes nested within ZF+CH universes, but it is perhaps best to think of these universes as existing side by side—or more generally, to think of the universes that are characterized by the theories

ZF+CH

ZF+'the size of the continuum is $\aleph_2$'

ZF+'the size of the continuum is $\aleph_3$'

and so on.

as existing side by side.

Objection 2: FBP entails that all consistent purely mathematical theories truly describe parts of the mathematical realm. Thus, it entails that among purely mathematical theories, consistency is sufficient for truth. But this seems to represent a shift in the meaning of the word 'true', as it is used by mathematicians, and so FBP seems to fly in the face of mathematical practice.

Reply: FBP does not entail that among purely mathematical theories, consistency is sufficient for truth. (It does entail that all purely mathematical theories truly describe parts of the mathematical realm, but as we will see, it does not follow from this that all such theories are *true*.) More importantly, FBP does not bring with it a shift in the meaning of the word 'true', as it is used by mathematicians. What mathematicians standardly mean when they say that a sentence is true is that it is true in the *standard model,* or the *intended structure* — or as we'll see, the class of intended structures — for the given branch of mathematics. It seems to me that this fits perfectly well with FBP. Indeed, it seems to me that FBP-ists can explain *why* mathematicians use 'true' to mean 'true in the standard model'.

Let me begin my argument for these claims by pointing out that talk of *truth in a model* dovetails with FBP. Models are just parts of the mathematical realm, so to say that a sentence S is true in a model M is just to say that S is true of some particular part of the mathematical realm. But if talk of truth in a model dovetails with FBP, then talk of truth in the standard model dovetails with FBP as well. The only thing that FBP-ists will want to emphasize in this connection is that there is nothing *metaphysically special* about standard models. Now, this is not to say that there can be no good reason for singling out a model (or class of models) as standard; it simply means that such models do not enjoy any privileged ontological status. The claim that a model (or class of models) is standard is a claim about *us* rather than the model; what is being claimed is that this is the model (or class of models) that is *intended*, that is, that we *have in mind* with respect to the given theory. Thus, for instance, a model of set theory is standard if and only if it jibes with *our notion of set*;[18] and a model of arithmetic is standard if and only if it jibes with *our conception of the natural numbers*; and so on. (There are also cases, I think, in which we want to say that a model is standard because it is *inclusive*, but I think that whenever this is true, the inclusive model is also what we *have in mind*.)

These remarks show that FBP-ists can account for talk of truth in the standard model. But FBP-ists can also account for why 'true in the standard model (or models)' is more or less synonymous with 'true' . This might seem surprising, for FBP-ists maintain that all consistent purely mathematical theories truly describe some collection of mathematical objects, but they do not claim that all such theories are true in a standard model. But FBP-ists can make sense of this by maintaining that not all theories that truly describe parts of the mathematical realm are true. And they can do this by appealing to a certain, fairly standard, way of thinking about truth that distinguishes the notion of *truth*, or *truth simpliciter,* from the notion of *truth in a language L* (where a language is an abstract object that, at the very least, maps sentence types onto truth conditions) . The fact that every consistent purely mathematical theory truly describes a collection of mathematical objects shows that every such theory is true in some language L. (Actually, it shows more than this; it shows that every such theory is true in a language L that interprets the given theory in a "natural way", that is, a way that takes the given theory to be about the objects that, intuitively, it *is* about.) But none of this shows that all consistent purely mathematical theories are true simpliciter. Indeed, insofar as many of these theories have never been tokened, the notion of truth simpliciter does not even make sense in connection with them. For on the present view, the notion of truth simpliciter is defined only for sentence tokens (and collections of sentence tokens) and not for sentence types. In particular, and very roughly, a sentence token is *true simpliciter*, on this view, if and only if it is true in the *intended* language (or rather, if and only if it is a token of a type t that is true in the intended language) . This is obviously very rough, but given the present view of what a language is, it is clear that we have to define 'true simpliciter' in some such way, because every sentence type is true in some languages and false in others. For instance, the sentence type 'Snow is white' is true in English but false in all languages that map it onto the truth condition of grass being orange.

In any event, it should be clear that if this view of the notion of truth simpliciter is at least roughly correct, then the notion of truth in the standard model *is* a notion of truth simpliciter. For as we've seen, to say that a model is standard is just to say that it's *intended*. But to say that a sentence is true in the intended model is essentially equivalent to saying that it is true in the intended *interpretation*, and so it's also more or less equivalent to saying that it is true in the intended *language*. Thus, I conclude that by appealing to the above view of the notion of truth simpliciter, FBPists can account for why mathematicians use 'true' to mean 'true in the standard model'.

It is important to note here that, according to FBP, none of this provides any *metaphysical* distinction to the mathematical theories that happen to be true simpliciter. Take any consistent purely mathematical theory T. If mathematicians became interested in the structure that T describes and formulated T in an effort to describe that structure, then according to FBP, T would be true simpliciter. But it doesn't follow from this that T is true simpliciter right *now*. Thus, whether a mathematical theory is true simpliciter depends partially upon facts about us. But this is just what we want. For in general, whether our utterances are true depends partially upon our intentions, upon what we intend these utterances to mean. For instance, part of the reason that our utterances of 'Snow is white' are true is that when we utter this sentence, we intend to be saying that snow is white, as opposed to, say, that grass is orange. (Of course, this isn't the *whole* reason that our utterances of 'Snow is white' are true; part of the reason is that snow is white.) In any event, my point here is that, according to FBP, mathematical truth works in essentially the same way as ordinary truth.

(One might object here as follows: "Given the above remarks, it's not clear that FBP succeeds in marking any important difference between mathematics and empirical science; after all, every consistent physical theory is true in some language L." My response is that by maintaining that the mathematical realm is plenitudinous, FBP-ists obtain the result that every consistent purely mathematical theory is true in a language L *that interprets the theory in a natural way*. This guarantees that whenever mathematicians think of a mathematical structure and formulate a theory that characterizes that structure, the theory will be true. But of course, the corresponding claim about physical reality is false. It is simply not the case that whenever somebody dreams up a physical situation and formulates a theory that characterizes it, the theory is true. If this were the case, then all logically consistent novels would be literally true stories.)

Before going on, I should point out that some of the remarks in the last few paragraphs might be a bit misleading, because they might lead one to think that FBP-ists are committed to the claim that, for each branch of mathematics, there is a *unique* intended model. As we will soon see, this is not true. To take the case of set theory, FBP-ists allow that it *may* be that there are multiple models of set theory that are not isomorphic to one another and that are all perfectly consistent with all of our set-theoretic intentions and, indeed, with the totality of all of our thoughts about sets. Thus, to leave room for this possibility, FBP-ists maintain that a mathematical sentence is *true simpliciter*, or *correct*, if and only if it is true in *all* of the standard models for the given branch of mathematics; and it is *incorrect* if and only if it is false in all of these models; and if it is true in some of these models and false in others, then it is neither correct nor incorrect. I will discuss this in more detail in my reply to objection 3. We will see there that this fits very well with mathematical practice.

(In response to the arguments of this section, one might wonder how human beings could succeed in mentally picking out a particular model, or class of models, as standard. I will address this worry in my reply to objection 4.)

Objection 3: FBP seems to sacrifice the *objectivity* of mathematics. Now, it does entail that mathematical theories are objectively true in the sense that they are true of an objective mathematical realm and, hence, true independently of us and our mathematical theorizing. Nonetheless, it seems that FBP-ists cannot salvage the objectivity of certain open questions. For instance, FBP seems to entail that undecidable sentences like CH do not have determinate truth values. Once it has been established that CH and ~CH are both consistent with the set theories that we currently accept, all we can say is that CH is true of some kinds of sets and false of others; we cannot maintain that there is any interesting mathematical question left to answer. But this flies in the face of mathematical practice, because there are a good many set theorists who think that CH does have a determinate truth value, that is, that there is an objectively and uniquely correct answer to the question 'How big is the continuum?' (Moreover, if one were inclined to agree with Kreisel that it is the *objectivity* of mathematics, and not its *ontology*, that is the really important issue, one might be inclined to conclude that FBP is actually not a very platonistic view.)[19,20]

Reply: The claim that FBP-ists cannot salvage the objectivity of undecidable open questions is simply false. Most mathematical disputes can be interpreted as disputes about what is true in the standard model (or models). Consider, for instance, arguments over the truth or falsity of CH. When people argue about whether some axiom candidate that's supposed to settle the CH question is true, what they are really arguing about is whether the given axiom candidate is inherent in *our notion of set*. In other words, they're arguing about whether the axiom candidate is true in the standard model (or class of models) of set theory. Thus, FBP-ists claim that CH and ~CH are both true in various set-theoretic hierarchies and that arguments over the truth of CH are arguments over its truth value in the intended hierarchy (or hierarchies).

Now, it *may* be that *our notion of set* is non-categorical, that is, that there are numerous models of set theory that are not isomorphic to one another but are, nonetheless, standard—or *as* standard as any other model. In other words, it may be that the totality of our set thoughts fails to pick out a unique model (or more precisely, a unique class of mutually isomorphic models). If this is the case, then for *some* open set-theoretic questions, there is no objectively correct answer. FBP-ists can easily account for this: to say that there is no objectively correct answer to, for instance, the CH question, is just to say that our notion of set isn't strong enough to settle that question, that is, that neither CH nor ~CH is inherent in our notion of set, that is, that CH is true in some standard models of set theory and false in others. It seems to me that this is an extremely important point, because traditional platonists *cannot* account for the existence of open questions without correct answers. If there is only *one* universe of sets, then CH is either true or false. But this is a problem for traditional platonism, because one of the dominant opinions about the CH question among contemporary set theorists —if not *the* dominant opinion—is that it doesn't have an objectively correct answer. The problem is that traditional platonists cannot account for how this could be so.

Thus, far from providing an *objection* to FBP, considerations involving objectivity and methodology actually provide us with a reason to *favor* FBP over traditional platonism. For FBP-ists can account for *more* of mathematical practice in this connection than traditional platonists can. In particular, they can account for the existence of undecidable open questions with objectively and uniquely correct answers *and* undecidable open questions *without* objectively correct answers. Most philosophies of mathematics *dictate* that we take one stance or the other here with respect to *all* open questions. But FBP allows mathematicians to say whatever they *want* to say in this connection with respect to each different open question. This, I think, is an extremely appealing feature of FBP. I say this for two reasons. First, a good philosophy of mathematics should not dictate things like this to mathematicians; the point of the philosophy of mathematics is to *interpret* mathematical practice, not to place metaphysically based *restrictions* on it. And second, the FBP-ist stance here just seems intuitively pleasing. It just seems right to say that it *may* be that some open mathematical questions have objectively correct answers whereas others do not. Moreover, it seems very plausible to suppose that what determines whether a given open question has an objectively correct answer is whether it is independent not just of the currently accepted theory in the given area of mathematics, but also of what we *have in mind* with respect to this theory, that is, our notion of set, or our conception of the natural numbers, or whatever. If multiple answers to an open question are consistent with our intentions and concepts and intuitions, then different answers to the question will be true in different standard models, and so the question will not have a unique, objectively correct answer. But if one answer to an open question is, in some sense, already contained in our intentions or concepts or intuitions, then the question does have a unique, objectively correct answer.[21]

Now, actually, this picture of things is a bit oversimplified. In the first place, there are surely going to be cases in which there is no clear fact of the matter as to whether a given answer to some open question is "inherent in our concepts". For insofar as our concepts can be vague and fuzzy, there can be answers to open questions that are "borderline inherent in these concepts". And in the second place, even if we assume that our concepts are always precise and well-defined, it is not the case that the *only* way an answer to an open question can be correct is if it is, in some sense, inherent in these concepts. For even if no answer to a given open question is inherent in our concepts, it may be that good reasons—for instance, aesthetic or pragmatic reasons—can be given for *revising* (or perhaps, *refining*) our concepts in a way that would settle the question. And in some cases of this sort, we might still want to say that the question had a correct answer. (Cases like this suggest that there is a relationship of back-and-forth influence between theory and intuition. It is obvious that our theories are influenced by our intuitive pre-theoretic concepts, but cases of this sort suggest that our concepts are also influenced by our theorizing. And this, in turn, suggests that which models count as standard is influenced by our theorizing as well.)

One might wonder what my FBP-ists would say about Euclid's fifth postulate, for we have here an undecidable proposition that seems a bit different from CH. What I would say is this: we know in exactly which kind of geometrical space this postulate is true and in which kinds of spaces it is false; moreover, we know which of these spaces corresponds to our pre-theoretic intuitions, and so there is simply no mystery here at all. That is, there is no mathematical question left to answer. The only interesting question is whether *physical* space is Euclidean, and that is a non-mathematical, empirical question.

As for open *arithmetical* questions, I think we can safely say that *all* of these have unique, objectively correct answers. If Q is a question about the natural numbers, then even if it were shown that all answers to Q were undecidable in a theory as strong as ZFC, we would still maintain that Q has an objectively correct answer, because we're convinced that *our conception of the natural numbers* is categorical. That is, we're convinced that the totality of our natural-number thoughts picks out a unique model, or at worst, a unique class of models that are all isomorphic to one another. This, at any rate, is what *mathematicians* would say. But there is at least one philosopher—namely, Putnam[22]—who has argued that our concept of number *isn't* categorical. There is no reason to go into this here, though, because even if Putnam is right about this, it is not a problem for FBP because, again, that view is compatible with the claim that our mathematical notions and conceptions—such as our notion of set and our conception of the natural numbers—are non-categorical. (I will say a bit more about Putnam's argument, and the point I'm making here, at the end of chapter 4.)

I want to make one more point before going on. I have claimed that it may be that our notion of set is non-categorical. But I want to emphasize that FBP-ists are not *committed* to this. If it turns out that our notion of set picks out a unique universe of sets (or at least does this up to isomorphism), that will not be a problem for FBP, for as the above remarks already make clear, FBP is neutral as to whether or not this is the case.

Objection 4: The appeal to standard models in the reply to objections 2 and 3 seems to give rise to an epistemic problem for FBP-ists about how human beings could acquire *knowledge* of what the various standard models are like.

Reply: In fact, there is no epistemic problem here at all. This is simply because standard models aren't metaphysically special. They're only *sociologically* special, or *psychologically* special. To ask whether some proposition is true in, for example, the standard model (or class of models) of set theory is just to ask whether it is inherent in *our* notion of set. Thus, since our notion of set is clearly accessible to us, questions about what is true in the standard model (or models) of set theory are clearly within our epistemic reach.

Thus, the answer to the question 'How do we know what the various standard models of mathematics are like?' is just this: we formulate axioms that are intuitively pleasing (that is, that jibe with our notion of set, or number, or whatever) and then we prove theorems. This, of course, is exactly true to mathematical practice. Mathematicians try to settle open questions by constructing proofs that rely only upon currently accepted propositions, that is, propositions that we already believe hold in the standard model. And if a question *cannot* be answered in this way—that is, if the propositions that answer the question are undecidable in the current theory—then mathematicians seek new axioms that are (a) powerful enough to entail an answer to the question and (b) intuitively pleasing. (Or if they can't find any axioms that are intuitively pleasing, they might use an axiom that is pragmatically appealing; I mentioned this above, and I'll say more about it below.) This is exactly what set theorists have tried to do in connection with CH, or at any rate, it's what has been attempted by those set theorists who think that CH has a determinate truth value.

The worry behind objection 4 can also be put in this way: "How could human beings mentally pick out a unique model (or class of models) to call standard?" My response to this way of putting the point is similar to my response to the other way of putting it. We do not do anything special here that involves some sort of *connection* between our heads and standard models. We just have our intuitions and notions and conceptions, and we slowly build theories out of them. Since these theories are consistent, it follows (on the assumption that FBP is true) that these theories truly describe parts of the mathematical realm. But some of our theories aren't categorical, that is, they have multiple models that aren't isomorphic to one another. Moreover, in some such cases, we're inclined to say that one of the models of the given theory (or one class of these models) is *standard*, whereas the others are not. But in such cases, standardness is determined not by any sort of *contact* that we have with the mathematical realm, but by the simple fact that our intuitions, notions, and conceptions happen to jibe more with one of the models (or class of models) than any of the others. Our intuitions, notions, and conceptions "pick out" one of the models (or class of models), but they do this only in a *thin* way; they are not "about" the standard model (or class of models) in any *thick* way. (I will elaborate on this picture, and justify it more thoroughly, in chapter 4.)

Objection 5: FBP seems to forbid us to speak of *all* sets. For it seems that according to FBP, every set theory is about a restricted universe of sets. But there doesn't seem to be any good reason for this; we ought to be able to develop a theory of *all* sets and say whether CH is true in this theory.

Reply: In fact, FBP *doesn't* forbid the development of such a universal set theory. If somebody came up with a set theory—call it ST—such that (a) each of the axioms of ST seemed intuitively plausible, that is, seemed to jibe with our notion of set, and (b) ST settled all important open questions of set theory and, indeed, picked out a *unique* universe of sets that seemed intuitively to correspond to our notion of set, then it would be reasonable to maintain that ST was a theory about *all* sets and that it told us once and for all whether CH is true. Now, there might still be other consistent theories, incompatible with ST, that purported to be about sets, and of course, FBP would entail that these other theories truly described parts of the mathematical realm; but we could simply maintain that these other theories weren't about *the universe of sets*, that is, that all the models of these other theories either contained some things that weren't really sets, or didn't contain some things that *were* sets, or both.

Now, at this point, one might be inclined to raise an objection that is, in a sense, the *opposite* of objection 5. In particular, one might argue as follows. "FBP-ists speak of various universes of sets. But we can surely *amalgamate* all these universes to form a single universe of sets. But if this is true, then the various open questions of set theory ought to be taken as being uniquely about this particular universe. Thus, it seems that FBP-ists are committed to the claim that open set-theoretic questions, such as the CH question, have unique, objectively correct answers. But this is problematic, for as we've seen, FBP-ists want to claim that their theory allows that it *might* be that some such questions don't have objectively correct answers."

The problem with this objection is that any FBP-ist who denies that CH has a determinate truth value (i.e., that CH has the same truth value in all of the standard models of set theory) will also deny that there is a unique amalgamated universe that clearly contains all of the things that legitimately count as sets and none of the things that don't. Moreover, if there *is* a unique amalgamated universe of this sort, then this shows not just that *FBP-ists* ought to say that CH has a determinate truth value, but that *everyone* ought to say this. In other words, it shows that CH does have a determinate truth value. The important point to note here is that by *itself*, FBP is *neutral* with respect to the question of whether there is a unique amalgamated universe that contains all and only things that legitimately count as sets; that is, it's neutral as to whether there is a unique universe that corresponds to our notion of set. Therefore, it's also neutral as to whether all of the open questions of set theory have unique, objectively correct answers.

So neither objection 5 nor its "opposite" succeeds: FBP doesn't entail that there *isn't* a theory of all and only sets (or a unique *universe* of all and only sets), and it doesn't entail that there is. It remains neutral here, so that mathematicians can settle this question however they want to.

Objection 6: Let's take objection 5 one step farther. FBP seems to prohibit us from making claims about the *entire mathematical realm*.

Reply: Again, this is just false. The sentence 'All mathematical objects are abstract objects' is about the entire mathematical realm, and it is presumably true. Now, it may be that there is nothing *mathematically interesting* to say about the entire mathematical realm, but that's just because the mathematical realm is so vast.

Objection 7: This reply misses the point of objection 6. The problem is that there are *some* things that we might want to say about the entire mathematical realm such that FBP prohibits us from saying *them*. For instance, suppose that

Scottie, a mathematical lunatic, believes that there is no such thing as the number 7, that the natural-number sequence goes straight from 6 to 8. If he utters the sentence 'There is no number 7', then since this is *consistent*, FBP entails that what Scottie said is true of part of the mathematical realm. But this seems to get things wrong. Scottie was talking about the *entire* mathematical realm, and so what he said is surely false.

Reply: FBP tells us that the sentence 'There is no number 7' truly describes *part* of the mathematical realm, but it *doesn't* tell us that it truly describes the *entire* mathematical realm. Thus, there is simply no problem here: if Scottie was talking about the entire mathematical realm when he uttered this sentence, then he was simply wrong, and FBP-ists can *say* that he was wrong. Why can't they? They never said that all consistent purely mathematical sentences and theories truly describe the *entire* mathematical realm.

Objection 8: Let's think a bit more about sentences like 'There is no number 7', or '$2 + 2 = 5$'. FBP entails that such sentences are true of part of the mathematical realm. But this seems wrong; it seems that sentences like these are just false. Now, of course, you might claim that what we *mean* when we say that sentences like '$2 + 2 = 5$' are false is that they are false in the *standard model*. But it's not clear that this is acceptable. After all, we seem to think that these sentences are false in some *absolute* sense.

Reply: FBP-ists can account for the intuition we have that sentences like '$2 + 2 = 5$' are false in some absolute sense. We could construct a consistent purely mathematical theory in which '$2 + 2 = 5$' was a theorem, but to do this, we would have to use at least one of the terms in this sentence in a non-standard way. For instance, we might simply use the symbol '5' to denote the number 4, or we might use '+' to express some unusual operation. But if we interpret the terms of this sentence in a non-standard way, then it would not really say that $2 + 2 = 5$. As long as we interpret '$2 + 2 = 5$' in the standard way, that is, according to *English*, it will be false. Now, of course, this is just to say that '$2 + 2 = 5$' is false in the standard model, but I think this way of putting the point explains why the fact that '$2 + 2 = 5$' is false in the standard model leads to the intuition that it is false absolutely.

Similar remarks can be made with respect to the sentence 'There is no number 7'. I could construct a consistent purely mathematical theory that had this sentence as a theorem. Indeed, I could construct *many* such theories, and according to FBP, they would all truly describe parts of the mathematical realm. For example, one such theory would characterize a part of the mathematical realm that is just like the natural-number sequence except that it has a sort of *hole* in it where 7 is in the natural-number sequence. But, of course, this weird quasi-sequence[23] is not the natural-number sequence; thus, while we can use the sentence 'There is no number 7' to say something true about this quasi-sequence, in doing this, we would be using the sentence in a non-standard way, and so we would not really be saying that there is no number 7. So long as 'There is no number 7' is taken to mean that there is no number 7, it is, according to FBP-ists, false.

Objection 9: We normally think that in order for a person S to know that p, there has to be a counterfactual relationship between S's belief that p and the fact that p, so that if things would have been different (that is, if it wouldn't have been the case that p), then S would have believed differently (that is, he or she wouldn't have believed that p). But the FBP-ist epistemology described here does not salvage this.

Reply: This objection is based on a worry that can be lumped together with the original Benacerrafian worry that human beings could not acquire knowledge of abstract mathematical objects, because they do not have any information-gathering *contact* with such objects. Both worries arise from taking epistemic principles that seem applicable (to at least a limited extent) in empirical contexts and applying them in mathematical contexts. Now, prima facie, it might seem that these principles *are* applicable in mathematical contexts — that is, it might seem that we couldn't have knowledge of mathematical objects without having any contact with such objects and without there being a counterfactual relationship here of the above sort — but one of the main points of the present chapter is precisely that these principles are *not* applicable in mathematical contexts. That is, the arguments that I'm developing in this chapter suggest that human beings could have knowledge of mathematical objects even if they don't have any contact with such objects and even if there isn't a counterfactual relationship here of the above sort. Thus, since we never had any good *argument* for thinking that these principles *are* applicable in mathematical contexts,[24] we can conclude that the present chapter provides a good response to our two worries here, that is, the worry behind objection 9 and the original Benacerrafian worry.

Objection 10: FBP-ists claim that our mathematical singular terms refer to mathematical objects. But *which* objects do they refer to? It seems pretty clear that if FBP is true, then our mathematical theories do not describe *unique* parts of the mathematical realm. Thus, it seems that singular terms like '3' and 'the null set' do not pick out unique objects. But on the standard view of reference, this is just to say that they suffer a kind of reference *failure*.

Reply: This objection is deeply related to the Benacerrafian non-uniqueness objection to platonism. Thus, since chapter 4 is going to be entirely devoted to providing an FBP-ist reply to the non-uniqueness objection, I want to put the present objection on hold for now and respond to it in chapter 4. To tip my hand a bit, though, my strategy will be to *embrace* the thesis that our mathematical singular terms do not uniquely refer. I should say, however, that the non-uniqueness I embrace will be very *limited*. It might seem that FBP-ists could be forced into the result that all mathematical singular terms refer (non-uniquely) to all mathematical objects, but we'll see that, in fact, they cannot be forced into this or, indeed, anything like it.

In addition to fending off the objections to FBP, I would also like to argue in its *favor*; that is, I would like to argue that it is the best version of platonism there is. The most important argument here is the one I have been developing over the last two chapters: FBP survives the Benacerrafian epistemological attack, whereas non-full-blooded, or non-plenitudinous, versions of platonism do not. If non-plenitudinous platonism were correct, it would be a mystery how we could ever know what the universe of sets was like. Since, in FBP-ist terms, there are infinitely many different universes of sets, traditional platonists have to allow that *the* universe of sets could correspond to any of these FBP-ist universes. But given all these possibilities, it's totally unclear how spatiotemporal creatures like ourselves could discover the nature of *the* universe of sets.[25]

But there are also *independent* reasons for favoring FBP over other sorts of platonism. Indeed, I already gave one such reason in connection with objection 3: FBP-ists can account for the existence of open questions with correct answers *and* open questions without correct answers, whereas traditional platonists can account only for the former.

A second independent argument for FBP is that it reconciles the objectivity of mathematics (to which all platonists are committed) with the legitimacy in mathematics of pragmatic modes of justification, that is, with the fact that the adoption of a new axiom for a mathematical theory can be justified pragmatically, for instance, because it solves certain open questions or simplifies the theory. We saw in chapter 2 (sub-section 5.3) that non-full-blooded platonists cannot account for the legitimacy of pragmatic modes of justification: since, according to their view, an axiom candidate (that has been shown to be independent of the other axioms of the given theory) could very easily turn out to be false of the given domain of objects, it is unclear why pragmatic modes of justification should be legitimate. Why should the fruitfulness of a claim about *the* universe of sets have anything to do with its truth?[26] FBP-ists, on the other hand, can easily explain the legitimacy of pragmatic modes of justification. Suppose that a sentence A is an axiom candidate for a purely mathematical theory T and that A is independent of the other axioms of T. If we assume that FBP is true, then even if A can be justified only pragmatically — that is, even if we do not have any intuition as to whether or not A is true — there is nothing wrong with adopting A, or T+A, because according to FBP, there do exist objects for which T+A holds. Of course, there are also objects for which T+~A holds, but that is irrelevant. The point is that the decision to adopt T+A can simply be seen as a decision to study a certain kind of object (or perhaps, as a decision to refine our concepts in a certain way).

A third (related) advantage of FBP is that it reconciles the objectivity of mathematics with the extreme *freedom* that mathematicians have.[27] As I have already pointed out, mathematicians cannot be legitimately criticized on the grounds that the objects of their (consistent and pure) theories do not exist. Indeed, just the opposite seems true: one way for a mathematician to become famous is to develop an interesting theory about a kind of mathematical entity or structure of which no one has yet conceived. (Now, of course, a physicist could also become famous in this way, but before we would accept the new physical theory, we would demand independent evidence that the objects in question exist.)

5. Consistency

It remains only to justify premise (ii) of my argument. To this end, I need to argue that FBP-ists can account for the fact that human beings can — without coming into contact with the mathematical realm — know of certain purely mathematical theories that they are consistent. Let me begin my argument here by stating a reason one might give for being *skeptical* of premise (ii). One might reason as follows.

"Look, there are two different notions of consistency: a theory T is *semantically consistent* (or satisfiable) iff it has a model, and it is *syntactically consistent* iff there is no derivation of a contradiction from T in any logically sound derivation system. But insofar as models and derivations are abstract objects, these are both platonistic notions. Thus, knowledge of consistency is going to be knowledge of abstract objects, namely, models and derivations. Indeed, Gödel has shown that knowledge of syntactic consistency is essentially equivalent to *arithmetical* knowledge. Thus, FBP-ists have not accomplished *anything* by reducing the question of how we could know that our mathematical theories are true to the question of how we could know that they are consistent."

FBP-ists can avoid this worry by merely claiming that the notion of consistency at work in (ii) — and, more generally, in (i)–(vi) — is an anti-platonist notion of consistency. One anti-platonist notion of consistency that FBP-ists can use here is suggested in the work of Kreisel and discussed recently by Field.[28] The main idea here is that 'consistent' is simply a *primitive* term. More precisely, the claim is that in addition to the syntactic and semantic notions of consistency, there is also a primitive or intuitive notion of consistency that is not defined in any platonistic way. Now, the standard view here is that the semantic notion of consistency can be thought of as a definition (or perhaps a reductive analysis) of our intuitive notion of consistency, but according to the Kreisel-Field view, this is wrong. On this view, the intuitive notion is related to the two formal notions in analogous ways: neither of the formal notions provides us with a *definition* of the primitive notion, but they both provide us with information about the *extension* of the primitive notion. More specifically, it follows from the definitions of the two formal notions, and from our intuitive understanding of the primitive notion, that (a) if a theory T is semantically consistent, then it is intuitively consistent; and (b) if T is syntactically inconsistent, then it is intuitively inconsistent. Moreover, if we combine these two points with the completeness theorem — or more precisely, with the Henkin theorem that (among first-order theories) syntactic consistency implies semantic consistency — we arrive at the result that (among first-order theories) the intuitive notion of consistency is coextensive with both formal notions of consistency.

Advocates of the Kreisel–Field view might want to claim that the primitive notion of consistency is equivalent to a primitive notion of *possibility*. Now, there are, of course, many different *kinds* of possibility, but this fits perfectly well with the present view. To see this, consider the fact that for each different kind of possibility, we can define formal notions of syntactic and semantic consistency. Here are two examples:

A theory T is *semantically conceptually consistent* iff the union T+C of T and the set C of all conceptual truths has a model; and T is *syntactically conceptually consistent* iff there is no derivation of a contradiction from T+C in any logically sound derivation system.

A theory T is *semantically physically consistent* iff the union T+P of T and the set P of all physical laws has a model; and T is *syntactically physically consistent* iff there is no derivation of a contradiction from T+P in any logically sound derivation system.

Now, given this, we can say that there is an intuitive notion of possibility, or consistency, corresponding to each such pair of formal notions. Thus, the Kreisel–Field intuitive notion is simply the *broadest* of these notions; it is a notion of *logical* possibility.[29] All of the other intuitive notions of possibility can be defined in terms of the Kreisel–Field intuitive notion. For example, a theory T is *intuitively physically possible* iff T+P is intuitively possible, or consistent, in the Kreisel–Field sense.

At any rate, in order to use all of this to motivate premise (ii), I need to argue two points. First, I need to argue that it is acceptable for me to use the Kreisel–Field primitive notion of consistency here, that is, that this notion is a genuinely *anti-platonist* notion. And second, I need to argue that if we insert this notion of consistency into premise (ii), then that premise is true; that is, I need to argue that FBP-ists can account for the fact that human beings can — without coming into contact with the mathematical realm — know of certain purely mathematical theories that they are intuitively consistent, in the sense developed by Kreisel and Field.

Now, actually, the first thesis here is stronger than what I really need to establish. All I really need here is that there is *some* legitimate anti-platonist account of consistency. Whether it is the account provided by the Kreisel–Field view is irrelevant; for so long as there is some legitimate anti-platonist account of consistency, I will be able to run the argument in (i)–(vi) and simply understand the word 'consistent' there in the given anti-platonist way. But it seems to me that the claim that there is *some* legitimate anti-platonist account of consistency is extremely weak. If there were *no* legitimate anti-platonist account of consistency, then anti-platonists wouldn't even be able to account for the simple fact that some of our theories are consistent, and so their view would be totally unacceptable. Thus, all of the arguments that I am considering in this book would be moot, because we would know that platonism was correct.[30]

But in any event, it is not hard to motivate the first thesis of the paragraph before last, that is, the thesis that the Kreisel–Field primitive notion of consistency is a genuinely anti-platonist notion. For since that notion is a *primitive* notion, it is entirely obvious that it isn't defined in terms of abstract objects, because it doesn't have any definition at all.

Now, I suppose that one might try to argue here that we ought not to think of our intuitive notion of consistency as a primitive notion, that we ought to take the semantic notion as providing a definition (or at least a reduction) of the intuitive notion. But I have no idea how one might proceed in trying to argue this point. Indeed, it seems to me that there is no reason to think that the intuitive notion is even *coextensive* with the semantic notion. Henkin's proof shows that they are coextensive in connection with first-order theories, but that argument doesn't extend to higher-order theories.[31] Moreover, even if we assume, for the sake of argument, that these two notions are coextensive, there are good reasons for thinking that the semantic notion doesn't provide a definition (or reduction) of the intuitive notion. Field argues this point very convincingly by showing that the semantic notion doesn't capture the "essence" of the intuitive notion. He does this by pointing out that there are certain theories for which it is *obvious* that they are intuitively consistent but *not* obvious that they are semantically consistent. For instance, the theory S consisting of all the truths about sets that are statable in the language of set theory is obviously consistent in the intuitive sense, but it is not at all obvious that S is semantically consistent, that is, that it has a model. For intuitively, it seems that a model of S would have the set of all sets as its universe, but we know that there is no such thing as the set of all sets.[32] Now, if the language of S is *first-order*, then by Henkin's theorem, S does have a model. But (a) the model produced by this proof is extremely unnatural; and (b) this result doesn't extend to cases where the language of S is higher-order; and most important, (c) the mere fact that this result is non-trivial, that it has to be *proven*, shows that the semantic notion doesn't capture the "essence" of the intuitive notion.

One might object as follows. "Even if the semantic notion doesn't capture the 'essence' of the intuitive notion, and indeed, even if it's not coextensive with the intuitive notion, there is still something illegitimate about FBP-ists claiming that we use platonistic notions to help us get a grip on the extension of the intuitive notion of consistency. For according to FBP-ists, mathematical knowledge is supposed to arise out of knowledge that certain sentences and theories are intuitively consistent. But given this, how can they also claim that knowledge of the extension of the intuitive notion of consistency is obtained, or partially obtained, by means of an appeal to the platonistic notions of syntactic and semantic consistency? Isn't this circular?" This objection would be cogent only if it were impossible to know that a sentence or theory was intuitively consistent without having some knowledge involving the syntactic or semantic notion of consistency. But this is clearly false: anyone who has taught an introductory logic course can attest that students can be pretty reliable judges of whether a set of sentences is consistent, even if they have no conception whatsoever of syntactic or semantic consistency. Thus, the idea here is that before we developed the notions of syntactic and semantic consistency, our knowledge of intuitive consistency was good enough to give rise to some mathematical knowledge. Then, once the "ball of mathematical knowledge was rolling", so to speak, we developed the formal notions of consistency, acquired some knowledge of them, and in this way, increased our knowledge of the extension of the intuitive notion of consistency. (It should be noted that this picture of things doesn't just refute the above objection—it also jibes with the historical facts.)

In any event, I now want to move on. Assuming that there *is* a legitimate anti-platonist notion of consistency, what I need to argue in order to motivate premise (ii) is this: FBP-ists can account for the fact that human beings can—without coming into contact with the mathematical realm—know of certain purely mathematical theories that they are consistent, where 'consistent' is understood anti-platonistically. It seems to me, however, that as soon as we realize that we are working with an anti-platonist notion of consistency here, this premise becomes pretty trivial. If the fact that a sentence or theory is consistent is an anti-platonistic fact, then that fact isn't about any abstract objects, and so it would seem that we don't need any contact with any abstract objects in order to know that the fact obtains, that is, that the given sentence or theory is consistent.

Now, one might object to this on the grounds that sentences and theories are abstract objects. But FBP-ists can simply restrict their attention here to concrete *tokens* of sentences and theories (where it is understood that a "token of a mathematical theory" includes only tokens of the *axioms* of the theory—or more precisely, the axiom schemata and the axioms that aren't instances of axiom schemata). If FBP-ists can explain how human beings could know that concrete tokens of our mathematical theories are consistent, that is all they need to do, because they can claim that these tokens truly describe parts of the mathematical realm in the same way that types do.

A second objection that one might raise here is this. "If T is a purely mathematical theory, then although the claim that concrete tokens of T are consistent isn't about abstract objects, T itself *is* about abstract objects; thus, it may be that we need contact with abstract objects in order to know that T is consistent, because it may be that we need contact with T's own ontology in order to know that T is consistent." But this worry is misguided. For in general, knowledge of the consistency of a set of sentences—whether the sentences are purely mathematical, purely physical, mixed, or whatever—does *not* require any sort of epistemic access to, or contact with, the objects that the sentences are about. For instance, I do not need any access to the seventh child born in 1991 in order to know that the sentences asserting it to be female and Italian are consistent with each other; likewise, I don't need any access to this child to know that the sentences asserting it to be male and not male are inconsistent with each other. And the same is true of mathematical sentences: I do not need any access to the number 4 in order to know that '4 is even' and '4 is positive' are consistent with each other, or that '4 is odd' and '4 is not odd' are inconsistent with each other.

I take it that this point is entirely obvious, but it is worth mentioning because it provides a clear picture of the intuitive idea behind my epistemology. If FBP is true, then knowledge of the mathematical realm falls straight out of knowledge of the consistency of mathematical theories. But knowledge of the consistency of a theory does not require any contact with the objects of that theory, and so the Benacerrafian lack-of-contact worry about platonism has vanished completely.

Now, I suppose that one might press me here to actually explain how human beings arrive at knowledge of consistency. But it would be entirely inappropriate to dive into this here, because this issue is irrelevant to the question of whether platonism is true. There may be a deep and important question about how we come to know that various sentences and theories are consistent, but it is no more pressing for FBP-ists than it is for anyone else. Everyone has to account for knowledge of consistency, and FBP-ists can accept any explanation here that anyone else can accept. In particular, they can accept any explanation that anti-platonists can accept, because consistency—or rather, the sort of consistency we're discussing here—is an anti-platonist notion. Moreover, the question of how we acquire knowledge of consistency is no more pressing in connection with our mathematical theories than with our empirical theories. But this means that platonists do not have to address this issue in order to respond to the Benacerrafian epistemological argument, for as I've already pointed out, if that argument is to succeed, it cannot work equally well against physical and mathematical objects. It can succeed only if it shows that there is a *special* epistemological problem with platonism that arises as a result of the inaccessibility of mathematical objects.

In the early sections of this chapter, I tried to reduce the question of how we could acquire knowledge of abstract mathematical objects to the question of how we could acquire knowledge that some of our mathematical sentences and theories are consistent. In this section, I have been trying to argue that this latter sort of knowledge is not problematic. That is, I have been trying to argue that platonists will not encounter any special problems in accounting for our knowledge of mathematical consistency. I think I can provide additional support for this claim by pointing out that knowledge of consistency is *logical* knowledge.[33] We wouldn't expect platonists to have any more trouble than anti-platonists in accounting for our logical knowledge because, intuitively, logical knowledge doesn't seem to be platonistic knowledge at all. This is perhaps the central point of this chapter: if FBP is true, then mathematical knowledge can arise directly out of logical knowledge. Platonists who do not endorse FBP cannot make this claim, because they have to account for how people could know which of our consistent purely mathematical theories truly describe mathematical objects and which do not, and this could not be logical knowledge. But FBP-ists do not have to account for this sort of knowledge, because according to them, *all* of our consistent purely mathematical theories truly describe mathematical objects.[34]

All of this should be reminiscent of Field's view. He argues that anti-platonists can take mathematical knowledge to be logical knowledge.[35] If I'm right, then FBP-ists can do the same thing, although I think the point is better put by saying that mathematical knowledge *can arise directly out of* logical knowledge. And it is worth noting that this doesn't commit FBP-ists to logicism any more than Field's view commits *him* to logicism. Mathematical truth is not logical truth, because the existence claims of mathematics are not logically true. More precisely, if T is a purely mathematical theory implying the existence of various mathematical objects, then (a) if FBP is true, then knowledge of the logical fact that T is consistent can give rise to knowledge of the mathematical fact that T truly describes part of the mathematical realm; but (b) 'T is consistent' is not *equivalent* to 'T truly describes part of the mathematical realm', because whereas the latter can be true only if there are mathematical objects, the former can be true even if there are no mathematical objects. What we can say, however, is that 'T truly describes part of the mathematical realm' follows from the conjunction of FBP and 'T is consistent'.

I end by tying up a loose end. In chapter 1, I said that FBP is (roughly) the view that all the mathematical objects that logically possibly could exist actually do exist. But I noted there that more needed to be said about exactly what is meant here by 'logically possible'. In this section, I have cleared this up: 'logically possible' just means 'consistent, in the primitive, intuitive sense'. (Or at any rate, this is the stance that FBP-ists should tentatively endorse. If it turns out that there is an anti-platonist account of consistency that is superior to the view that 'consistent' is a primitive term, then FBP-ists might want to change what they say here.) Of course, this means that 'logically possible' can be applied only to whole sentences (or collections of sentences, or sentential components of sentences), and so the above definition of FBP will have to be reworded; but as I showed in chapter 1, this is not a serious problem.

Non-Uniqueness Embraced

1. Introduction

So the best argument against platonism — Benacerraf's epistemological argument —
fails. It succeeds in refuting non-full-blooded, or non-plenitudinous, versions of
platonism, but it does not refute FBP. Now, the natural question to ask at this
point is whether any of the *other* arguments against platonism refute FBP. In
chapter 3, I defended FBP against a number of different criticisms, but they were
all aimed at FBP in particular, rather than at platonism in general. The question
I want to ask now is whether any of the traditional arguments against platonism
are capable of refuting FBP. Now, there is really only *one* argument here, aside
from the epistemological argument, that is considered important, namely, the argument from multiple reductions, or non-uniqueness. In section 5, I will suggest
that there are two other problems that platonists need to deal with (and I will
eventually show that FBP-ists *can* deal with these problems), but for now, I want
to concentrate on the non-uniqueness problem.

In a nutshell, the non-uniqueness problem is this: platonism suggests that our
mathematical theories describe *unique* collections of abstract objects, but in point
of fact, this does not seem to be the case. But let me spell this argument out in
more detail. I will state the argument in terms of arithmetic, as is commonly done,
but it should be noted that analogous arguments can be given in connection with
other mathematical theories. The argument proceeds as follows:

(1) If there are any sequences of abstract objects that satisfy the axioms of
Peano Arithmetic (PA), then there are infinitely many such sequences.

(2) There is nothing "metaphysically special" about any of these sequences that makes it stand out from the others as *the* sequence of natural
numbers.

Therefore,

(3) There is no unique sequence of abstract objects that is the natural numbers.

But

(4) Platonism entails that there *is* a unique sequence of abstract objects that is the natural numbers.

Therefore,

(5) Platonism is false.

(Let me make a historical point about this argument. As was the case with the epistemological argument, discussions of the non-uniqueness argument trace to Benacerraf, the important work here being his 1965 paper, "What Numbers Could Not Be". It should be noted, however, that the argument in (1)–(5) is not explicitly formulated in Benacerraf's paper. The sub-argument in (1)–(3) is pretty clearly contained in that paper, but (4) is not. Now, most commentators seem to think that this premise is more or less implicit in Benacerraf's paper, but it seems to me equally likely that Benacerraf never meant to commit to (4) — that he only meant to establish (3) and not (5). In any event, I will not be concerned with this exegetical issue here. I am simply going to respond to the argument in (1)–(5).[1])

It seems to me that the only vulnerable parts of the non-uniqueness argument are (2) and (4). The two inferences — from (1) and (2) to (3) and from (3) and (4) to (5) — are both fairly trivial. Moreover, as we will see, (1) is virtually undeniable. (And it should be noted that we cannot make (1) any less trivial by taking PA to be a second-order theory and, hence, categorical. This will only guarantee that all the models of PA are isomorphic to one another. It will not deliver the desired result of there being only one model of PA.) So it seems that platonists have to attack either (2) or (4). In what follows, I will attack (4). But before I do that, I want to say a few words about the strategy of attacking (2).

2. Trying to Salvage the Numbers

I begin by sketching Benacerraf's argument in *favor* of (2). He proceeds here in two stages. First, he argues that no sequence of *sets* stands out as *the* sequence of natural numbers, and second, he extends the argument so that it covers sequences of other sorts of objects as well. The first claim, that is, the claim about sequences of sets, is motivated by reflecting on the numerous set-theoretic reductions of the natural numbers. Benacerraf concentrates, in particular, on the reductions given by Zermelo and von Neumann. Both of these reductions begin by identifying o with the null set, but Zermelo identifies $n + 1$ with the singleton $\{n\}$, whereas von Neumann identifies $n + 1$ with the union $n \cup \{n\}$. Thus, the two progressions proceed like so:

$$\varnothing, \{\varnothing\}, \{\{\varnothing\}\}, \{\{\{\varnothing\}\}\}, \ldots$$

and

$\emptyset, \{\emptyset\}, \{\emptyset, \{\emptyset\}\}, \{\emptyset, \{\emptyset\}, \{\emptyset, \{\emptyset\}\}\}, \ldots$

Benacerraf argues very convincingly that neither of these progressions provides a *better* reduction than the other, that there is no non-arbitrary reason for identifying the natural numbers with one of these sequences rather than the other or, indeed, with any of the many other set-theoretic sequences that would seem just as good here, such as the sequence that Frege suggests in his reduction.

Having thus argued that no sequence of sets stands out as *the* sequence of natural numbers, Benacerraf extends the point to sequences of other sorts of objects. His argument here proceeds as follows. From an arithmetical point of view, the only properties of a given sequence that *matter* to the question of whether it is the sequence of natural numbers are *structural* properties. In other words, nothing about the individual objects in the sequence matters—all that matters is the structure that the objects jointly possess. Therefore, any sequence with the right structure will be as good a candidate for being the natural numbers as any other sequence with the right structure. In other words, any *ω-sequence* will be as good a candidate as any other. Thus, we can conclude that no one sequence of objects stands out as *the* sequence of natural numbers.

It seems to me that if Benacerraf's argument for (2) can be blocked at all, it will have to be at this second stage, for I think it is more or less beyond doubt that no sequence of *sets* stands out as *the* sequence of natural numbers. So how can we attack the second stage of the argument? Well, one strategy here is to argue that all Benacerraf's argument shows is that the natural numbers cannot be *reduced* to anything else. On this view, the first part of the argument shows that they can't be reduced to sets, and the second part shows that they can't be reduced to anything else. But the possibility remains that numbers are simply irreducible entities. In other words, it may be that while there *are* numerous sequences of sets and functions and properties that satisfy PA, there is also a sequence of irreducible natural *numbers* that satisfies PA. And if there is such a sequence, then it certainly does stand out from all other sequences as *the* sequence of natural numbers. (Michael Resnik has made a similar point. He maintains that while Benacerraf has shown that numbers aren't sets or functions or chairs, he hasn't shown that numbers aren't objects, because he hasn't shown that numbers aren't *numbers*.[2])

Now, one problem with this response is that Benacerraf did not formulate the second stage of his argument for (2) in terms of reductions. The first stage of his argument was formulated in terms of reductions, but the second stage wasn't; it was based upon the observation that only structural facts about a sequence of objects are relevant to the question of whether that sequence is the sequence of natural numbers. But one might think that we can preserve the *spirit* of the response given in the last paragraph—that is, the one formulated in terms of reductions—while responding more directly to the argument that Benacerraf actually used. In particular, one might try to do this in something like the following way.

"There is some initial plausibility to Benacerraf's claim that only structural facts are relevant to the question of whether a given sequence of objects is the sequence of natural numbers. For (a) only structural facts are relevant to the question of whether a given sequence is *arithmetically adequate*, that is, whether it satisfies PA; and (b) since PA is our best theory of the natural numbers, it would seem that it captures *everything we know* about those numbers. But a moment's reflection reveals that this is confused, that PA does *not* capture everything we know about the natural numbers. There is nothing in PA that tells us that the number 17 is not the inventor of Cocoa Puffs, but nonetheless, we know (pre-theoretically) that it isn't. And there is nothing in PA that tells us that numbers aren't sets, but again, we know that they aren't. Likewise, we know that numbers aren't functions or properties or chairs. Now, it is true that these facts about the natural numbers aren't *mathematically important* — that's why none of them are included in PA — but in the present context, that is irrelevant. What matters is this: while Benacerraf is right that if there are any sequences of abstract objects that satisfy PA, then there are many, the same cannot be said about our *full conception of the natural numbers* (FCNN). We know, for instance, that no sequence of sets or functions or chairs satisfies FCNN, because it is built into our conception of the natural numbers that they do not have members, that they cannot be sat on, and so forth. Indeed, we seem to know that no sequence of things that aren't natural numbers satisfies FCNN, because part of our conception of the natural numbers is that they are natural numbers. Thus, it seems that we know of only *one* sequence that satisfies FCNN, namely, the sequence of natural numbers. But, of course, this means that (2) is false, that one of the sequences that satisfies PA stands out as *the* sequence of natural numbers."

Before saying what I think is really wrong with this argument, let me set a couple of worries aside. First, one might be a bit uneasy about the appeal to FCNN here; one might think that before platonists can rely upon any claims about FCNN, they need to say exactly what this "theory" (or whatever it is) consists in. Does it have axioms and theorems? Is it first-order? Is it second-order? Can it be formalized at all? And so on. It seems to me, however, that the appeal to FCNN is rather uncontroversial and that to ask these sorts of questions is to miss the point of this appeal. There are, of course, controversial questions about exactly what is contained in FCNN and what is not; but the basic idea behind FCNN — that we have beliefs about the natural numbers that are not captured by PA — seems relatively uncontroversial. Just about everyone agrees, for instance, that the number 3 is non-red; even mathematical fictionalists, who deny that there is any such thing as 3, agree that non-redness is built into our "conception of 3". Now, I do not mean to suggest that *no one* would take issue with the idea of FCNN; but it seems to me that there is nothing problematic about *platonists* appealing to FCNN, for the idea here goes hand in hand with the platonistic conception of mathematics. Moreover, given that we are allowing platonists to speak of FCNN, it would seem inappropriate to demand that they get very precise about its nature. FCNN is just the collection of everything that we, as a community, believe about the natural numbers. It is not a formal theory, and so it is not first-order or second-order, and it does not have any axioms in anything like the normal sense. Moreover, it is likely that there is no clear fact of the matter as to precisely which sentences are contained in FCNN (although for *most* sentences, there *is* a clear fact of the matter—for instance, '3 is prime' and '3 is not red' are clearly contained in FCNN, whereas '3 is not prime' and '3 is red' are clearly not). So it seems to me that to get precise about FCNN would do violence to the very idea of FCNN.

A second worry that one might have concerns the *details* of FCNN. More specifically, one might grant the general idea behind the appeal to FCNN but take .issue with the particular claim that it is built into FCNN that numbers aren't, for example, sets or properties. But I don't think there is much to motivate this; it seems pretty clear to me that it *is* built into FCNN that numbers aren't sets or properties (although I should note here that nothing I am going to say will depend on this claim).

So what *is* wrong with the above response to the non-uniqueness argument? In a nutshell, the problem is that this response begs the question against Benacerraf, because it simply helps itself to "the natural numbers". We can take the point of Benacerraf's argument to be that if all the ω-sequences were, so to speak, "laid out before us", we could have no good reason for singling one of them out as *the* sequence of natural numbers. Now, the above response does show that the situation here is not as grim as Benacerraf has made it seem, because it shows that *some* ω-sequences can be ruled out as definitely *not* the natural numbers. In particular, any ω-sequence that contains an object that we recognize as a non-number—such as a function or a chair or (on the view in question here) a set—can be ruled out in this way. In short, any ω-sequence that doesn't satisfy FCNN can be so ruled out. But platonists are not in any position to claim that all ω-sequences but one can be ruled out in this way; for since they think that abstract objects exist *independently of us*, they must admit that there are very likely numerous kinds of abstract objects that we've never thought about and, hence, that there are very likely numerous ω-sequences that satisfy FCNN and differ from one another only in ways that no human being has ever imagined. I don't see any way for platonists to escape this possibility, and so it seems to me very likely that (2) is true and, hence, that (3) is also true.[3]

There are, of course, various responses that platonists might make to this argument, but I do not want to pursue this any further, because the solution that I am going to give (in section 4) to the non-uniqueness problem does not depend upon the attitude I have taken here toward (2) and (3). That is, my response is consistent with the *falsity* of (2) and (3), although I will be assuming from here on out that they are true.[4]

3. Structuralism

If (2) is true, then platonists must either abandon their view or find some plausible way to reject (4). Now, there is one very famous way of rejecting (4) that, I think, does *not* provide an adequate solution to the non-uniqueness problem. What I have in mind here is the view that platonists can solve the non-uniqueness problem by merely adopting a platonistic version of Benacerraf's own view, that is, a platonistic version of *structuralism*.[5] The idea here, I suppose, is that since structuralists do not maintain that arithmetic is about some particular sequence of objects, the non-uniqueness problem just doesn't arise for them.

The trouble with this response to the non-uniqueness problem isn't that structuralism is false; it's that it doesn't solve the problem. This can be appreciated by merely noting that we can reformulate the non-uniqueness argument in (1)–(5) so that it applies to structuralism as well as to object-platonism. We can do this as follows:

(1') If there are any parts of the mathematical realm that satisfy the axioms of PA, then there are infinitely many such parts.

(2') There is nothing "metaphysically special" about any of these parts of the mathematical realm that makes it stand out from the others as *the* sequence of natural numbers (or natural-number positions or whatever).

Therefore,

(3') There is not a unique part of the mathematical realm that is the sequence of natural numbers (or natural-number positions or whatever).

But

(4') Platonism entails that there *is* a unique part of the mathematical realm that is the sequence of natural numbers (or natural-number positions or whatever).

Therefore,

(5') Platonism is false.

So platonists cannot solve the non-uniqueness problem by merely adopting structuralism and rejecting the thesis that mathematics is about objects, because the problem remains even after we make the switch to a structuralistic platonism.

But we cannot yet close the book on structuralism. Before we do that, we need to ask whether there is any way of responding to this new version of the argument that's available to structuralists but not to object-platonists. More specifically, we need to ask whether there's any way of refuting (2') that's available to structuralists but not to object-platonists, because this is how structuralists will want to respond to the new version of the argument. (It might seem surprising that structuralists would respond in this way, since, as we've seen, they respond to the original version of the argument by rejecting (4). But if we think of the strategies of rejecting (2') and (4') as the strategies of trying to *salvage* uniqueness and *abandon* uniqueness, respectively, then it makes perfectly good sense to think of structuralists as rejecting (2'). For despite their rejection of (4), they do not want to abandon uniqueness. They reject (4) because of the role played in that sentence by the word 'object' — not because of the role played by the word 'unique'. As far as uniqueness is concerned, structuralists want to *salvage* it: their claim is that arithmetic is about *the* structure that all ω-sequences have in common. Or at any rate, this is the *standard* structuralist view.[6] Of course, the possibility remains that *some* structuralists might want to respond to the non-uniqueness problem by *aban-*

doning uniqueness, that is, by rejecting (4'). I will say a few words about this later, but first, I want to discuss (2'); in particular, I want to argue that structuralists are no better off with respect to the strategy of rejecting (2') than object-platonists are.)

It seems to me very unlikely that there is a plausible way of refuting (2') that's available to structuralists but not to object-platonists. For the claim that there is a unique structure — that is, a sequence of positions — that stands out as *the* sequence of natural numbers seems just as implausible as the claim that there's a unique sequence of *objects* that stands out as *the* sequence of natural numbers. And, indeed, it seems implausible for the same reason: since structures exist independently of us in an abstract mathematical realm, it seems very likely that there are numerous things in the mathematical realm that count as structures, that satisfy FCNN, and that differ from one another only in ways that no human being has ever imagined. (And this, by the way, shows not just that structuralists are as bad off as object-platonists with respect to (2'), but also that (2') is just as well motivated as (2). In other words, the point here is that (2') can be motivated in the same way that (2) was motivated in section 2.)

Structuralists might try to respond here by arguing for

(A) There exists a *unique* structure — or sequence of positions — that satisfies FCNN

in something like the following way. "Any two structures that are structurally equivalent, that is, isomorphic, are identical with one another. But it seems safe to assume that any two structures that satisfy FCNN are isomorphic to one another, that is, that FCNN is categorical, that is, that non-standard models of arithmetic do not satisfy FCNN. Therefore, it seems to follow that there is only *one* structure that satisfies FCNN."

The problem with this argument is the claim that any two structures that are isomorphic to one another are identical. If structuralists endorse this thesis, then they also have to endorse

(S) There is no more *to* a structure than the relations that hold between its positions; that is, positions do not have any properties other than those they have in virtue of the relations that they bear to other positions in the structure.

But we have already seen (chapter 1, sub-section 2.1) that (S) is untenable and, indeed, that it leads to a contradiction.[7] Now, I suppose that structuralists might try to come up with an argument here that doesn't rely upon (S), but I don't see how they could do this. It seems to me that without (S), structuralists won't be able to get what they need here. For if (S) is false, then it is possible for structures to differ from one another in non-structural ways, and so it is possible for two structures that are isomorphic to one another to differ. And, presumably, it's possible for them to differ in ways that we've never thought about. Thus, given the vastness and metaphysical independence of the mathematical realm, it seems very likely that if (S) is false, then there are at least two structures that satisfy FCNN and differ from one another only in ways that no human being has ever imagined.

Therefore, it seems to me that as long as we reject (S), we ought to maintain that (A) is false and that the above argument for (2') goes through.[8]

That's *one* problem with the argument of the paragraph before last. A second problem is that even if structuralists could find some way to motivate (A), this would *not* provide them with an adequate response to the non-uniqueness problem. They would also need to motivate

(B) The unique sequence of positions mentioned in (A) stands out from all sequences of *objects* as *the* sequence of natural numbers.

But (B) seems very implausible. For even if (A) were true, there would still be numerous sequences of objects that satisfied FCNN, and these sequences would all have as much claim to being the natural numbers as the sequence of positions mentioned in (A) would have, and so the non-uniqueness problem would still remain. I don't see any plausible way for structuralists to avoid this. It seems that the only thing they could argue here — the only thing that would single out their sequence of positions as *the* sequence of natural numbers — is that it's built into FCNN that numbers are positions in structures. But this seems utterly implausible. (Alternatively, structuralists might try to argue that something like

(N) There is no more to the numbers than the relations that hold between them

is built into FCNN. But in the first place, this is just as prima facie implausible as the bare claim that it's built into FCNN that numbers are positions in structures; indeed, it's even more implausible, for in this case, it actually seems that the *negation* of (N) is built into FCNN, because it seems to be built into FCNN that numbers are, for example, *non-red*, and non-redness doesn't have anything to do with the relations that hold between the numbers. And in the second place, (N) leads to the same contradiction that (S) leads to.)

I conclude, then, that as was the case with (2) and (3), it is very likely that (2') and (3') are true. And so I also conclude that platonists cannot solve the non-uniqueness problem by merely adopting structuralism. (Actually, this second conclusion hasn't really been established yet, because the possibility still remains that structuralism could provide platonists with a solution to the non-uniqueness problem via the strategy of rejecting (4'). We're going to see in section 4, however, that *all* platonists can solve the problem by rejecting (4'), regardless of whether they endorse structuralism. I'm going to develop this solution in object-platonist terms, but one could also develop a structuralist version of the solution. But even if we did this, structuralism wouldn't play any *role* in the solution; that is, the solution would still be the same — it would just be stated in structuralist terms. Thus, what we can say is this: the arguments of this section and section 4, taken together, show that the question of whether platonists endorse structuralism is wholly irrelevant to the question of whether they can solve the non-uniqueness problem.[9])

I end with the same remark I made at the end of section 2: while there are certainly responses that one might offer to the argument of this section, I do not want to pursue any of them here, because the solution that I will give (in section

4) to the non-uniqueness problem doesn't depend upon the cogency of my refutation of the structuralist solution.

4. The Solution

Having dispensed with the idea that structuralism might provide us with a solution to the non-uniqueness problem, I want to go back to speaking in terms of the argument in (1)–(5) and forget about the argument in (1')–(5'). I do this merely for reasons of elegance: it is simply less cumbersome to speak in terms of mathematical *objects* than of parts of the mathematical realm.

In any event, it seems to me that the only remaining platonist strategy for responding to the non-uniqueness argument is to reject (4). That is, platonists have to give up on uniqueness. And they have to do this in connection not just with arithmetical theories like PA and FCNN, but with all of our mathematical theories. They have to claim that while such theories truly describe collections of abstract mathematical objects, they do not pick out *unique* collections of such objects. (Or at the very least, platonists have to claim that if any of our mathematical theories does describe a unique collection of abstract objects, it is only by blind luck that it does.)

Now, this stance certainly represents a departure from traditional versions of platonism. But it cannot be seriously maintained that in making this move, we *abandon* platonism. For since the core of platonism is the belief in abstract objects — and since the core of mathematical platonism is the belief that our mathematical theories truly describe such objects — it follows that the above view is a version of platonism. Thus, the only question is whether there is some reason for thinking that platonists cannot make this move, that is, for thinking that platonists are *committed* to the thesis that our mathematical theories describe unique collections of mathematical objects. In other words, the question is whether there is any *argument* for (4) — or for a generalized version of (4) that holds not just for arithmetic but for all of our mathematical theories.

It seems to me — and this is the central claim of my response to the non-uniqueness objection — that there *isn't* such an argument. First of all, Benacerraf didn't give any argument at all for (4).[10] Moreover, to the best of my knowledge, no one else has ever argued for it either. But the really important point here is that, prima facie, it seems that there couldn't *be* a cogent argument for (4) — or for a generalized version of (4) — because, on the face of it, (4) and its generalization are both highly implausible. The generalized version of (4) says that

(P) Our mathematical theories truly describe collections of abstract mathematical objects

entails

(U) Our mathematical theories truly describe *unique* collections of abstract mathematical objects.

This is a *really* strong claim. And near as I can tell, there is absolutely no reason to believe it. Thus, it seems to me that platonists can simply accept (P) and reject (U). Indeed, they can endorse (P) together with the *contrary* of (U); that is, they can claim that while our mathematical theories do describe collections of abstract objects, none of them describes a unique collection of such objects. In short, platonists can avoid the so-called non-uniqueness "problem" by simply *embracing* non-uniqueness, that is, by adopting *non-uniqueness platonism* (NUP).

One might respond here as follows. "Your argument is too quick. You are right that in order to really show that platonists *cannot* endorse NUP, we would have to provide an argument for (4) (and/or its generalization). And you are also right that the entailment claims inherent in (4) and its generalization are extremely implausible. But we might be able to grant that (4) and its generalization are false — that is, that (P) doesn't *entail* (U) — but still maintain that those who endorse (P) ought to endorse (U) as well. In other words, we might be able to grant that NUP is *intelligible* but still maintain that platonists ought not to endorse it. For it may be that NUP can be refuted, or made to seem implausible, on independent grounds."

This worry is related to a second worry, namely, that the adoption of NUP is an ad hoc device, that is, that the only reason for platonists to endorse NUP is that it solves the non-uniqueness problem. Thus, while the first worry is that there may be good reasons for favoring traditional (U)-platonism over NUP, the second worry is that there doesn't seem to be any *independent* reason for favoring NUP over (U)-platonism. Now, this second worry can be dispensed with very quickly: platonists do have independent reasons for favoring NUP over traditional (U)-platonism, because (a) FBP is a version of NUP, and (b) we have already seen that FBP is the best version of platonism there is; indeed, we've seen that FBP is the only tenable version of platonism, because non-full-blooded (i.e., non-plenitudinous) versions of platonism are refuted by the epistemological argument. (It should be clear that FBP really is a version of NUP, that is, that FBP-ists would reject (U). For if the mathematical realm is as populated as FBP would have it, then it seems extremely unlikely that any of our mathematical theories — even those that include pre-theoretical claims, such as FCNN — are uniquely satisfied. To take the example of FCNN, it seems overwhelmingly likely that there are numerous ω-sequences that satisfy FCNN and differ from one another only in ways that no human being has ever thought about. Thus, while FBP doesn't *entail* NUP, it seems that once we adopt FBP, we ought to adopt NUP as well.)

So we appear to have good independent reasons for favoring NUP over traditional (U)-platonism. But in order to block the *first* worry discussed above — that is, the worry of the paragraph before last — I need to argue the opposite point; that is, I need to argue that there are no good reasons for favoring (U)-platonism over NUP, or FBP–NUP. Now, I think there are a number of arguments that one might attempt here, but most of these emerged in chapter 3 as arguments against FBP. For instance, one might try to argue that (U)-platonism is superior to NUP on the grounds that it guarantees that propositions like the continuum hypothesis (CH) have determinate truth values. But I argued in chapter 3 that the FBP–NUP-ist view of propositions like CH is not only acceptable, but actually *superior* to the traditional (U)-platonist view of such propositions. (I argued this point in purely FBP-ist terms, but it is obvious that the same things could be said from an FBP–NUP-ist point of view.)

But there was *one* objection to FBP that I put on the back burner in chapter 3, and I would now like to discuss it as an argument for the claim that (U)-platonism is superior to NUP, or rather, to FBP–NUP. The argument can be stated as follows. "We should take our mathematical theories as being about unique collections of mathematical objects, because we use *singular terms* in these theories, and this would be acceptable only if there were unique referents for these terms. After all, if a singular term doesn't have a unique referent, we are inclined to say that it doesn't refer at all, that it suffers some sort of reference *failure*."

It seems to me that the central premise here — the claim that the use of mathematical singular terms would be acceptable only if there were unique referents for these terms — requires *argument*. For this is precisely what NUP-ists deny. To deny that our mathematical theories are descriptions of unique collections of mathematical objects just *is* to deny that our mathematical singular terms have unique referents. Moreover, NUP-ists do not just deny that our mathematical singular terms have unique referents and leave it at that. They have a story to tell about why this is acceptable, or unproblematic. The reason, in a nutshell, is that the internal properties of mathematical objects are mathematically unimportant. As structuralists are quick to point out, all mathematically important facts are structural facts, that is, facts about the relations between mathematical objects, as opposed to facts about the internal properties of mathematical objects.[11] Because of this, it simply doesn't *matter* if our mathematical theories fail to pick out unique collections of objects (or if our mathematical singular terms fail to pick out unique referents), because we can capture the structural facts that we are really after *without* picking out unique collections of objects (or unique referents).

So the first point to note here is that NUP-ists have a reason for thinking that it would be acceptable to use singular terms in mathematics without there being unique referents for those terms. But we ought to ask whether (U)-platonists have any argument for the opposite conclusion. Is there any reason for thinking that it would be *unacceptable* to use singular terms in mathematics without there being unique referents for those terms? Or ignoring the issue of acceptability, is there any reason for thinking that, in point of actual fact, our mathematical singular terms do have unique referents? I can think of three arguments that (U)-platonists might offer here. They can be formulated as follows:

> *Argument 1*: In abandoning unique reference, platonists abandon the ability to adopt a *standard semantics* for mathematese, that is, a semantics that parallels the one we use for ordinary discourse. But the ability to adopt such a semantics for mathematese has always been one of the main motivations for mathematical platonism.

> *Argument 2*: Mathematicians seem to have unique objects *in mind* when they use singular terms. Indeed, considerations of this sort can be used to argue against NUP directly, for it also seems that mathematicians have

unique *collections* of objects in mind when they construct their *theories*, for example, arithmetic.

Argument 3: Given the right background, any mathematical object can play the role of any position in any mathematical structure. Therefore, NUP-ists have to allow that every mathematical singular term refers (non-uniquely) to every mathematical object. But this *vicious* sort of non-unique reference is surely unacceptable.

In response to argument 3, I simply deny that NUP-ists are committed to this vicious sort of non-unique reference. This goes back to a point I made in section 2: just because all mathematically important facts are structural facts, it does not follow that these are the only facts relevant to the determination of mathematical reference. To take an example, NUP-ists can maintain that we know '3' doesn't refer to any function, because it is built into our conception of the natural numbers — that is, FCNN — that numbers aren't functions. More generally, the point here is that the vast majority of ω-sequences fail to satisfy FCNN, and so our numerals do not refer to the objects in those sequences. They refer only to the objects in those ω-sequences that satisfy FCNN. Of course, this is all completely standard; the only non-traditional claim that NUP-ists make is that there may be numerous ω-sequences that satisfy FCNN.

One might object as follows. "Your argument here shows that we cannot assign to the term '3' any object that is in the extension of the predicate 'function'. Thus, given that the extension of 'function' is *fixed*, it follows that '3' does not refer to any object in this extension. But if we are allowed to reinterpret 'function' and '3' at the same time, then things change. Indeed, if we think of interpretations as applying to the language of mathematics as a *whole*, then it seems that '3' could refer to any mathematical object whatsoever. For we could, so to speak, "begin" each interpretation by assigning an object to '3', and then construct the rest of the interpretation around this, being careful that the referent of '3' is in the extension of 'number', not in the extension of 'function', and so on."

The author of this objection seems to think of mathematical objects as, so to speak, "bare particulars". That is, the objection seems to assume something like

(I) Taken *in themselves*, that is, without any interpretation present, mathematical objects are all indistinguishable from one another.

Now, I grant that if (I) were true, then NUP-ists would have to admit that '3' could refer to any mathematical object whatsoever. But this wouldn't be a *problem* for NUP, because if (I) were true, then '3' *really could* refer to any mathematical object whatsoever, because all these objects would be indistinguishable from one another. Thus, if (I) were true, then we would have a refutation not of NUP but of (U)-platonism! But it seems to me that (I) doesn't fit very well with platonism anyway. Consider, for instance, $\emptyset$ and $\{\emptyset\}$. Is it in the spirit of platonism to claim that these two objects are indistinguishable and that we just happen to assign the former to '$\emptyset$' and the latter to '$\{\emptyset\}$'? I think it is better (and more in the spirit of platonism) to say that it is part of the *nature* of $\{\emptyset\}$ that it contains $\emptyset$ (or in NUP-ist terms, if x is a referent of '{∅}', then it is part of x's nature that it contains an object that is a referent of '∅'). (Moreover, FBP seems to entail that there *are* mathematical objects with such natures, because it says that all the mathematical objects that possibly could exist actually do exist, and intuitively, it seems that there could exist mathematical objects with such natures.) But if mathematical objects have distinct natures in this way, then it is surely not the case that the term '3'—or more precisely, *our* term '3', that is, the '3' of FCNN—could refer to any mathematical object at all.

Moving on to argument 2, my response here is to deny that there is a unique sequence of objects such that mathematicians have *that sequence in mind* when they are doing arithmetic, or talking about "the numbers". Given the platonist thesis that the mathematical realm exists independent of us and our theorizing, we arrive at the result that there may be numerous ω-sequences that satisfy FCNN and differ from one another only in ways that no human being has ever imagined. Moreover, if there *are* numerous ω-sequences that satisfy FCNN, then they are all on a par with respect to our arithmetical thoughts and beliefs; that is, none of them stands out from the others as somehow "uniquely connected" to our mental states so that those mental states are *about* that ω-sequence, where 'about' is understood here in the metaphysically *thick* sense discussed above.[12] We can say that our arithmetical beliefs are *thinly* about *all* of these ω-sequences, but it is wrong to claim that there is some particular one of these sequences that is such that we have *it* in mind. This is simply because FCNN is *all* we have in mind when we do arithmetic. FCNN gives us a list of desiderata that need to be satisfied by an ω-sequence in order for it to be a candidate for being the sequence of natural numbers; but if several different sequences satisfy the list of desiderata, then none of them is *the* sequence of natural numbers, because there is nothing *more* that we have in mind, over and above the list of desiderata contained in FCNN, that could settle the matter. Thus, if FCNN doesn't pick out a unique ω-sequence, then we simply don't have a unique ω-sequence in mind when we do arithmetic.

Now, in *empirical* contexts, when there is no unique object answering to a singular term, we often want to say that something has gone *wrong*—that the singular term suffers a reference failure, or something to that effect. But I have already argued that in mathematical contexts, there is no need to make such a claim. If FCNN doesn't pick out a unique ω-sequence and, hence, the numerals don't pick out unique objects, it is simply not a problem, because we can accomplish what we want to accomplish in arithmetic—in particular, we can succeed in characterizing the structural facts that we want to characterize—even if FCNN fails to pick out a unique ω-sequence and the numerals fail to denote unique objects. And it's not just that there's no *need* to consider non-unique reference problematic; the fact is that mathematicians *wouldn't* consider it problematic. In other words, it seems to me that the above stance is perfectly consistent with mathematical practice. Now, in saying this, I do not mean to deny that there are a lot of mathematicians who naively think that the numerals have unique referents. What I mean is this: if we pointed out to these mathematicians that it may be that there are numerous ω-sequences that satisfy all of FCNN and differ from one another only in ways that no human being has ever imagined, they would not see this as a problem. Most of them, I think, would say something like the following. "Oh, come on. None of this matters in the least bit, because all of these sequences will serve our needs perfectly well. If they all satisfy FCNN, that's all that matters. There doesn't have to be a *unique* sequence that satisfies FCNN."[13,14]

What about argument 1? Well, I suppose the least misleading way to express my response to this argument is as follows: I deny that the NUP-ist's appeal to non-unique reference brings with it an abandonment of standard semantics. In giving a standard semantics for the language of arithmetic, what we do is assign objects to the singular terms, sets of objects to the one-place predicates, sets of ordered pairs of objects to the two-place predicates, and so on. NUP-ists do *not* want to abandon this practice. They merely want to claim that in using singular terms in arithmetic and providing them with a standard semantics, we make an assumption that is, strictly speaking, false, but nevertheless, very convenient and completely harmless. The assumption is just that there is a unique ω-sequence that satisfies FCNN, or in other words, that numerals have unique referents. The reason this assumption is convenient should be obvious: it's just intuitively pleasing to do arithmetic in this singular-term, standard-semantics way. And the reason the assumption is *harmless* is that we simply aren't interested in the differences between the various ω-sequences that satisfy FCNN. In other words, all of these sequences are indistinguishable with respect to the sorts of facts and properties that we are trying to characterize in doing arithmetic, and so no harm can come from proceeding as if there were only *one* sequence here.

One might object as follows. "I'm wondering what you think the *truth conditions* of, say, '3 is prime' are. Of course, you might just say that this sentence is true iff 3 is prime, and you might add that it's "convenient" to take this as being about a particular object, but you don't think that it's *really* about a particular object. On your view, there might be many 3s. Moreover, some of these "3s" might be "4s" in other ω-sequences — indeed, in other ω-sequences that satisfy FCNN. And of course, in the setting of these other ω-sequences, these "3s" will not be prime. So in asking what the truth conditions of '3 is prime' are, what I'm asking is this: According to FBP–NUP, what does the world really need to be *like* in order for it to be the case that '3 is prime' is true?"

Before I say what FBP–NUP-ists take the truth conditions of '3 is prime' to be, let me say that I think there is a mistake in this objection. FBP–NUP-ists admit that there might be many 3s, but they do *not* admit that one of these 3s could be a "4" in another ω-sequence that satisfied FCNN. Now, of course, *all* of these 3s appear in the "4 position" in other ω-sequences, but none of these other ω-sequences satisfies FCNN, because they all have objects in the "4 position" that have the property *being 3*. And we know that these objects have the property *being 3* because (a) by hypothesis, they appear in the "3 position" in ω-sequences that do satisfy FCNN, and (b) they couldn't do this without having the property *being 3*, because it is built into FCNN that the number 3 has the property *being 3*.

Given this, I can answer the above question — that is, "What does the world need to be like in order for it to be the case that '3 is prime' is true?" — in the obvious way. In order for '3 is prime' to be true, it needs to be the case that (a) there is at least one object that satisfies all of the desiderata for being 3, and (b) all objects that satisfy all of these desiderata are prime. Or more simply, it needs to be the case that (a) there is at least one standard model of arithmetic, and (b) '3 is prime' is true in all of the standard models of arithmetic. This, of course, is very similar to what traditional (U)-platonists say about the truth conditions of '3 is prime'. The only difference is that FBP-NUP-ists allow that it may be that there are numerous standard models of arithmetic and, hence, numerous objects that satisfy all of the desiderata for being 3.

So it seems to me that none of the three arguments shows that it would be unacceptable to use singular terms in mathematics without there being unique referents for these terms (or that, in point of actual fact, our mathematical singular terms do have unique referents). Therefore, this whole reference-based argument for (U) — or for the superiority of (U)-platonism over NUP — fails. Moreover, I can't think of any other arguments that traditional (U)-platonists might use against NUP (or more precisely, I can't think of any argument here that isn't more or less equivalent to one of the arguments against FBP that I discussed in chapter 3). Now, I might be overlooking some argument here, but I think this is unlikely, because we've already seen that there are good reasons for favoring NUP over (U)-platonism and, moreover, that (U) is at odds with the platonistic view that mathematical objects exist independently of us in an abstract mathematical realm. (This last point suggests that NUP is actually more in the spirit of platonism than traditional platonism is. For when NUP-ists allow that our mathematical theories might not capture unique parts of the mathematical realm, they are merely acknowledging that the mathematical realm is, in some sense, "beyond us" and that there may be parts and facets of the mathematical realm that we've never thought about. And it's also worth pointing out here that FBP is very much in the spirit of platonism. For in allowing that all the mathematical objects that possibly could exist actually do exist, FBP-ists eliminate any *arbitrariness* from the mathematical realm.)

In brief, then, my response to the non-uniqueness objection to platonism is this: the fact that our mathematical theories fail to pick out unique collections of mathematical objects (or *probably* fail to do this) is simply not a problem for platonists, because they can endorse NUP. Moreover, the version of platonism that I introduced and defended in chapter 3, namely, FBP, dovetails very nicely with NUP, and so there is no non-uniqueness problem with FBP.

5. Two Loose Ends

I would like to end with two more or less tangential points. The first point, which I actually touched on in chapter 3, is that FBP-ists can extend the stance of this chapter by embracing non-categoricity as well as non-uniqueness. In other words, the point is that FBP is consistent not just with the thesis that our mathematical theories do not describe unique parts of the mathematical realm but also with the thesis that our mathematical theories are not categorical. Now, I remarked above that I think that FCNN *is* categorical, but the point I'm making now is that even if I'm wrong about this, it wouldn't be a problem for FBP, because that view is perfectly compatible with the thesis that FCNN is *not* categorical. (This is an important point, for I think it's fairly likely that our "full conception of the universe of sets" (FCUS) is not categorical. Again, this is a point that I made in chapter 3.)

These remarks suggest that Putnam's Löwenheim–Skolem argument[15] does not raise any problem for FBP, for they suggest that FBP-ists can respond to this argument in essentially the same way that they respond to the non-uniqueness argument. Now, one might respond here by claiming that Putnam's worry is not so easily answered, because the Löwenheim–Skolem theorem can be brought to bear not just on our *mathematical* theories but on the FBP-ist's *own* theory as well. A detailed discussion of this problem would be out of place here, because it is really a problem for realism in *general*, as opposed to mathematical platonism in particular. But let me make a few points here. First of all, one might argue that, in fact, the Löwenheim–Skolem theorem doesn't apply to FBP, because FBP cannot be formulated in a first-order language. Moreover—and this is the most important point here—even if the Löwenheim–Skolem theorem does apply to FBP, it seems very plausible to suppose that FBP-ists could provide good reasons for maintaining that the models generated in this way are *unintended*. And finally, even if there are denumerable models of FBP that FBP-ists *cannot* argue are unintended, it's not clear that this is a problem. That is, it may be that FBP-ists can simply continue their strategy of embracing things here, that is, that they can say something like the following. "So what? So our theory has denumerable models that we can't prove are unintended. What's *wrong* with that?"

The second point that I want to make in this section is something of a segue into part II of this book. I have now argued that FBP-ists can adequately respond to both of Benacerraf's objections to platonism, that is, the epistemological objection and the non-uniqueness objection. Thus, since these two objections are widely considered to be the only objections that really challenge mathematical platonism, one might be inclined to conclude that FBP is home free. But I think there are some other objections to platonism, in addition to the two Benacerrafian objections, that FBP-ists need to address. Now, I have responded to several of these objections in chapter 3 and the present chapter,[16] but there are still two important problems with platonism that I haven't yet discussed. The first is the problem of explaining the usefulness, or applicability, of mathematics,[17] and the second is based upon Ockham's razor. I want to put these two problems on hold for now, because they will become easily solvable in the wake of the arguments of part II. I will give my solutions to them in the final section of chapter 7.

In any event, it is time now to turn our attention from the problems with platonism to the problems with anti-platonism.

ANTI-PLATONISM

There's no place like home.

—Dorothy Gale (late)

The Fregean Argument Against Anti-Platonism

1. Introduction

So far, I have tried to show that there is a version of mathematical platonism that avoids all of the important objections to that view. I will now try to do the same for mathematical anti-platonism. This will occupy me for all but the last few pages of part II.

Now, I suppose that there are numerous arguments against mathematical anti-platonism (or, what comes to the same thing, in favor of mathematical platonism), but it seems to me that there is only one such argument with a serious claim to cogency. Thus, I will ignore all other arguments and consider only this single line of attack. The argument I have in mind is due to Frege. My presentation will be somewhat different from Frege's, but the spirit of the argument is essentially the same.

2. The Argument

The Fregean argument is best understood as a pair of embedded inferences to the best explanation. In particular, the argument proceeds as follows:

(i) The only way to account for the truth of our mathematical theories is to adopt platonism.

(ii) The only way to account for the fact that our mathematical theories are applicable and/or indispensable to empirical science is to admit that these theories are true.

Therefore,

(iii) Platonism is true and anti-platonism is false.

Prima facie, it might seem that (i) is sufficient to establish platonism by itself. But (ii) is needed to block a certain response to (i). Anti-platonists might claim that the alleged fact to be explained in (i) — that our mathematical theories are true — is really no fact at all. In other words, they might respond to (i) by denying that our mathematical theories are true and endorsing *fictionalism*.[1] The purpose of (ii) is to argue that this sort of response is unacceptable, the idea being that our mathematical theories have to be true, because if they were fictions, then they would be no more useful to empirical scientists than, say, the novel *Oliver Twist* is. (This argument — that is, the one contained in (ii) — is known as the *Quine–Putnam indispensability argument*, but it does trace to Frege.[2])

I am going to respond to this argument by pursuing the fictionalist strategy of rejecting (ii). Now, there are two different ways for fictionalists to attack (ii). First, they can admit that there *are* indispensable applications of mathematics to empirical science and simply account for these applications from a fictionalist point of view. And second, they can argue that, in fact, there *aren't* any indispensable applications of mathematics to empirical science. Now, of course, this second strategy does not involve the claim that mathematics isn't applicable to empirical science at all; the idea is, rather, to argue that

(NI) Mathematics is *not indispensable* to empirical science,

and

(AA) The mere fact that mathematics is applicable to empirical science — that is, applicable in a dispensable way — can be accounted for without abandoning fictionalism.

This second strategy is the one that Hartry Field has pursued.[3] The hard part here is motivating (NI).[4] To do this, one has to argue that all of our empirical theories can be *nominalized*, that is, reformulated in a way that avoids reference to, and quantification over, abstract objects. Field tries to do this by simply carrying out the nominalization for one empirical theory, namely, Newtonian Gravitation Theory. But there have been a number of objections raised against Field's construction,[5] and the consensus opinion among philosophers of mathematics seems to be that his nominalization program cannot be made to work.

I am inclined to disagree with this consensus, however, and in chapter 6, I will try to provide some motivation for my disagreement. In particular, I will block what I think is the most pressing objection to Field's program, namely, Malament's objection that it cannot be extended to cover quantum mechanics. But I will not address any of the other worries that people have raised about Field's program, and so chapter 6 does not provide a complete response to (ii). This doesn't matter, though, because in the end, I do not want to respond to (ii) via this Fieldian strategy. Instead, I want to use the other strategy: I want to *grant* (for the sake of argument) that there *are* indispensable applications of mathematics to empirical science — that is, that mathematics is hopelessly and inextricably woven into some of our empirical theories — and I want to simply *account* for these indispensable applications from a fictionalist point of view. To the best of my knowledge, no one has pursued this strategy before, but in chapter 7, I will show that it can be

made to work. I will do this by simply providing the required fictionalist explanation of indispensable applications.

(Given that I think both of these strategies of responding to (ii) can succeed,
one might wonder why I favor my own response over Field's. One reason is that
my response is simply less controversial: the arguments I give in chapter 7 show
pretty clearly, I think, that fictionalists can account for indispensable applications
and, hence, that they can sidestep the Fregean argument. But this is not the only
reason for favoring my response over Field's. A second reason is that my response
fits better with mathematical and scientific practice. A third reason is that whereas
Field's strategy could yield only a piecemeal response to the problem of the applications of mathematics, I account for all applications of mathematics at the
same time and in the same way. And a fourth reason is that my response can be
generalized so that it accounts not just for the use made of mathematics in empirical science, but also for the use made there of *non-mathematical*-abstract-object
talk—for instance, the use made in belief psychology of 'that'-clauses that pur-
portedly refer to propositions.[6])

Chapters 6 and 7, then, will be concerned with the fictionalist attempt to
attack (ii), that is, the fictionalist attempt to block the Quine–Putnam argument.
Before I embark on this, however, I want to argue (in the present chapter) that
(i) is true, that we cannot admit that our mathematical theories are true without
believing in abstract mathematical objects. Now, given that I am going to argue
in chapter 7 that (ii) is false, it might seem pointless to argue here that (i) is true.
But it is not pointless. For in chapter 8, when I discuss the implications of the
philosophical "tie" between FBP and fictionalism, I am going to rely upon
the result that FBP is the *only* tenable version of platonism and fictionalism is the
only tenable version of anti-platonism. Now, I have already argued (in chapter 2)
that non-full-blooded (that is, non-plenitudinous) versions of platonism are untenable. What I want to argue now is that non-fictionalistic versions of anti-platonism
are untenable. But in arguing this, I will also be arguing for (i); for if all non-
fictionalist versions of anti-platonism are untenable, then all of the various
anti-platonist attempts to salvage mathematical truth are untenable.

Let me make two points about all of this. First, in order to show that fictionalism is the only tenable version of anti-platonism, I need to argue not just that
non-fictionalistic versions of anti-platonism are untenable, but also that fictionalism is itself tenable. But in order to do this, I need to defend fictionalism against
not just the Quine–Putnam attack discussed above, but *all* attacks. It seems to me,
however, that aside from the Quine–Putnam worry, there are really only three
worries that one might reasonably have about fictionalism, and in section 3 of this
chapter, I will argue that all of these worries can be answered rather easily.

Second, since there are so many different *kinds* of non-fictionalistic anti-
platonism, it might seem that it would take a huge amount of work to show that
all of these views are untenable. But I am going to reduce the amount of work
that needs to be done here by arguing that most versions of anti-platonism are *not*
importantly different from fictionalism. More specifically, I will argue (in section
4) that no version of *anti-realistic* anti-platonism possesses any important advantage
over fictionalism and that, in the present context, it would be acceptable to treat

all of these views together, as a *single* view. Once this has been established, all I will need to do is refute *realistic* anti-platonism. I will do this in section 5. (Recall from chapter 1 that *realistic* anti-platonism is the view that our mathematical singular terms refer to spatiotemporal objects and that our mathematical theories are about such objects, whereas *anti-realistic* anti-platonism is the view that our mathematical singular terms do not refer at all and that our mathematical theories are not about any objects at all.)

(I should note here that while it would be acceptable for me to treat all versions of anti-realistic anti-platonism together, I am not going to do this. I am going to take fictionalism as a *representative* of anti-realism and concentrate solely on it. This is simply because I think fictionalism is the *best* of these views. I will explain why in section 4.)

3. In Defense of Fictionalism

Aside from the Quine–Putnam worry, I can think of only three worries that one might reasonably have about fictionalism. (This might seem surprising; it might seem that there are a *lot* of problems that fictionalists need to address, for the simple reason that there have been so many different objections to Field's program. But almost all of the objections that have been raised against Field's view have been concerned with his particular way of responding to the Quine–Putnam argument. Very few of them have been attempts to construct independent arguments against the thesis that our mathematical theories are fictional. Thus, insofar as I am not going to rely upon Field's response to the Quine–Putnam argument, I do not need to address the worries that are concerned with that response.) In any event, the three worries that one might have about fictionalism, aside from the Quine–Putnam worry, are (a) that it cannot account for the objectivity of mathematics; (b) that it is not genuinely anti-platonistic, that is, that any plausible formulation of the view will involve a commitment to abstract objects; and (c) that it flies in the face of mathematical and scientific practice, that is, that the thesis that mathematics consists of a body of truths is inherent in mathematical and scientific practice.

It seems to me that all three of these worries can be answered rather easily. Indeed, responses to the first two worries were inherent in the discussions of previous chapters. In connection with the objectivity worry, I explained in chapter 3, section 4, how FBP-ists can account for the objectivity of mathematics, and it seems to me that fictionalists can say essentially the same thing here. The problem of objectivity is essentially equivalent for FBP and fictionalism: both views entail that from a purely *metaphysical* point of view, all consistent purely mathematical theories are equally "good" — FBP says that all such theories truly describe some part of the mathematical realm, and fictionalism says that all such theories are fictional — and so FBP-ists and fictionalists both need to find some way of accounting for the fact that some of our mathematical sentences and theories do seem to stand out as being somehow "better" than various other ones. More specifically, it seems that sentences like '2 + 1 = 3' are objectively correct, whereas sentences like '2 + 1 = 4' are objectively incorrect, and fictionalists and FBP-ists have to account for this. Now, in chapter 3, I argued that FBP-ists can do this by claiming that sentences like '2 + 1 = 3' are true in the *standard model* of arithmetic, whereas sentences lik '2 + 1 = 4' are not. But it seems to me that fictionalists can say essentially the same thing; they can say that sentences like '2 + 1 = 3' are part of the *standard story* of arithmetic, whereas sentences like '2 + 1 = 4' are not. More-over, fictionalists can follow FBP-ists in maintaining that arithmetical standardness is ultimately determined by what is, and what is not, "built into" *our full conception of the natural numbers*.

To make a more general point here, it seems to me that fictionalists can maintain that even if all the answers to some open mathematical question Q are undecidable in our current theories, Q could still have an objectively correct answer, because it could be that one of the answers to Q is "built into", or follows from, the intentions, notions, conceptions, intuitions, and so on that we have in the given branch of mathematics. This shows that fictionalists can account for the existence of open mathematical questions with objectively correct answers. But like FBP-ists, fictionalists can also account for the existence of open questions *without* objectively correct answers (although, like FBP-ists, they do not have to *commit* to the existence of such questions). For fictionalists can maintain that it *may* be that, in some branches of mathematics, there are some open questions that have multiple answers that are all perfectly consistent with all of the inten-tions, notions, conceptions, intuitions, and so on that we have in the given branch of mathematics.

Now, at this point, there are a number of questions that one might raise, and so I think it's fair to say that in order to really lay the worry about objectivity to rest, fictionalists would have to say a lot more than I have said here. But I am not going to pursue this any farther, because I already discussed this in connection with FBP, and I would make essentially the same points here that I made there.

Let me move on to consider the second worry that one might have about fictionalism, that is, the worry that that view cannot be adequately formulated without committing to abstract objects. In particular, one might claim that fic-tionalists are committed to *stories* and that these are abstract objects. But I ad-dressed this worry in chapter 1, sub-section 2.2, and so I don't need to discuss it here. Are there any *other* reasons for thinking that fictionalism isn't a genuinely anti-platonistic view? Well, fictionalists who rely upon Field's response to the Quine–Putnam argument are committed to spacetime points and, moreover, they need to use second-order logic; thus, one might think that, for these reasons, their view is not genuinely anti-platonistic. But we needn't worry about this here be-cause, again, I am not going to rely upon Field's response to the Quine–Putnam argument. Given this, it seems to me that there is only one other worry that one might reasonably have about the nominalistic acceptability of fictionalism: one might think that (a) fictionalists need to appeal to modal notions like *necessity* and *possibility* (or perhaps, *consistency*) and (b) the only plausible ways of interpreting these notions involve appeals to abstract objects, such as possible worlds. But, again, I have already dealt with this worry: I argued in chapter 3, section 5, that modal notions like these can be understood anti-platonistically.[7]

Finally, I turn to the worry that it is inherent in mathematical and scientific practice that our mathematical theories are true. It seems to me that this is just wrong, that there is nothing in mathematical or scientific practice that suggests our mathematical theories are true. Now, I admit that mathematicians utter sentences like " '3 is prime' is true", but the problem is that it's totally unclear how the word 'true' should be interpreted here. Should we take it to mean something like 'true description of reality', or something more like 'true in the story of mathematics' (or perhaps 'true in the story of arithmetic')? I do not think there is anything in mathematical practice that suggests an answer to this question, because I do not think there is anything in mathematical practice that suggests an answer to the question 'Are there really any such things as mathematical objects?' In other words, if an answer to the question of whether there really exist any mathematical objects were inherent in mathematical practice, then it would be clear how the 'true' of mathematical practice ought to be interpreted; but since no answer to the question of the existence of mathematical objects is inherent in mathematical practice, it seems to me that there is nothing in mathematical practice that dictates how we should interpret the word 'true' as it is used by mathematicians.[8,9]

These remarks suggest that the only really important problem with fictionalism is the Quine–Putnam problem of applicability and indispensability. For unlike the problems discussed in this section, the Quine–Putnam problem cannot be solved very easily. Indeed, as I have already pointed out, I am going to dedicate two whole chapters to this problem.

4. Non-Fictionalistic Versions of Anti-Realistic Anti-Platonism

Given the result that the Quine–Putnam worry is the only important worry about fictionalism, it is easy to show that no version of anti-realistic anti-platonism possesses any advantage over fictionalism. For it seems to me that all versions of anti-realism encounter the same worry about applicability and indispensability that fictionalism encounters. Consider, for example, *deductivism* (or *if-thenism*).[10] Unlike fictionalists, deductivists try to salvage mathematical truth. But the truths they salvage cannot be lifted straight off our mathematical theories. That is, if we take the theorems of our various mathematical theories at *face value*, then according to deductivists, they are *not* true. What deductivists claim is that the theorems of our mathematical theories "suggest" or "represent" certain closely related mathematical assertions that *are* true. For instance, if T is a theorem of Peano Arithmetic (PA), then according to deductivists, it represents, or stands for, the truth 'AX $\rightarrow$ T', or '$\Box$(AX $\rightarrow$ T)', where AX is the conjunction of all of the axioms of PA used in the proof of T. Now, it should be clear that deductivists encounter the same problem of applicability and indispensability that fictionalists encounter. For while sentences like 'AX $\rightarrow$ T' are true, according to deductivists, AX and T are *not* true, and so it is still mysterious how mathematics could be applicable (or indeed, indispensable) to empirical science.

Now, one might object here that the problem of applicability and indispensability that deductivists face is *not the same* as the problem that fictionalists face, because deductivists have their "surrogate mathematical truths", that is, their conditionals, and they might be able to solve the problem of applicability by appealing to these truths. But this objection is confused. If these "surrogate mathematical truths" are really *anti-platonistic* truths — and they have to be if they are going to be available to deductivists — then fictionalists can endorse them as easily as deductivists can, and moreover, they can appeal to them in trying to solve the problem of applicability. The only difference between fictionalists and deductivists in this connection is that the former do not try to use any "surrogate mathematical truths" to *interpret mathematical theory*. But they can still *endorse* these truths and appeal to them in accounting for applicability and/or indispensability. More generally, the point is that deductivism doesn't provide anti-platonists with *any* truths that aren't available to fictionalists. Thus, deductivists do not have any advantage over fictionalists in connection with the problem of applicability and indispensability.[11]

Similar remarks can be made in connection with *all* non-fictionalist versions of anti-realistic anti-platonism. Consider, for instance, *conventionalism*.[12] Advocates of this view actually try to salvage *face-value* mathematical truth. But it turns out to be an *empty* sort of face-value truth — in particular, conventionalists hold that the sentences of mathematics are *analytic*, or true by convention — and it is no less mysterious how a collection of factually empty sentences could be applicable to empirical science than how a collection of false sentences could be applicable to empirical science. In general, it seems that (a) all versions of anti-realistic anti-platonism are going to give rise to a prima facie worry about applicability and indispensability, because all such views make the sentences and theories of mathematics empty in a certain way, since they all maintain that the singular terms in these sentences and theories are *vacuous*, that is, fail to refer; and (b) no such view is going to have any advantage over fictionalism in connection with the attempt to *solve* the problem of applications, because insofar as these views deny the existence of mathematical objects, their proponents do not have available to them any means of solving the problem that aren't also available to fictionalists.

These remarks suggest that all versions of anti-realistic anti-platonism ought to be understood as attempts to reject (ii) rather than (i). This might seem a bit surprising, because non-fictionalistic anti-realists try to salvage mathematical truth,[13] and so they *seem* to be attacking (i). But if the Fregean argument is properly understood, it becomes clear that they aren't really attacking (i) at all. It seems to me that the word 'true' appearing in the Fregean argument, that is, in (i) and (ii), should be taken to mean something like 'true in a *non-empty, face-value* way'. Platonists who endorse the Fregean argument do not claim that we need to countenance mathematical objects in order to endorse the truth of "surrogate mathematical theorems" like 'AX → T'. They simply maintain that in endorsing such sentences, we do not *really* endorse the truth of mathematics. Their claim is that we need to countenance mathematical objects in order to maintain that our mathematical theories are true in a *non-empty* way. And they claim that we have to maintain that these theories are true in a non-empty way, because this is the only way to account for their applicability and/or indispensability to empirical science. Once the Fregean argument is understood in this way, it becomes clear that *all* anti-realists — whether they accept fictionalism or not — would accept (i) and reject (ii). And, of course, this means that in order to motivate (i), all we have to do is refute realistic anti-platonism. I will do this in section 5, but first, I need to say a few more words about anti-realism.

The above remarks suggest that, for the present purposes, we could lump all versions of anti-realistic anti-platonism together and treat them as a single view, which we could simply call *anti-realism*. But I am not going to do this here; I am going to take fictionalism as a *representative* of this view and concentrate on it. In a moment, I will explain why I am going to do this, but first, I want to emphasize that I could have done things in this other way. If I replaced the word 'fictionalism' with the expression 'anti-realistic anti-platonism' throughout the last three chapters of this book, I would have to make a few stylistic changes, but nothing substantive would have to be changed, because all of the important features of fictionalism that are relevant to my arguments are shared by all versions of anti-realistic anti-platonism. The important features of fictionalism that will be relevant to my arguments are (a) that it is anti-realistic; (b) that it gives rise to a prima facie problem of applicability and/or indispensability; and (c) that it is committed to the thesis that every consistent purely mathematical theory is, from a metaphysical or onto-logical point of view, as good as every other such theory (i.e., that such theories can be judged superior or inferior to one another only for aesthetic or pragmatic reasons, or because some of them "dovetail with our intuitions", whereas others do not). But it is entirely obvious that all versions of anti-realistic anti-platonism have these three features.[14]

In any event, let me say a few words about why I am going to concentrate on fictionalism, that is, why I think fictionalism is the best version of anti-realistic anti-platonism. The various versions of anti-realistic anti-platonism do not differ from one another in any metaphysical or ontological way, because they all deny the existence of mathematical objects. (This, by the way, is precisely why they don't differ in any way that will be relevant to the arguments that I develop in later chapters.) They differ only in the interpretations that they provide for math-ematical theory and practice. But as soon as we appreciate this point, the beauty of fictionalism and its superiority over other versions of anti-realism begin to emerge. For whereas fictionalism interprets our mathematical theories in a very standard, straightforward, face-value way, other versions of anti-realism — such as deductivism, formalism, and conventionalism — advocate controversial, non-standard, non-face-value interpretations of mathematics that seem to fly in the face of actual mathematical practice.

Now, of course, this last claim would have to be defended in connection with each different version of non-fictionalistic anti-realism. I don't want to go into this in any real depth, however, because I don't need to refute these various versions of anti-realism here because, as we've seen, it would be acceptable for me to lump all of these views together with fictionalism. But I would like to say just a few words here because, frankly, it seems to me that in each case, the point is fairly obvious. Look, for instance, at conventionalism. Isn't it obvious that our mathe-matical theories are not true by convention? After all, these theories have existen-tial import. How could it be true by convention that there exists a prime number between 2 and 4? Or consider formalism. Mathematicians just don't seem to be playing games with symbols, as game formalists suggest. They seem to be making assertions. And these assertions aren't always metamathematical claims of the form 'The sentence S is a theorem of the formal system T', as Curry's formalism suggests.[15] Likewise, they aren't always conditionals, as deductivism suggests. Rather, mathematicians seem very often to make straightforward categorical assertions about objects. For instance, they say things like 'There exists a prime number between 2 and 4'. And there doesn't seem to be anything in mathematical practice that suggests that we ought to understand this assertion as really meaning that *if* the axioms of PA are true, *then* there exists a prime number between 2 and 4, or that the sentence 'There exists a prime number between 2 and 4' is a theorem of PA. On the contrary, it seems that the best interpretation of the mathematician's utterance of 'There exists a prime number between 2 and 4' is that it means that there exists a prime number between 2 and 4. And this is just what fictionalists say.

I do not want to pretend that this discussion is really sufficient to dispense with all non-fictionalist versions of anti-realistic anti-platonism. In the first place, I haven't gone into any depth in connection with any of these views; I have only given very quick sketches of the views and "one-liner" objections. Moreover, I haven't addressed *all* versions of anti-realism; I have said nothing, for instance, about the views of Chihara and Wittgenstein. But while I acknowledge these points, I would like to make three counterpoints. First, as I have already pointed out, I don't need to provide any more than a cursory discussion here, because in the present context, it would be acceptable for me to treat all versions of anti-realism together. Second, most of the views that I have been discussing here have been more or less abandoned, and what's more, the reasons for this are well known. Thus, since I have nothing particularly important to add to the well-known problems with these views, it would be rather pointless to rehearse the arguments again here. I refer the reader to the literature.[16] Third, as for the versions of anti-realism that I have ignored, I think it is pretty clear that the "one-liner" objection I raised against the above views applies to *all* versions of anti-realism. This is simply because all such views involve non-standard, non-face-value interpretations of mathematical theory. Chihara and Wittgenstein, for example, do not think that sentences like 'There exists a prime number between 2 and 4' express truths about numbers. Chihara takes such sentences as making assertions about what *open-sentence tokens* it is *possible to construct*, and Wittgenstein seems to think that such sentences express *rules*.[17] These are surely non-standard interpretations. They are also counterintuitive, and they seem to fly in the face of mathematical practice. Thus, since these views have no advantage over fictionalism, they are inferior to that view.

One might object to the argument that I have given here—that is, the argument for the supremacy of fictionalism over other versions of anti-realism—on the grounds that fictionalism *also* runs counter to mathematical practice. But I have already argued (in section 3) that this is not the case, that there is nothing in mathematical practice that runs counter to fictionalism. Moreover, it is worth pointing out here that even if it *were* the case that mathematical practice ran counter to fictionalism as well as the other versions of anti-realism, we would still have reason to favor fictionalism over these other views, because it would still be true that fictionalism provides a *standard semantics* for the language of mathematics. In other words, whereas non-fictionalistic versions of anti-realism provide non-standard views of the truth conditions of mathematical sentences, fictionalism provides a standard view here. Thus, even if it provides a non-standard view of whether or not these truth conditions are actually *satisfied*, fictionalism jibes with mathematical practice more than other versions of anti-realism do.

I end with a historical remark. It seems to me that history supports the choice of fictionalism as the representative of anti-realistic anti-platonism. For I think it is correct to say that Putnam created his deductivism in an effort to solve the problems with old-style formalism and that Field created fictionalism in an effort to solve the problems with deductivism. As for conventionalism and Wittgensteinianism, those views had been pretty much abandoned by the time fictionalism was born. But, of course, this picture isn't entirely accurate, as is clear from Hellman's recent defense of deductivism and Chihara's recent defense of anti-realistic constructivism.

5. The Refutation of Realistic Anti-Platonism

I still have to motivate (i). To do this, I need to refute realistic anti-platonism, that is, the view that our mathematical singular terms refer to spatiotemporal objects and that our mathematical theories are about such objects. Now, at first blush, it seems that there are two kinds of realistic anti-platonism, one that claims our mathematical theories are about *physical* objects and one that claims they're about *mental* objects. But it seems to me that the second of these views — *psychologism* — ought to be interpreted as a version of anti-realistic anti-platonism. For while this view yields the result that our mathematical singular terms refer, the objects that serve as referents here do not exist objectively, that is, they do not exist "out there in the world", independently of us. Because of this, it seems to me that psychologism is no more realistic than fictionalism. Fictionalism holds that our mathematical theories are fictional stories and, hence, not true, whereas psychologism allows that these theories are true, because the "characters" of these stories exist in the mind. But this is a rather *empty* sort of truth, and so psychologism is not a genuinely realistic view. Moreover, it encounters the same worry about applicability and indispensability that fictionalism encounters. For it is no less mysterious how a story about ideas in our heads could be applicable to empirical science than how a fictional story could be so applicable.

Another way to appreciate the fact that psychologism is best interpreted as a version of anti-realism is to notice that (a) mathematical realists, whether they are platonists or anti-platonists, claim that mathematicians *discover* facts about objective entities, whereas (b) proponents of psychologism agree with fictionalists and other anti-realists that mathematicians are primarily *inventors*, free (within certain limits) to construct as they please.

What, then, does the distinction between psychologism and fictionalism really come to? Well, the difference certainly *doesn't* lie in the assertion of the *existence* of the mental entities in question. Fictionalists admit that human beings do have ideas in their heads that correspond to mathematical singular terms. They admit, for instance, that I have an idea of the number 3. Moreover, they admit that we can make claims about these mental entities that correspond to our mathematical claims; corresponding to the sentence '3 is prime', for instance, is the sentence 'My idea of 3 is an idea of a prime number'. The only difference between fiction-alism and psychologism is that the latter, unlike the former, involves the claim that our mathematical theories are *about* these ideas in our heads. In other words, advocates of psychologism maintain that the sentences '3 is prime' and 'My idea of 3 is an idea of a prime number' say essentially the *same thing*, whereas fiction-alists deny this. Therefore, it seems to me that the relationship between fiction-alism and psychologism is essentially equivalent to the relationship between fic-tionalism and the versions of anti-realistic anti-platonism that I discussed in section 4. In short, psychologism interprets mathematical theory in an empty, non-standard way in an effort to salvage mathematical truth, but it still leads to the same Quine–Putnam indispensability problem that fictionalism leads to, and moreover, it doesn't provide anti-platonists with any means of solving this problem that aren't available to fictionalists, because it doesn't provide anti-platonists with any entities or truths that aren't available to fictionalists.

It follows from all of this that psychologism can be handled in the same way that I handled all of the other non-fictionalist versions of anti-realism and, hence, that I do not really need to refute the view. But as I did in connection with the other non-fictionalist versions of anti-realism, I would like to say just a few words about why I think the psychologistic interpretation of mathematical theory and practice is implausible. The arguments here have been well known since Frege destroyed this view of mathematics in 1884. First of all, psychologism seems in-capable of accounting for any talk about the class of *all* real numbers, since human beings could never construct them all. Second, it seems to entail that assertions about very large numbers (in particular, numbers that no one has ever thought about) are all untrue; for if none of us has ever constructed some very large number, then any proposition about that number will, according to psychologism, be vacuous. Third, psychologism seems incapable of accounting for mathematical *error*: if George claims that 4 is prime, we cannot argue with him, because he is presumably saying that *his* 4 is prime, and for all we know, this could very well be *true*.[18] And finally, psychologism turns mathematics into a branch of psychol-ogy, and it makes mathematical truths contingent upon psychological truths, so that, for instance, if we all died, '2 + 2 = 4' would suddenly become untrue. As Frege says, "Weird and wonderful . . . are the results of taking seriously the sug-gestion that number is an idea."[19]

I should emphasize here that I do not take these elementary arguments to have any force against any serious contemporary philosophy of mathematics, such as the intuitionistic view of Michael Dummett.[20] They are intended to apply only to the view that our mathematical singular terms refer to mental objects and that our mathematical theories are descriptions of such objects. But I do not think that very many people have seriously believed this view since Frege refuted it.[21]

In any event, given that we're grouping psychologism together with anti-realism, we are left with only *one* kind of realistic anti-platonism, namely, the kind that holds that mathematics is about ordinary physical objects. The most famous advocate of this view is John Stuart Mill.[22] According to his view, mathematics is the most general of the natural sciences. Just as astronomy gives us laws concerning all astronomical bodies, so arithmetic and set theory give us laws concerning all objects and piles of objects. The sentence '2 + 1 = 3', for instance, says that whenever we add one object to a pile of two objects, we end up with a pile of three objects. Calculations involving large numbers, on this view, are abstractions from simple facts like this one. We learn that '2 + 1 = 3' is true from our manipulations of physical objects, and we then abstract away from these objects to form ideas about pure mathematics. Thus, we can know that '17,000 + 1 = 17,001' is true, without actually checking it out, by simply extending the practice of addition in the obvious way; but what this sentence really *means*, according to Mill's view, is that whenever we add one object to a pile of 17,000 objects, we get a pile of 17,001 objects.

The first point I want to make here is that we have finally come to an anti-platonist view of mathematics that is *genuinely* realistic and that really ought to be seen as rejecting (i) rather than (ii). According to Mill, sentences like '2 + 1 = 3' are true in a non-empty way, for they are true of things that exist objectively and independently of us. Because of this, Mill's view does not encounter the Quine–Putnam worry that anti-realists encounter; there is no mystery, on this view, about how mathematics could be applicable to empirical science because, according to Mill, mathematics and empirical science have the same subject matter. Indeed, on this view, mathematics just *is* an empirical science.

The upshot of this, for our purposes, is that we have finally come to a version of anti-platonism that I actually have to refute. I will start by giving some standard reasons for rejecting Mill's view. Then I will consider Philip Kitcher's recent attempt to resurrect the Millian view and respond to it.

Let me begin here by reminding the reader that in chapter 2, sub-section 5.1, I gave two criticisms of Mill's view that zeroed in on the fact that Mill has no option but to identify sets of physical objects with aggregates of physical matter. Thus, for instance, if I have three eggs in a carton, then according to Mill, the set of eggs is identical to the aggregate of all the physical "egg-stuff" in the carton. Frege's objection to this view is that aggregates do not have determinate number properties, whereas sets do. But the more penetrating objection, in my opinion, is that Mill cannot countenance the existence of sets of higher rank. The reason is simple: if sets are aggregates of physical matter, then every higher-rank set will be identical to some rank-one set. For instance, the rank-two set {{Mars, Ralph Macchio}} will be identical to the rank-one set {Mars, Ralph Macchio}, because both sets will consist of the same matter, namely, the aggregate of all the physical "Mars-stuff" and all the physical "Macchio-stuff". But if Mill cannot countenance the existence of higher-rank sets, then he cannot account for the truth of hierarchical set theories like ZF.

In addition to arguing this point, I also argued in chapter 2 that there is no way for Mill to avoid this criticism without abandoning his realistic anti-platonism. Since {{Mars, Macchio}} and {Mars, Macchio} are made of the same matter, it follows that in order to claim that they are distinct, we need to maintain that there is more to them than there is to the aggregate of physical matter that makes up

Mars and Macchio. But I argued in chapter 2 that as soon as we make this claim, we have no choice but to allow that {{Mars, Macchio}} and {Mars, Macchio} are *abstract*, in some relevant sense of the term, even if they exist in spacetime. In other words, in claiming that there is more to a set than the corresponding physical aggregate, we already commit ourselves to some version or other of platonism.

A related problem with Mill's view is that there simply isn't enough physical stuff in the universe to satisfy our mathematical theories. In order for PA to be true in the way that Mill thinks it's true, there would have to be infinitely many physical objects in the world.[23] Now, I suppose one might try to claim that, in fact, there *are* infinitely many physical objects in the world — for instance, one might try to do this by endorsing substantivalism about spacetime points — but this wouldn't solve the problem. For even if there are infinitely many physical objects in the world, it should be clear that the truth of PA isn't *contingent* upon this controversial claim.[24]

This last point is related to yet another problem with Mill's view. The suggestion that mathematics is a branch of empirical science seems to entail that it is contingent on physical facts and susceptible to empirical falsification. But we do not think that the truths of mathematics can be empirically falsified. No amount of empirical evidence could ever persuade us to abandon '2 + 1 = 3'. Mill responds to this criticism by claiming that mathematical truths like '2 + 1 = 3' only *seem* necessary and a priori because we see them confirmed so frequently.[25] But this response just doesn't ring true. On the one hand, some physical claims (e.g., 'if a human being throws a baseball into the air and nothing obstructs its course, then it will come back down') are just as frequently confirmed as '2 + 1 = 3', but they don't seem necessary or a priori. And on the other hand, some mathematical claims (e.g., the axiom of infinity) are *never* confirmed and would, if taken empirically, be highly controversial.

Some of the problems with Mill's view that I have been discussing here are avoided by Kitcher's version of empiricism.[26] But I would like to argue that Kitcher has managed to do this only by collapsing back into an *anti-realistic* version of anti-platonism. According to Kitcher, our mathematical theories are about the activities of an ideal agent. In the case of arithmetic, the activities involve the ideal agent pushing blocks around, that is, making piles of blocks, adding blocks to piles, taking them away, and so on. Now, in taking this line, Kitcher manages to side-step some of the above problems.[27] Most important, there is no problem for Kitcher's view in connection with the infinite nature of arithmetic, because insofar as his version of arithmetic is about an *ideal* agent, he can just stipulate that, for instance, this agent can always add one block to any pile of blocks that he or she has already created.

The problem with all of this, in the context of our discussion, is that Kitcher's version of arithmetic is *vacuous*, because (a) it is about an ideal agent, and (b) there are no such things as ideal agents. Kitcher readily admits this. He says, "there is no commitment to the existence of an ideal agent. . . . Statements of arithmetic . . . turn out to be vacuously true."[28] Now, it's actually not clear that *all* of the statements of Kitcher's arithmetic will be true. Many of them will be true, because they have logical forms similar to '$(\forall x)(Fx \rightarrow Gx)$', and so, assuming there are no

Fs, these statements will be vacuously true. But not all of the statements of Kitcher's arithmetic have logical forms like this. For instance, one of Kitcher's axioms is that there *is* a one-operation, and this has '$(\exists x)(Fx)$' as its logical form. If this axiom is taken to be about an ideal agent, it will simply be false. Perhaps Kitcher could say that this axiom can be understood as being about *actual* agents, but it would seem odd for him to maintain that some of his axioms are about ideal agents while others are about actual agents. But in the present context, none of this matters. It doesn't matter whether Kitcher's view is a sort of fictionalism (holding that arithmetic makes fictional claims about non-existent ideal agents) or a sort of deductivism (holding that arithmetic makes vacuously true conditional claims about non-existent ideal agents) or some sort of hybrid view. For whatever line Kitcher takes here, it is clear that his view will be a version of *anti-realism*. And it follows from this that I can handle Kitcher's view in the same way that I handled all of the other versions of anti-realism above. In particular, I do not have to provide a refutation of Kitcher's view, because it would be acceptable to lump it together with fictionalism; but we nevertheless have reason to favor fictionalism over Kitcher's view, because the latter involves a non-standard, non-face-value interpretation of mathematese that seems to fly in the face of mathematical practice.

Now, I think that Kitcher would respond to this argument by claiming that (a) my position with respect to the various versions of non-fictionalistic anti-realism was based upon the fact that all of these views encounter the same problem of applicability and indispensability that fictionalism encounters; and (b) his view (i.e., Kitcher's view) does *not* encounter this problem. The reason Kitcher thinks that his view doesn't have a problem with respect to the applicability of mathematics is that while his axioms are, strictly speaking, about the activities of ideal agents, we arrive at these axioms by reflecting upon the activities of actual human agents and abstracting away from their accidental limitations. Thus, arithmetic is *grounded*, so to speak, in *our* activities. But to say that arithmetic is grounded in "what we can do to the world" is essentially equivalent to saying that it is grounded in "what the world will let us do to it". In other words, it's grounded in the "structural features of the world in virtue of which we are able to segregate and recombine objects".[29] But given this, it should not be surprising that arithmetic is applicable to empirical science.

The problem with this argument is that fictionalists can say essentially the same thing in response to the problem of applications. In particular, they can say that (a) we arrive at our mathematical theories by reflecting upon certain structural features of the physical world, extending them in various ways, and abstracting away from their particularities; and (b) our mathematical theories are applicable to empirical science, because they describe certain (non-existent, idealized) structures that are partially and imperfectly instantiated in the physical world. Now, of course, fictionalists can't solve the problem of applicability by *merely* saying this; as we will see in chapter 7, they need to explain why it doesn't matter that the structures described by our mathematical theories don't really exist. But, of course, Kitcher has to do the same thing: he has to explain why it doesn't matter that the ideal agents described by his versions of our mathematical theories don't really exist.

Thus, no matter how much Kitcher *says* that there is no problem with his view in connection with applicability, the fact is that since mathematics is *vacuous* on his view, he has the same problem that fictionalists have. And what's more important here, Kitcher doesn't have any way of solving this problem that isn't already available to fictionalists. (For the record, I think that Kitcher can solve the problem of applicability, but this is irrelevant, because I'm going to argue that *fictionalists* can solve it too.) In any event, it should now be clear that the problem with Kitcher's view is the same as the problem with all the other non-fictionalist versions of anti-realism. He goes to a lot of trouble in an effort to salvage a non-standard, non-face-value sort of mathematical truth, but this doesn't supply him with any advantage over fictionalism, and indeed, it creates a *problem*, because his non-standard interpretation of mathematical theory seems to fly in the face of mathematical practice; that is, it seems far-fetched and at odds with what mathematicians actually think they're doing.

Returning to Mill's view, I don't see any way of avoiding the sorts of problems that I've described here without doing something along the lines of what Kitcher has done, that is, without retreating into some sort of empirically minded anti-realism. For in order to hang on to a genuinely *realistic* version of anti-platonism, we need to maintain that our mathematical theories are about ordinary physical objects. But as long as we make this claim, our view will encounter all of the problems that Mill's view encounters. In particular, there will be all sorts of sentences that mathematicians accept but that we won't be able to handle, such as 'There are infinitely many transfinite cardinals'.

Now, again, I have been fairly brief in dispensing with Mill's view, and I do not want to pretend that there are no replies a Millian could make. But I do not think we need to explore all the routes that a Millian might pursue here, because there are already a good many critical discussions of Mill's view in the literature,[10] and there is a strong consensus that the view is untenable. We might be able to come up with ingenious ways to sidestep *some* of the above problems, but almost everyone agrees that, in the end, the view cannot be salvaged. This, I suppose, is partly because most people think that the empiricist view just completely misconceives the nature of mathematics. And this, I think, is right. One needn't listen to mathematicians for very long before one gets the impression that they are simply *not* concerned with physical objects like eggs and biscuits and blocks.

6. Platonism and the Issue of Applicability and Indispensability

If the arguments of sections 3–5 are sound, then fictionalism is the best version of anti-platonism. There are several other views that are similar in certain ways to fictionalism, but they are inferior to that view, because they provide (implausible) non-standard interpretations of mathematical theory. From here on out, I will assume that my arguments *are* sound and, hence, that fictionalism is the only version of anti-platonism still standing.

Now, we've also seen in this chapter that the only serious problem for fictionalism is the Quine–Putnam problem of applicability and indispensability. Thus, what we need to do is consider whether fictionalists can solve this problem. I will do this in chapters 6 and 7, but first, I want to address the question of whether *platonists* can solve it, that is, whether they can adequately account for the applicability of mathematics. The traditional wisdom is that they can, that the Quine–Putnam argument raises a problem for anti-platonism *only*. But I will argue in this section that the traditional wisdom is confused here. In particular, I will argue that there is as much (or almost as much) reason to doubt that platonists can account for applicability as there is to doubt that anti-platonists can.[31] (This discussion will also provide us with a clearer picture of exactly what needs to be accounted for in connection with applicability; but we will not get totally clear on this point until chapter 7.)

Many platonists write as if they can explain the applicability of our mathematical theories by merely pointing out that, on their view, these theories are *true*. But this is wrong. To account for applicability, we have to account for *relevance*, and a mere appeal to truth doesn't do this. If I have a theory of Mars that makes indispensable use of facts about Charles Manson, I cannot account for this by merely pointing out that all my claims about Manson are true. I have to say what Manson has to do with Mars. Likewise, platonists have to say what mathematical objects have to do with the physical world; that is, they have to account for the *relevance* of mathematical theory to physical theory. But there is a prima facie reason for thinking that it will be very difficult for platonists to do this. For since platonists maintain that mathematical objects exist outside of spacetime, they endorse what we might call the *principle of causal isolation* (PCI), which says that *there are no causal interactions between mathematical and physical objects*. But this gives rise to the following question: If there are no mathematical facts that are causally relevant to any physical facts, why is mathematical *theory* (which presumably is concerned with mathematical facts) relevant to physical theory (which presumably is concerned with physical facts)?

It is worth noting here that PCI is behind not just the *platonist's* problem of applicability, but the anti-platonist's problem of applicability as well. This can be appreciated by noting that (a) anti-platonists who endorse PCI — namely, anti-realistic anti-platonists (e.g., fictionalists)[32] — encounter the worry about the relevance of mathematical theory expressed at the end of the last paragraph, whereas (b) anti-platonists who reject PCI — namely, realistic anti-platonists like Mill — do *not* encounter this worry. Moreover, the same goes for platonists here: those who take mathematical objects to exist *within* spacetime, such as Maddy (or rather, the early Maddy), will *reject* PCI, and for this reason they will *not* encounter the worry of the last paragraph. In other words, there is no reason to think that Maddy will have a problem accounting for the applicability of mathematics, because, like Mill, she thinks that mathematics is concerned with causally efficacious, spatiotemporal entities. The upshot of all of this is that the Quine–Putnam argument should be construed as an argument not for platonism or the truth of mathematics but, rather, for the *falsity of PCI*.[33] It is a challenge to people who deny that mathematics is about causally efficacious, empirical objects to account for the relevance of mathematics to empirical science. (And I should note that it is very important that we find a response to this challenge to PCI, because we've already seen that both versions of anti-PCI-ism, namely, Maddian physicalistic platonism and Millian realistic anti-platonism, are untenable.)

So let us turn to the question of whether platonists can answer this challenge, that is, whether they can account for the applicability of mathematics. It seems to me that the acceptance of PCI already rules out one strategy that platonists might be inclined to attempt, namely, the strategy of claiming that the reason mathematics is relevant to empirical science is that many of the facts with which empirical science is concerned are not purely physical facts but, rather, *mathematico-physical* facts. To give an example here, when we say that a physical system, say S, is forty degrees Celsius, we are expressing a mathematico-physical fact, namely, the fact that S stands in a certain relation (viz., the Celsius relation) to the number 40. The problem with this account of applicability is that while this relational fact — let's call it $C(S,40)$ — is surely a mixed fact, that is, a mathematico-physical fact, PCI entails that it is not a *bottom-level* mixed fact; in other words, PCI entails that $C(S,40)$ supervenes on a purely physical fact about S and a purely mathematical fact about the number 40.[34] Thus, it seems that this account of applicability just moves the problem back a step; the challenge now becomes that of explaining what $C(S,40)$ has to do with the purely physical fact of S's temperature state.

But while this account of applicability fails, there is another fairly obvious account that platonists might offer here, one that is, I think, a bit more subtle. The account I have in mind proceeds as follows. "We *admit* that facts like $C(S,40)$ are not bottom-level facts. The reason the real number line is useful in making temperature ascriptions is not that numbers are causally relevant to the temperatures of physical systems, but that they provide a convenient way of *representing*, or *expressing*, purely physical temperature facts. To give a bit more detail, what we do here is define a function Φ that maps physical objects into real numbers, so that for any physical object x and any real number r, if $\Phi(x) = r$, then x is r degrees Celsius. Thus, what's going on here is that we use the numbers to *represent* (or to *name*) the purely physical temperature states. The reason this is convenient is that (a) the various temperature states are related to one another in a way that is analogous to the way in which the real numbers are related to one another,[35] and (b) it is simply easier to say that $\Phi(x) = 40$ — or more colloquially, that x is forty degrees Celsius — than to describe the purely physical bottom-level fact of x's temperature."

This account of applicability — let's call it the *representational account* — seems to be exactly what PCI-platonists need: it explains how talk of mathematical objects is relevant to describing the physical world without violating PCI. (PCI is not violated because the only relations between physical and mathematical objects that the representational account alludes to — e.g., the relation corresponding to the fact that $\Phi(x) = 40$ — are *non-causal* relations.) But there is a problem with the representational account: it might not be able to explain *all* applications of mathematics to empirical science. The easiest way to appreciate this is to notice that any application of mathematics that can be explained by the representational account can be dispensed with. Thus, insofar as we're not sure that all uses of mathematics in empirical science are dispensable, we're not sure that the representational account can explain all uses of mathematics.

But why should we believe that any application of mathematics that can be explained by the representational account can be dispensed with? Well, whenever the representational account can be used to explain a given application of mathematics, we will be able to define a function Φ, of the sort discussed above, from the physical objects that the assertions in question (that is, the assertions of the given empirical theory that refer to mathematical objects) can be taken to be *about*, to the mathematical objects of the mathematical theory being applied. But to define such a Φ is just to prove a *representation theorem* for the given use of mathematics. That is, the Φ here is going to be exactly the sort of function that's constructed by a representation theorem: it's going to be an appropriate sort of homomorphism mapping an appropriate sort of empirical structure (which the assertions in question can be taken to be about) into the mathematical structure that we're applying. But as Field has shown,[36] once we've proved a representation theorem, it is not hard to nominalize the assertions in question. All we have to do is restate these assertions solely in terms of the empirical structure that we defined along with the homomorphism Φ. I will explain how this works in chapter 6.

So it seems that PCI-platonists are in the same boat that fictionalists are in. They need to either (a) argue that all of our empirical theories can be nominalized, thus clearing the way for the representational account of applicability (but also clearing the way for fictionalists to solve the indispensability problem via Field's strategy) or else (b) admit that some applications of mathematics are indispensable — and, hence, that some applications cannot be explained by the representational account — and provide an alternative explanation of these indispensable applications. Now, as I have already pointed out, chapters 6 and 7 are concerned, respectively, with the *fictionalist's* attempt to do these two things, that is, to deny the existence of indispensable applications and to account for indispensable applications. What I plan to do, then, is simply let PCI-platonists ride on the coattails of fictionalists. After explaining how fictionalists can solve the Quine–Putnam problem, I will simply point out that PCI-platonists can solve it in the same way.

(I probably should also note here, to avoid misunderstanding, that the account of applicability that I provide in chapter 7 is not completely unlike the representational account. It is similar in spirit to that account, but it is more general; in particular, it can handle *all* applications of mathematics to empirical science, including indispensable ones.)

Denying the Existence of Indispensable Applications

Toward a Nominalization of Quantum Mechanics

1. Introduction

We saw in chapter 5 that fictionalism is the best version of anti-platonism, that if fictionalism cannot be made to work, then anti-platonism cannot be made to work. But we also saw that there is a very serious argument against fictionalism, namely, the Quine–Putnam indispensability argument, which maintains that fictionalism cannot be right, because it is incompatible with the fact that there are indispensable applications of mathematics to empirical science. Finally, we also saw in chapter 5 that there are two strategies fictionalists can use to try to rebut this argument: they can either (a) admit that there *are* indispensable applications of mathematics to empirical science and simply *account* for these applications from a fictionalist point of view, or else (b) argue that, in fact, there *aren't* any indispensable applications of mathematics to empirical science. To the best of my knowledge, no one has ever attempted strategy (a) before, but I will argue in chapter 7 that it can be used to refute the Quine–Putnam argument.

Before I do this, however, I want to consider the more widely discussed strategy (b). This, of course, is the strategy that Field pursues in *Science Without Numbers*. His idea is to block the indispensability argument by showing how to *nominalize* our empirical theories, that is, how to restate them so that they do not contain any reference to, or quantification over, abstract objects. Now, there are several different worries about Field's program, but the most pressing of these, in my opinion, is that Field has only shown how to nominalize *one* physical theory, namely, Newtonian Gravitation Theory, and that he hasn't shown how to extend his strategy to some of our more fundamental physical theories, most notably, quantum mechanics (QM). Moreover, David Malament has turned this worry into a bona fide objection, for he has given reasons for thinking that Field's strategy *cannot* be extended to cover QM.[1] In this chapter, I will respond to Malament's objection. I will do this by simply explaining how we can nominalize QM in a way that avoids Malament's problem and by doing much of the work needed to provide the nominalization. Now, I will not *completely* nominalize QM, but I will provide what I think is the most important part of such a nominalization, namely, a nominalistic recovery of the algebraic structure of Hilbert spaces.

But insofar as I don't completely nominalize QM, and insofar as I do not address any of the other objections that have been raised against Field's program,[2] this chapter cannot be seen as an attempt to completely refute the Quine–Putnam argument. I won't do that (i.e., completely refute the Quine–Putnam argument) until chapter 7, where I argue that it doesn't matter if there are any indispensable applications of mathematics to empirical science, because fictionalists can *account* for such applications. My aim in the present chapter is merely to show that the Fieldian strategy of *denying* indispensability is more promising than most philosophers of mathematics seem to think.

2. How Field Nominalizes

The first thing to do is explain Field's method of nominalization. I will concentrate on his nominalization of physical quantities, such as temperature and length.[3] For the sake of simplicity, my presentation will differ somewhat from Field's. For example, I concentrate on length instead of temperature, and I take physical objects rather than spacetime points as the basic entities of my nominalistic structures; but the basic strategy is identical to Field's. I also note (as Field himself did) that my account depends heavily upon work carried out by Krantz, Luce, Suppes, and Tversky on the foundations of measurement.[4]

For those who have worries about the nominalistic acceptability of spacetime points, my approach might seem superior to Field's. But, ultimately, we might have to use spacetime points anyway. That is, because I use physical objects rather than spacetime points, there are certain aspects of my construction — such as the fact that I appeal to concatenations of physical objects that, it would seem, haven't *actually* been performed — that might generate worries about nominalistic acceptability. In this section, I will gloss over such worries, because the reason I use physical objects rather than spacetime points is *not* that I think spacetime points are nominalistically unacceptable; it's merely that I think Field's strategy of nominalization can be more easily understood in terms of physical objects. Now, I *will* consider several worries about nominalistic acceptability that arise from *other* sources, but I will not consider all the worries that one might reasonably have in this connection; there is no need to consider all such worries, however, because the central aim of this section is not to provide a complete justification of Field's method of nominalization, but simply to familiarize the reader with his general strategy, so that, in later sections, I can address Malament's worry about QM.

In any event, I now turn to the task at hand. Ordinarily, when we state the lengths of physical objects, we do so in platonistic terms. We say, for instance, that Ralph's boat is fifty feet long. Thus, we seem to be committed here to the number 50 and also, perhaps, to a numerical functor. That is, length-in-feet can be thought of as a function f from physical objects to real numbers: to say that a boat b is fifty feet long is to say that $f(b) = 50$. And we also *quantify* over numbers in such settings: we say things like 'Boat b is more than 50 feet long', which can be symbolized as $(\exists x)(x > 50 \,\&\, f(b) = x)$.

The basic idea behind Field's strategy for nominalizing such length assertions is to show how to state the length of a physical object by specifying relations it bears not to numbers but to other physical objects. Thus, we would say not that Ralph's boat stands in the foot relation to the number 50, but that it stands in the longer-than relation to Wanda's boat and the shorter-than relation to Warren's boat. Now, of course, this is not enough; if all we could do was compare two physical objects and say which was longer, we would not be able to reproduce what the numbers do for us; this would only give us an *ordering* of physical objects. To get the equivalent of exact length readings, we need to be able to say *how much* longer Ralph's boat is than Wanda's boat. To do this, we are going to have to construct an empirical structure that can be embedded in the mathematical structure we're using here—that is, the real number line—and then replace the latter with the former. I will now go through this slowly.

The first thing we need to do is define a *concatenation* operation $\circ$ on physical objects, which works in the obvious additive way; thus, if b and c are foot-long rulers, then $b \circ c$ is two feet long. This gives us a nominalistic way of saying that Ralph's boat is fifty feet long: if $a_1, \ldots, a_{50}$ are foot-long rulers, and b is Ralph's boat, then we can say that $(a_1 \circ a_2 \circ \ldots \circ a_{50}) \sim b$, where '$\sim$' means 'is the same length as'. Now, we can make things easier by choosing some physical object u— for instance, the king's foot or a stick in Paris—as the *unit* object. Thus, to say that Ralph's boat is fifty units long, we need merely say that it is the same length as u concatenated with itself forty-nine times; symbolically, this can be expressed as '$b \sim 50u$', where '$50u$' is just shorthand for '$u \circ u \circ \ldots \circ u$', (where the concatenation operation is performed here forty-nine times). Finally, we can get more fine-grained length readings of physical objects by merely switching to a shorter unit object. For instance, to say that b is 50.5 u's long, we need merely define one of the halves of u as u' (that is, $u \sim 2u'$) and say that $b \sim 101u'$. Or if we want to say that b is 50.346 feet long, we just find a unit object c that is .001 feet long, and claim that b is the same length as $c \circ c \circ \ldots \circ c$ (where the concatenation operation is performed 50,345 times), that is, that $b \sim 50{,}346c$. Now, obviously, there are pragmatic constraints on how small we can make the unit object; but this is irrelevant, because we are only trying to give a nominalistic treatment of the mathematics that we *actually* apply, and it's clear that our apparatus is going to give us a nominalistic way of expressing any length assertion that we could ever make, for any such claim will always be in terms of some unit that we actually use.

I've just claimed that our nominalistic apparatus is sufficient for our purposes. But this result can also be *proven* (in a metalanguage that allows platonistic terminology). The general strategy is as follows. First, we take the empirical structure consisting of (i) the set D of all physical objects and all finite concatenations of such objects, and (ii) the concatenation operation $\circ$ and the longer-than relation $>$, both of which are defined on D, and we call it E. That is, $E = \langle D, >, \circ \rangle$. To show that our nominalistic apparatus is acceptable, we have to construct a homomorphism[5] Φ that takes E into R—where R = $<$Re, $>$, $+>$, Re is the set of real numbers, $>$ is the usual greater-than relation, and $+$ is the usual addition operation—in such a way that $>$ preserves the important properties of $>$, and $+$ preserves the important properties of $\circ$. The main property of $>$ that needs to be preserved is this: for all b,c such that b $>$ c, there is some (sufficiently short) object u such that b $>$ nu $>$ c, where 'nu' is shorthand for 'u $\circ$ u $\circ$ ... $\circ$ u' (where the concatenation operation is performed here n $-$ 1 times).[6] For our Φ to preserve this, it must be that in any such situation, Φ(b) $>$ nΦ(u) $>$ Φ(c). As far as $\circ$ is concerned, what we need to demand is that Φ(b $\circ$ c) = Φ(b) + Φ(c). To construct a homomorphism Φ that satisfies these constraints is to prove a *representation theorem*; the name is supposed to suggest that once the proof is carried out, facts about R can be used to represent facts about E, that is, that purely physical length facts about the physical objects in D can be stated in terms of real numbers.

There are many different homomorphisms that would serve our needs here, that is, satisfy the constraints mentioned in the last paragraph. A *uniqueness theorem* tells us what all of these homomorphisms have in common; more precisely, it tells us which sorts of *transformations* of our homomorphism Φ are acceptable. It turns out that, in the case of length, all and only *similarity* transformations are permissible; in other words, if Φ is a homomorphism from E into R that satisfies the constraints discussed above, then if Φ' is also such a homomorphism, then there is some positive real number c such that Φ' = cΦ. (With different physical quantities, different sorts of transformations are permissible; with temperature, for instance, *affine* transformations are permissible; that is, for any two acceptable homomorphisms Φ and Φ', there is a real number b and a positive real number c such that Φ' = cΦ + b. All of this is just a technical way of stating the obvious facts that (a) any two acceptable length scales, such as the foot and inch scales, differ only in the length of the unit, and (b) any two acceptable temperature scales, such as Celsius and Fahrenheit, differ only in the size of the degree and the zero point.)

In a nutshell, then, to prove that my nominalization of length is acceptable, I would have to state intuitively plausible axioms about E that would enable me to prove a representation theorem between E and R and a corresponding uniqueness theorem. I will not discuss exactly how this is to be done. It is discussed by Field and, in much more detail, by Krantz, Luce, Suppes, and Tversky.

Once these theorems are proven, we can use real numbers to state facts about length without believing in the numbers. For we can treat 'b is 50 feet long' as shorthand for 'b is the same length as a foot-long ruler concatenated with itself forty-nine times'. In short, the point is that if we wanted to, we could say everything we need to say about the lengths of physical objects in nominalistic terms, that is, by referring only to physical objects and using only nominalistic vocabulary, such as '$>$', '$\circ$', and '$\sim$'. (Of course, it's easier to speak in platonistic terms, but from an ontological point of view, that is irrelevant.)

Now, one might object here that the function Φ, the set D that forms the domain of our nominalistic structure E, and indeed, E itself—which is just an ordered triple—are abstract objects. But this is irrelevant, because nominalists need not believe that any of these things really exist, since they need not believe that their representation theorems, or the proofs of these theorems, are true. All they need to believe is their nominalistic reconstruction of science. But Φ, D, and E do not appear in this reconstruction; they appear only in the proof of the representation theorem for length. In other words, our various representation theorems are not part of our nominalistic reconstruction of science; they are only part of the argument for the claim that that reconstruction is adequate. In other words, representation theorems are designed to convince *platonists* of the adequacy of a given nominalization; they are not *part* of that nominalization.

Now, nominalists might try to salvage a nominalistic structure that they can believe in by using Goodmanian sums. They could define E_G as the Goodmanian-sum ordered triple $[D_G, >, \circ]$, where D_G is the Goodmanian sum of all physical objects and all finite concatenations of such objects, and $>$ and $\circ$ are defined on the parts of D_G. But there doesn't seem to be any reason to go to this trouble, or to bring up the controversial issue of Goodmanian sums, because we are still going to have to take the attitude of the last paragraph with respect to the homomorphism Φ.[7] Thus, we might as well take the same attitude with respect to E and D, because nominalists have no need for a nominalistic structure that they can believe in. They can maintain that they only believe in the objects in D, and that talk of the *sets* D and E serves merely to aid the proof of the claim that it's acceptable to believe only in those objects.

I have spoken here only of the nominalization of physical quantities, such as length. Field did much more than this: he provided nominalistic statements of many *laws involving such quantities*.[8] I will not go into this here, because I have already given enough background to motivate Malament's objection to Field's program, that is, to see why Malament thinks that Field's method cannot be extended to cover QM.

3. Malament's Objection

Malament's argument for the claim that Field's program cannot be extended to QM is short enough to quote in its entirety:

> I do not see how Field can get started [nominalizing QM] at all. I suppose one can think of the theory as determining a set of models—each a Hilbert space. But what form would the recovery (i.e., representation) theorem take? The only possibility that comes to mind is a theorem of the sort sought by Jauch, Piron, *et al.* They start with "propositions" (or "eventualities") and lattice-theoretic relations as primitive, and then seek to prove that the lattice of propositions is necessarily isomorphic to the lattice of subspaces of some Hilbert space. But of course no theorem of the sort would be of any use to Field. What could be worse than *propositions* (or *eventualities*)?[9]

This objection might seem a bit obscure to those who don't know much about QM, but in this section I will explain exactly what Malament is worried about.

The most important mathematical structures used in QM are Hilbert spaces, and the main use of Hilbert spaces is for representation. For example, we represent the possible pure states of quantum systems with vectors in Hilbert spaces, and we represent observable quantities of quantum systems (e.g., position and spin) with Hermitian operators defined on the vectors of Hilbert spaces. But most important is the representation of *quantum events* (or *propositions*) with closed subspaces of Hilbert spaces: if we let 'A' denote some observable, 'Δ' denote some Borel set of real numbers that can be values of A, and '(A,Δ)' denote the quantum event of a measurement of A yielding a value in Δ (or equivalently, the proposition that asserts that this event has occurred, or perhaps will occur) then we can represent (A,Δ) with the closed subspace CS(A,Δ) of the Hilbert space H in which A is represented, where CS(A,Δ) is defined as follows: a vector v of H is in CS(A,Δ) iff there is a probability of 1 that a measurement of A, for a quantum system in the state represented by v, will yield a value in Δ.

Note the use of probabilities here. In classical mechanics, we can think of a state as a function from propositions of the above sort to truth values. QM, however, is a probabilistic theory: it does not (in general) predict with certainty how a quantum system in some given state will behave when we measure it. Thus, instead of thinking of quantum states as functions from propositions to truth values, we think of them as functions from propositions to *probabilities*, that is, to [0,1]. Thus, a given quantum state Ψ will assign to each proposition, or event, (A,Δ) a real number r in [0,1]; r is the probability that the event (A,Δ) will occur if a state-Ψ system is measured for A (or that the corresponding proposition will be true). Thus, each quantum state determines a probability function from quantum propositions (or events) to [0,1]. (The rule for calculating the exact probability r that a particular quantum state Ψ assigns to a particular proposition, or event, (A,Δ) is this: r is equal to the inner product of the vector v that represents Ψ and the vector v' that results from projecting v onto CS(A,Δ).)

Applying all of this to a concrete example, if we let 'z+' denote the spin-up-in-the-z-direction state, 'Sx' denote the spin-in-the-x-direction observable, and '+' denote the spin-up value, then (assuming that z is orthogonal to x) z+ determines a function p_{z+} such that $p_{z+}(Sx,+) = 0.5$. Thus, according to the above manner of correlating quantum events and closed subspaces of Hilbert spaces, we will associate the event (Sx,+) with the closed subspace CS(Sx,+) that contains a given vector v iff v represents a state Ψ that determines a probability function p_ψ such that $p_\psi(Sx,+) = 1$.

The last few paragraphs tell us that the following two sets are in one-one correspondence:

S(H), the set of closed subspaces of a Hilbert space H,

and

S(E), a certain set of quantum events (or propositions).

But more needs to be said about S(E), that is, about precisely which events are contained therein. S(E) is *not* the set of *all* quantum events of the form (A,Δ); rather, it is the set of events (A,Δ) *associated with a given set of mutually incompatible observables*. In the present context, it doesn't really matter what this comes to, because nothing important is going to hang on it. But loosely speaking, two observables are *incompatible* if and only if QM never assigns them determinate values for the same quantum system at the same time. An example of a pair of incompatible observables is position and momentum. But there are also larger sets of mutually incompatible observables, such as the set SPN of all of the infinitely many spin-1/2 observables. Now, of course, if we take one of these spin-observables out of SPN, the resulting set will still be a set of mutually incompatible observables; but let us ignore such sets and restrict our attention to classes of mutually incompatible quantum observables that are *maximal* in the sense that there are no observables that are *not* in the set but are incompatible with all the observables *in* the set. It turns out that the set S(E) of quantum events associated with a given class of this sort—that is, a (maximal) class of mutually incompatible quantum observables (e.g., the set SPN, or the set containing position and momentum)— is in one–one correspondence with the set S(H) of closed subspaces of the Hilbert space H in which the given class of observables is represented. Indeed, a much stronger relation holds here: we can define lattice-theoretic predicates on S(H) and S(E) and thereby construct *(non-distributive) orthomodular lattices* out of these two sets that are isomorphic to one another. We can call these orthomodular lattices L(H) and L(E), respectively.

It would take quite a bit of space to give a precise definition of 'orthomodular lattice', but in the present context, there is no need to be very precise here. All I will say is that an orthomodular lattice is a special sort of *partially ordered set*, where a partially ordered set is an ordered pair $<A, \leq>$, where A is a non-empty set, and $\leq$ is a reflexive, transitive, antisymmetric relation defined on A. (In our lattices, '$\leq$' will mean '*is included in*'; thus, if a and b are closed subspaces in S(H), then to say that a $\leq_H$ b is to say that all the vectors in a are also in b; and if a and b are events in S(E), then to say that a $\leq_E$ b is to say that whenever a occurs, b also occurs.) An orthomodular lattice is a partially ordered set that satisfies certain further conditions, such as having a maximum element and a minimum element, that is, an $\leq$-most element and an $\leq$-least element.[10]

How can we nominalize the parts of QM that use Hilbert spaces in the ways I have been describing? Well, in section 2, we saw that the strategy for nominalizing is to produce a nominalistic structure that can be embedded in the platonistic mathematical structure being used. Thus, in the present case, what we want to do is produce a nominalistic structure that can be embedded in L(H); doing this will show that we can take L(H) as a mere representational device, that is, as a means of representing various features of our nominalistic structure. Now, in this light, it is easy to appreciate Malament's worry. For as things have been set up, it seems that the closed subspaces that are the elements of L(H) are being used to represent things that are *not* nominalistically kosher, namely, quantum events (or propositions). In other words, the obvious representation theorem that suggests itself here is one that obtains between L(H) and L(E); but the problem is that L(E) is *not* a nominalistic structure, because the members of S(E)—whether we take them to be propositions or events—are *abstract objects*. (One might wonder why we cannot take events as nominalistically kosher, since they occur in spacetime. The reason is that there aren't *enough* events that have *already* occurred: in order to get the full structure of an orthomodular lattice, we are going to have to make use of *all* the events in S(E); but many of these events have never occurred, and so we are going to have to take the events in S(E) as abstract objects.) Thus, to replace L(H) with L(E) is just to replace one platonistic structure with another. This is Malament's worry.

What I need to do, then, is find a way of taking the closed subspaces of Hilbert spaces as representing *physical* phenomena of some sort or other; if I can do this, I should be able to construct nominalistic structures out of these physically real things and then prove representation theorems that enable me to replace the mathematical structures in question—that is, the orthomodular lattices built up out of closed subspaces of Hilbert spaces—with these new nominalistic structures.

4. The Strategy for Nominalizing QM

My thesis is that the closed subspaces of our Hilbert spaces can be taken as representing *physically real properties* of quantum systems. In particular, they represent *propensity* properties, for example, the r-strengthed propensity of a state-Ψ system to yield a value in Δ for a measurement of A (or, to give a more concrete example, the 0.5-strengthed propensity of a z+ electron to be measured spin-up in the x direction).

Does this mean that I am committed to a propensity interpretation of QM? No. First of all, the *most* I'm committed to here is the very broad claim—let's call it BC—that quantum probability statements are about physically real propensities of quantum systems; but BC can be understood in a very weak way, a way that makes it seem very plausible; in particular, it can be understood as saying simply that quantum systems are *irreducibly* probabilistic, or indeterministic; thus, it seems to me that BC is compatible with all interpretations of QM except for hidden-variables interpretations and, moreover, that at present it is very widely accepted. And second, I'm not even committed to BC; I'm merely giving a strategy for nominalizing QM that assumes BC; there may be other ways to nominalize QM that *don't* assume BC, and if QM experts rejected (the weak reading of) BC, we could try to find one. For now, I merely want to undercut Malament's worry by showing how *one* nominalization of QM would go.

In any event, I need to establish two different claims in order to justify my thesis; first, I need to establish either

(1a) Propensities are nominalistically kosher

or

(1b) References to propensities can themselves be nominalized away;

and second, I need to establish

(2) Propensities provide a means of nominalizing the parts of QM discussed in section 3; that is, the closed subspaces of our Hilbert spaces can be taken as representing quantum propensities.

In this section, I will argue for (2) by simply showing how the nominalization goes; in section 5, I will argue (very quickly and sketchily) that (1b) is true and that, even if it isn't, (1a) is true.

In order to establish (2), I have to find, for each Hilbert space H that we use in QM, a set of propensities that corresponds to the set S(H) of closed subspaces of H, and I need to construct a nominalistic structure out of this set of propensities and then prove a representation theorem showing that this nominalistic structure is homomorphic to the orthomodular lattice L(H) built up out of S(H). I am not going to do *all* of this here; instead, I will (a) do some of it and (b) motivate the claim that it can all be done.

I begin by recalling that each quantum state can be thought of as a function from events (A,Δ) to probabilities, that is, to [0,1]. Thus, each quantum state specifies a set of ordered pairs $<(A,Δ), r>$. The next thing to notice is that each such ordered pair determines a propensity property of quantum systems, namely, an r-strengthed propensity to yield a value in Δ for a measurement of A. We can denote this propensity with '(A,Δ,r)'.

Now, consider the set S(P) of propensities (A,Δ,r) associated with a particular quantum state Ψ (and a particular (maximal) class of mutually incompatible observables). I claim that from the set S(P) we can construct a nominalistic orthomodular lattice L(P) that is homomorphic to the orthomodular lattice L(H) constructed from the set S(H) of closed subspaces of the Hilbert space H in which the given observables are represented. This claim can be justified by arguing that L(P) is homomorphic to L(E), that is, the orthomodular lattice built up out of the set S(E) of quantum events associated with the given class of observables; for as we saw in section 3, L(E) is isomorphic to L(H). How, then, can I argue that L(P) is homomorphic to L(E)? Well, to really argue this point in the right way, I would need to provide precise characterizations of L(P) and L(E), and then state and prove a *representation theorem*. (Actually, I'd really need to prove *infinitely many* representation theorems here. For every (maximal) class of mutually incompatible observables will generate a new L(E), and every quantum state associated with that L(E) will generate a different L(P), and my claim is that each of these L(P)s will be homomorphic to that L(E). Thus, I would need to prove a different representation theorem for every L(E)–L(P) pair in QM.) I am not going to prove any of these theorems here. What I want to do instead is provide an informal argument for the claim that *all* of them do hold, that is, the claim that for each L(E)–L(P) pair in QM, L(P) is homomorphic to L(E). I will argue this point in two steps, one dealing with the *domains* of the two sorts of structures and one dealing with the *predicates* (or, to be more precise, the *non-logical expressions*).

The first step is to show that for any given L(E)–L(P) pair, there is a homomorphic correspondence between the domains of L(P) and L(E), that is, between S(P) and S(E). This can be seen in the following way. S(E) is a set of quantum events (A,Δ). Now, if we choose a particular quantum state Ψ, it will determine a probability function $p_Ψ$ that assigns to each (A,Δ) in S(E) a unique real number r in [0,1]. Thus, it seems clear that when we *fix* the state of the system, each event (A,Δ) in S(E) is going to be associated with a *unique* propensity (A,Δ,r) and vice versa; for (a) we can use the probability function associated with the state in question to assign a unique (A,Δ,r) to each (A,Δ), and (b) we can assign a unique (A,Δ) to each (A,Δ,r) — indeed, the very (A,Δ) to which (A,Δ,r) was assigned in (a) — by merely "erasing" the r.

Now, actually, this last sentence isn't exactly right, because it suggests that there is a one–one correspondence between $S(P)$ and $S(E)$ — that is, between the (A,Δ,r)s associated with a given state and the (A,Δ)s — but there's actually a many-one correspondence here. The reason is that *every* state-Ψ quantum system will have an (A,Δ,r)-type propensity. For instance, every state-z+ electron will have an $(Sx,+,o.5)$-type propensity. The reason this is relevant here is that in order to maintain that propensities are nominalistically kosher, I am going to have to treat the $(Sx,+,o.5)$s associated with different electrons as *different things*; but there is only *one* $(Sx,+)$, and so the correspondence between the (A,Δ,r)s associated with a given quantum state on the one hand, and the (A,Δ)s on the other, is going to be many–one rather than one–one. This is exactly analogous to the case of length, where the mapping from physical objects to real numbers is a homomorphism. I will return to this topic in section 5.

The second step of my argument for the claim that $L(P)$ is homomorphic to $L(E)$ is to show that there are nominalistic versions of our (platonistic) lattice-theoretic predicates and operator expressions. When we construct $L(H)$, we do so by defining certain non-logical expressions — most notably, the two-place-relation predicate 'is subspace-included in' and the unary-operation expression 'the sub-space-orthocomplement of' — on $S(H)$; and when we construct $L(E)$, we do so by defining analogous expressions — 'is event-included in' and 'the event-orthocomplement of' — on $S(E)$. Thus, if I can show that we can lift nominalistic propensity expressions directly off of these platonistic expressions — just as we did in the case of length, when we lifted '>' and '∘' off of '>' and '+' — then (given the result of the last two paragraphs) it would seem extremely plausible to suppose that we can use these predicates to build a lattice $L(P)$ out of the set $S(P)$ that is homomorphic to $L(E)$. Let me begin with the predicate 'is included in'.

Corresponding to the platonistic predicate 'is event-included in', or '$\leq_E$', we can introduce the nominalistic predicate 'is propensity-included in', or '$\leq_P$'. To say that one propensity is propensity-included in another — for instance, that (A,Δ,r) $\leq_P (A',\Delta',r')$ — is (on the definition I will propose) a *nominalistic* claim, because it is to say something *about quantum systems*; in particular, it is to state a *physical law* about quantum systems. But *what* law? Well, the first suggestion one might make here is that (A,Δ,r) $\leq_P (A',\Delta',r')$ iff it's a law of nature that any quantum system that has (A,Δ,r) also has (A',Δ',r'). But there is a technical difficulty with this definition of '$\leq_P$', and as a result, it does not capture the notion of propensity-inclusion that we want to capture. The problem here is generated by the fact that propensities are indexed to particular states — in other words, the elements of $L(P)$ are (A,Δ,r)s instead of (A,Δ)s. Because of this, there will be cases where it is a law of nature that any system that has (A,Δ,r) also has (A',Δ',r'), but where this law holds not because the one propensity is *included* in the other, in the sense we're interested in, but simply because (a) the *only* quantum state that generates the probability r for (A,Δ) is the state Ψ associated with the $L(P)$ we're currently working with, and (b) Ψ also happens to generate the probability r' for (A',Δ'). In other words, the law holds by *accident* in such cases, because the *only* L(P) in which (A,Δ,r) appears is the L(P) associated with Ψ.

What I propose is simply to ignore the r's in defining '$\leq_P$'. We can do this by simply lifting the definition of '$\leq_P$' directly off of the definition of '$\leq_E$'. '$\leq_E$' can be defined as follows: (A,Δ) $\leq_E$ (A',Δ') iff for every quantum state Ψ associated with the given L(E), p_ψ(A,Δ) $\leq p_\psi$(A',Δ'). Thus, we can define '$\leq_P$' as follows: (A,Δ,r) $\leq_P$ (A',Δ',r') iff it is a law of nature that every quantum system has a propensity to have a value in Δ for a measurement of the observable A that is weaker than, or equal in strength to, its propensity to have a value in Δ' for a measurement of the observable A'.[11] (It is, perhaps, more intuitive to define '$\leq_E$' by saying that (A,Δ) $\leq_E$ (A',Δ') iff whenever (A,Δ) occurs, (A',Δ') also occurs. Analogously, we can define '$\leq_P$' by saying that (A,Δ,r) $\leq_P$ (A',Δ',r') iff it is a law of nature that any quantum system that has a value in Δ for A also has a value in Δ' for A'.)

Let me explain my strategy here a bit more carefully. Every (maximal) class of mutually incompatible observables in QM generates an orthomodular lattice L(E), and corresponding to each such L(E) is a whole collection of L(P) lattices — in particular, there is one for each state Ψ associated with the given class of observables. Now, each of these L(P)s consists of a group of (A,Δ,r)s, and what's more, each (A,Δ) from the given L(E) appears in an (A,Δ,r) *exactly once* in each L(P). (We know this because the (A,Δ,r)s in a given L(P) are generated from the (A,Δ)s in L(E) by means of a probability function that assigns exactly one real number r to each (A,Δ) in L(E).) Thus, the *only* differences between the various L(P)s associated with a given L(E) are the r's that are attached to the various (A,Δ)s. But we can now see that the inclusion patterns in the given L(E) are going to be reproduced in each of the L(P)s; for on the above definition of '$\leq_P$', the r's appearing in the various (A,Δ,r)s don't play any role at all in determining what propensities are propensity-included in what other propensities. (And we know that this is acceptable, that is, that no confusion will arise from this, because in any given L(P), each (A,Δ,r) can be uniquely picked out by A and Δ alone.) So whether or not some propensity (A,Δ,r) is propensity-included in some other propensity (A',Δ',r') depends *solely* upon facts about A, Δ, A', and Δ'; indeed, it depends upon the *same* facts that the question of whether (A,Δ) $\leq_E$ (A',Δ') depends upon. Thus, it is clear that each L(P) associated with a given L(E) will have the same inclusion patterns as the given L(E); that is, for each such L(P), we will have (A,Δ,r) $\leq_P$ (A',Δ',r') iff we have (A,Δ) $\leq_E$ (A',Δ') in the given L(E). And so it should also be clear that the above definition of '$\leq_P$' succeeds in capturing the notion of inclusion that we're after, that is, it succeeds in capturing the right extension.

But even if all this is granted, one might have misgivings about my definition of '$\leq_P$', for one might doubt that it is really nominalistically kosher. Now, I mentioned one worry of this sort in note 11, but there are two other worries that one might have here. First, one might wonder whether it is nominalistically acceptable to speak of a quantum system *having a propensity*, or having one propensity that's *stronger* than another. I will address this worry in section 5. For now, I will concern myself only with the second worry I have in mind, that is, the worry that it is not nominalistically acceptable to appeal to *values in* Δ, because Δ is a *set* and values in Δ are *real numbers*. The reader may well have been worrying about the appeal to values in Δ all along, that is, since the first paragraph of this section, when I first began speaking of r-strengthed propensities for yielding values in Δ for measurements of A. And, of course, the reader might *also* be worried here about the real number r; I will address the worry about r in section 5, when I discuss the nominalistic acceptability of quantum propensities; right now, I will address only the worry about Δ.

It is not difficult to eliminate talk of values in Δ, because these values are values of a *physical quantity*—namely, A—and, therefore, we can dispense with them in the same way that we dispense with real numbers in connection with other physical quantities, such as temperature and length. In other words, we can construct a nominalistic structure consisting of a domain of quantum systems together with A-predicates (e.g., 'A-less-than') defined on this domain, and then formulate a set of axioms that enables us to prove a representation theorem between this structure and the ordinary platonistic one. Thus, what's going on here is that we have an ordinary Field-style nominalization of the observable A embedded within my nominalization of the probability claims of QM. So, for example, we will replace sentences like 'There is a probability of 0.75 that a state-Ψ electron will yield a value in the closed interval $[m_1, m_2]$ for a measurement of momentum' with sentences like 'A state-Ψ electron has a 0.75–strengthed propensity to be momentum-greater-than-or-equal-to a state-Ψ_1 electron and momentum-less-than-or-equal-to a state-Ψ_2 electron', where Ψ_1 is the state of having a momentum value of m_1 and Ψ_2 is the state of having a momentum value of m_2. And, of course, the same sort of thing can be done to eliminate the appeal to values in Δ from the definition of '$\leq_P$'.

Now, to be sure, there will be differences between the nominalization of length and the nominalization of various quantum observables. But none of these differences raises any impediment to nominalization. For instance, whereas physical objects can take any positive real number as a value of length, spin-1/2 particles can have only two different values of spin, namely, ½ and $-½$. Thus, in nominalizing spin-1/2 observables, the relevant platonistic structure is not going to be the real number line, and our nominalistic predicates are not going to be analogous to our nominalistic length predicates—for instance, we won't be using 'spin-less-than'. But this doesn't create any problem, because we can simply use *different* nominalistic predicates—for instance, for the observable Sx, we will want to use 'Sx-up' and 'Sx-down'—to build up a different sort of nominalistic structure.

So it seems to me that the above definition of '$\leq_P$' provides us with an acceptable nominalistic version of '$\leq_E$'. Now, aside from 'is included in', the only other lattice-theoretic non-logical expression for which we need to find a nominalistic version is the unary-operation expression 'the orthocomplement of'. (The binary operations 'join' and 'meet' can be defined in terms of inclusion; if a and b are elements of a lattice, then *a join b*—that is, a $\lor$ b—is the inclusion-least-upper-bound of a and b; and their meet is their inclusion-greatest-lower-bound.) I do not want to go into nearly as much detail in defining '$\perp^P$'—that is, 'the propensity-orthocomplement of'—as I did in defining '$\leq_P$'. I simply want to note that (a) 'the event-orthocomplement of', or '$\perp^E$', can be defined by saying that $(A,\Delta) = (A',\Delta')^{\perp E}$ iff for all states Ψ, $p_\Psi(A,\Delta) = 1$ iff $p_\Psi(A',\Delta') = 0$; and so (b) '$\perp^P$'

can be defined by saying that $(A,\Delta,r) = (A',\Delta',r')^{\perp P}$ iff it is a law of nature that a quantum system has the propensity $(A,\Delta,1)$ iff it also has the propensity $(A',\Delta',0)$.

This concludes my argument for the claim that the various L(P)s I have described are homomorphic to the L(E)s they're associated with. Now, again, to really *establish* that a given L(P) is homomorphic to its L(E), I would have to formally define a mapping Φ that took the given S(P) into the given S(E) and then prove that it was a homomorphism; that is, I would have to prove a representation theorem. I have not done this here, but it seems to me that I have shown that, in any given case, it could be done. For (a) I have made it very clear what the various Φs will look like — in any given case, Φ will take S(P) into S(E) by simply "erasing" the r's from the (A,Δ,r)s — and (b) I have given arguments that strongly suggest that these Φs will be homomorphisms. If all of this is correct — and if I can argue that either (a) propensities are nominalistically kosher, or (b) references to propensities can themselves be nominalized away — then Malament's worry has been refuted.

Now, this does not constitute a *complete* nominalization of QM; what is left unnominalized is the dynamics of the theory — in particular, the Schrödinger equation. But I don't see any reason why this can't be nominalized in the same general way that Field nominalizes the differential equations of Newtonian Gravitation Theory. Now, of course, it is not trivial that this can be done, but I do not foresee any impediments. In any event, Malament's worry has nothing to do with the dynamics of QM; indeed, I do not know of *any* arguments against the nominalizability of the dynamics of QM. Thus, it seems to me that if what I am suggesting in this chapter is correct, then it shows how the most important and problematic part of the nominalization of QM ought to go.

Any nominalization should come complete with a nominalistic *picture* of what is going on, and before I end this section, I would like to make sure that the picture I have in mind here is clear. My idea, in a nutshell, is this: every quantum system has a bunch of physically real propensities associated with various observables; moreover, since any quantum system is (at any given time) in some *particular* state Ψ, it will always be the case that the collection S(P) of propensities that it *actually, presently has* with respect to a particular (maximal) set of mutually incompatible observables can be formed into a lattice L(P) that is homomorphic to the lattice L(H) that can be constructed from the closed subspaces of the Hilbert space H in which these observables are represented. The important thing to notice here is the nominalistic benefit of switching from events (or propositions) to propensities. I pointed out above that if we're working with events, then in order to get the appropriate orthomodular lattice for a particular case (that is, for a particular set of mutually incompatible observables), we need to make use of the *complete* infinite set S(E) of events associated with these observables, and this will force us to speak of events that *haven't occurred* and, hence, to treat events as abstract objects. But when we make the switch from events to propensities, we hold the state fixed and claim that each such state already generates a set S(P) of propensities that gives rise to the appropriate sort of structure. And since any actual quantum system is always in a particular state, this enables us to claim that any such system already has an infinite collection of propensities that gives rise to an appropriate sort of structure, that is, a (nominalistic) orthomodular lattice. In other words, all the propensities needed to generate an orthomodular lattice are already contained in a *single* quantum system. (Actually, every quantum system generates *many* L(P)-style lattices, one for each of its states. For instance, every system has a spin state that generates one infinite collection of propensities that can be formed into an orthomodular lattice and also a position/momentum state that generates another.)

5. The Nominalistic Status of Propensities

I still need to argue that propensities are nominalistically kosher. (If they're not, then no progress will have been made — I will have merely replaced one platonistic structure with another.) The main worry that one might have here is, of course, that propensities are *properties*, and properties are abstract objects.

There are two strategies that nominalists can adopt here, and I think *both* are acceptable. The first strategy is to take quantum propensities of the form (A,Δ,r) as the basic entities of our nominalistic structures and simply argue that these things *are* nominalistically kosher. This is the strategy I have been assuming throughout. But there is another way of proceeding that, I think, most readers will find less controversial, and that is simply to nominalize away the commitment to propensities and build up our nominalistic structures out of quantum systems themselves. That this can be done can be seen in the following way.

Propensities are just physical properties, like temperatures and lengths, and so we can get rid of them in the manner of section 2. The strategy of section 2, recall, was not to introduce a continuum of *length properties* (e.g., being-5-feet-long, or being-17.3-feet-long) that is isomorphic to the real number line; it was, rather, to introduce the comparative length-relation $>$ and use this to order ordinary physical objects into a structure that can be embedded in the real number line. Thus, presumably, we can do the same thing here: we can eliminate references to r-strengthed propensities by introducing propensity-relations that hold between quantum systems. That is, rather than building up structures from things like $(Sx,+,0.5)$, we can build up structures from the quantum systems themselves. Thus, we will replace sentences like 'State-Ψ electrons have r-strengthed propensities to yield values in Δ for measurements of A' with sentences like 'State-Ψ electrons are (A,Δ)-*propensity-between* state-Ψ_1 electrons and state-Ψ_2 electrons'. Now, I do not want to suggest that it is trivial that talk of propensities can be eliminated in this way, but I do not foresee any real problems. Thus, in short, it seems to me reasonable to suppose that if we can nominalize length and temperature in the manner of section 2, then we can also nominalize propensities in this manner.

But while it seems clear to me that this strategy would work, it also seems to me that the *first* strategy would work, that is, the strategy of taking propensities of the form (A,Δ,r) as basic and arguing that they are nominalistically kosher. Now, to properly *argue* this point would take quite a bit of space, and it would, I think, be inappropriate to dive into this here, especially given that this whole chapter is something of an aside. But I would at least like to indicate the line of argument I would use. First, I would carefully distinguish *physical properties* — that is, properties of *particular* physical objects, such as the temperature of my tongue, or the 0.5-strengthed propensity of some particular z+ electron to be spin-up in the x direction — from *properties-in-abstraction*, that is, Platonic Forms. I would then admit that if there *are* any properties-in-abstraction, then they are abstract objects, but I would argue that (i) physical properties are *not* abstract objects, that is, they exist in spacetime and are, therefore, nominalistically kosher, and (ii) in order to nominalize QM by means of the first strategy, that is, the propensities-are-basic strategy, we only need to make use of physical properties, that is, we needn't appeal to any properties-in-abstraction.[12]

The argument for (ii) would be based upon the fact that all the propensity properties needed to generate an orthomodular lattice are already contained in a *single* quantum system. The argument for (i), on the other hand, would need to be quite long, but my general strategy would be two-pronged. First, I would try to show that all the arguments for thinking that properties are abstract — for example, that there are uninstantiated properties — apply only to properties-in-abstraction and not to physical properties. And second, I would provide positive argument for the claim that physical properties exist in spacetime by pointing out that they are *causally efficacious*. For instance, if we consider a particular particle b, it seems that b's charge *causes* b to move about in certain ways in a magnetic field; but given this, it seems obvious that b's charge exists *in* b (although it might not have any exact location in b) and it seems almost crazy to say that it exists outside of spacetime. What would it be doing *there*? And how could it have causal influence from there?

Accounting for Indispensable Applications from a Fictionalist Point of View

1. Introduction

We still need a response to the Quine–Putnam worry that fictionalists cannot account for the applications of mathematics to empirical science. In chapter 6, I provided some motivation for the claim that fictionalists can respond to this worry by arguing that none of these applications are *indispensable* to empirical science. But I did not give a complete argument for this claim, and so chapter 6 did not contain a complete response to the Quine–Putnam argument. In this chapter, I *will* provide a complete response to that argument, but I will do this by following a different strategy. In particular, I will (a) assume (for the sake of argument) that there do exist some indispensable applications of mathematics to empirical science, and (b) account for these applications from a fictionalist point of view.

(Actually, this will occupy me only in sections 2 and 3 of this chapter. In the last section (section 4) I will return to the topic of part 1. More specifically, I will try to solve two problems that still remain for FBP, namely, the applicability-indispensability problem and an Ockham's-razor-based problem. I will explain there why I take up this topic in the present chapter.)

2. What, Exactly, Needs to Be Accounted For?

I want to guard against a possible confusion. One might think that fictionalists have to account for the very fact of indispensability. But this is wrong; all that's needed is an account of applicability. The argument against fictionalism is that it leaves mysterious the fact that mathematical theory is *relevant* to empirical theory. Now, to eliminate this mystery, that is, to account for the relevance, it would be sufficient to account for the mere applicability of mathematics. It is not required that fictionalists provide an account of indispensability. Now, this is *not* to say that indispensability is unimportant in this connection. On the contrary, it is crucially important: by claiming that mathematics is indispensable to some of our empirical theories, we rule out a certain sort of account of applicability, namely, the sort of account that Field has tried to give (and for which I tried to provide some motivation in chapter 6). In other words, if all of our empirical theories can be nominalized, then the applicability (i.e., relevance) of mathematics can be accounted for in the way that Field suggests (namely, by appealing to the conservativeness of mathematics and the convenience of working with platonistic versions of empirical theories). But if some of our empirical theories *cannot* be nominalized, then Field-style explanations of applicability don't go through, and fictionalists have to go back to the drawing board.

Thus, while indispensability is certainly relevant to the challenge facing fictionalists, it is not indispensability that they need to explain. The point is that fictionalists have to account for *all* applications of mathematics to empirical science, including those that seem indispensable; but they have to account *only* for the *usefulness* of the mathematics in these cases; they do not have to account for its (seeming) indispensability. Now, this is not to say that indispensability *never* needs to be explained. My point is simply that our prima facie worry about fictionalism is a worry about mere applicability and not about indispensability. In other words, if we assume that everyone can account for the applicability of mathematics to empirical science — that is, that they can account for *all* applications of mathematics, including those that seem indispensable — then there is absolutely no reason to think that fictionalists will have more difficulty than anyone else explaining the (alleged) *further* fact that some uses of mathematics are indispensable to empirical science. In short, the point is this: if some of our empirical theories do make indispensable use of mathematics, then this fact needs to be explained; but everyone needs to explain it, and there is no reason to think that the acceptance of platonism, fictionalism, or PCI[1] will be relevant to our efforts to explain it.

Now, my own view is that it's not possible to account for the indispensability of mathematics to empirical science, because I do not think that mathematics *is* indispensable to empirical science. Moreover, even if it is indispensable, I do not think that anyone has ever said anything that could be considered an explanation of that fact. This prompts the question "What would an account of indispensability look like?" The answer depends upon what we mean by 'indispensable'. For it seems to me that there are (at least) two different ideas that one might have in mind in claiming that mathematics is indispensable to empirical science. We can separate these two ideas and, hence, disambiguate the claim that mathematics is indispensable to empirical science by saying that

> mathematics is *relatively indispensable* to empirical science iff at least one of the empirical theories that we currently accept makes indispensable use of mathematics,[2]

and

> mathematics is *absolutely indispensable* to empirical science iff it is indispensable to the very project of doing empirical science in a theoreti-

cally attractive way; that is, iff it is impossible to formulate a theory of the physical world that (a) is true, (b) is more or less complete (if not wholly complete) in its description of physical reality, (c) is theoretically attractive, and (d) doesn't use any mathematics.[3]

Now, again, I don't know what an explanation of either of these kinds of indispensability would look like, because I don't believe that mathematics is really indispensable in either of these two ways. But I think we can at least say this: if someone came up with a good reason for thinking that mathematics was indispensable to empirical science in one of these two ways, then the argument in question would probably bring with it an explanation of the given sort of indispensability.

(I have indicated that in my opinion, we don't have any good reason to believe that mathematics is indispensable in either of the two ways. Now, this might be controversial with respect to relative indispensability, but it's worth noting that it is not at all controversial with respect to absolute indispensability. For in order to motivate the thesis of absolute indispensability, one would have to look into a crystal ball, so to speak, and foresee *all* the ways in which one might try to construct a nominalistic empirical science and then explain why *none* of them could succeed. Thus, it's pretty clear, I think, that at present, we don't have any good reason to think that mathematics is absolutely indispensable to empirical science. Indeed, it seems to me that we have good reason to believe that it's *not*. For if PCI is true, that is, if there are no mathematical objects that are causally relevant to the physical world, then it seems that there should be an attractive way of describing the physical world that makes no reference to such objects. After all, doesn't it seem that God could describe the physical world and say how it "works" without making reference to any causally irrelevant (or non-existent) entities?)

3. A Fictionalist Account of the Applicability of Mathematics

In this section, I will provide a fictionalist account of the (dispensable and indispensable) applications of mathematics to empirical science.

3.1 *Nominalistic Scientific Realism*

I will assume here that in accounting for the applications of mathematics to empirical science, I need to maintain some sort of *realism* about empirical science. That is, I will assume that it is not acceptable for fictionalists to claim that the reason fictional platonistic theories are applicable to empirical science is that empirical science is *also* fictional. (The idea behind this unacceptable strategy is that there is no mystery about how one fiction could be applicable to another. All you have to do is make up the two fictions in the right way. Thus, within a general instrumentalism, the fact that mathematical theories are applicable to empirical theories is no more surprising than the fact that *Rambo II* is applicable to *Rambo III*.) I will not discuss *why* I think this response to the Quine–Putnam argument is unacceptable, but in a nutshell, the reason is that I think full-blown scientific anti-realism is just an untenable view.

But while I will assume that fictionalists need to maintain some sort of realism about empirical science, it is clear that they cannot endorse any *standard* version of scientific realism, because all such views entail that our empirical theories are true, and so they commit to the existence of mathematical objects. Thus, the challenge facing fictionalists is to locate an alternative form of scientific realism, one that is consistent with their anti-realism about mathematics. In other words, the challenge is to explain how we can maintain that our empirical theories are *strictly speaking* false without committing to the implausible claim that there are no truths "buried" in these theories. Now, Field's nominalization program offers one such form of scientific realism. But we are presently assuming that that program is unworkable. Thus, what I want to do is formulate another version of scientific realism.

My proposal is that fictionalists can endorse what I will call *nominalistic scientific realism*, the view that the nominalistic content of empirical science — that is, what empirical science entails about the physical world — is true (or *mostly* true — there may be some mistakes scattered through it), while its platonistic content — that is, what it entails "about" an abstract mathematical realm[4] — is fictional. The reason this view is a genuine form of scientific *realism* is that it endorses the "complete picture" that empirical science paints of the physical world, including the parts about so-called "theoretical entities", such as electrons.[5]

There is an immediate worry about nominalistic scientific realism that can be expressed in two different ways. First, one might claim that if *everything* empirical science says about the mathematical realm is fictional, then much of what it says about the physical world will come out false, and hence, even if we preserve *some* of what empirical science says about the physical world, we will not preserve it all, that is, we will not preserve the *complete picture* that empirical science paints of the physical world. Second, one might claim that if everything empirical science entails about the physical world is true, then what it entails about the mathematical realm must also be true. Both claims arise from the single worry that it is not possible to *separate* the nominalistic content of empirical science from its platonistic content. In sub-section 3.2, I will respond to both sides of this worry by arguing that it *is* possible to separate the nominalistic content of empirical science from its platonistic content. More specifically, I will argue that

(NC) Empirical science has a purely nominalistic content that captures its "complete picture" of the physical world

and

(COH) It is coherent and sensible to maintain that the nominalistic content of empirical science is true and the platonistic content of empirical science is fictional.

(It might seem that this stance commits me to the claim that empirical science can be *nominalized,* but we will see that it does not.)

In short, then, what I will be arguing in sub-section 3.2 is that nominalistic scientific realism is a coherent view, or perhaps a tenable or sensible view. Now, I will *not* argue that nominalistic scientific realism is *true*, because I am not trying to argue that *fictionalism* is true. All I'm trying to show is that fictionalism is *defensible* — in particular, that it can be defended against the Quine–Putnam worry that it is incompatible with the applicability of mathematics. But it should be clear that (NC) and (COH) are sufficient to establish this conclusion. One way to state the Quine–Putnam worry about fictionalism is as follows: we have to endorse the truth of mathematics, because our empirical theories have mathematical entailments, and we believe that these theories are true. But if (NC) and (COH) are true and, hence, nominalistic scientific realism is tenable, then the fact that our empirical theories have mathematical entailments does not show that we are committed to the truth of mathematics because we can simply maintain that we do not believe the mathematical entailments of empirical science. Or to put the point another way, if nominalistic scientific realism is tenable, then our mathematical theories can do the work they're supposed to do in empirical science, even if there are no such things as mathematical objects and, hence, our mathematical theories are fictional.

This argument shows that I do not need anything more than (NC) and (COH) here, because I need to show only that fictionalism and nominalistic scientific realism are coherent and tenable. But I do not want to rest content with this result. I also want to show that these views are *plausible*. More specifically, I want to show that, taken together, they are just as plausible as the conjunction of mathematical platonism and standard scientific realism. I will do this in sub-section 3.3 by describing the role that mathematics actually plays in empirical science and explaining how this dovetails with fictionalism and nominalistic scientific realism.

3.2 *The Coherence and Tenability of Nominalistic Scientific Realism*

My argument for (NC) and (COH) is based upon PCI, that is, the claim that there are no causally efficacious mathematical objects. (Notice that PCI is neutral as to whether platonism is true. The claim here is that *if* there exist any mathematical objects, then they are causally inert. And of course, the argument for this claim is that if there are any mathematical objects, then they exist outside of spacetime.) The first point that needs to be made here is that if we assume that (NC) is true, then PCI suggests that (COH) is also true, because it suggests that the truth value of the platonistic content of empirical science is simply irrelevant to the truth value of its nominalistic content. We can think of it this way: if all the objects in the mathematical realm suddenly *disappeared*, nothing would change in the physical world; thus, if empirical science is true right now, then its nominalistic content would remain true, even if the mathematical realm disappeared; but this suggests that if there never existed any mathematical objects to begin with, the nominalistic content of empirical science could nonetheless be true.

But the main point that needs to be made here is that PCI lends support to (NC) as well as to (COH). Let me begin my case for this claim with a very quick argument. Empirical science *knows*, so to speak, that mathematical objects are causally inert. That is, it does not assign any causal role to any mathematical entity. Thus, it seems that empirical science *predicts* that the behavior of the physical world is not dependent in any way upon the existence of mathematical objects. But this suggests that what empirical science says about the physical world—that is, its complete picture of the physical world—could be true even if there aren't any mathematical objects. That is, it suggests that (NC) and (COH) are both true.

Now, as a segue into a more complete and adequate statement of the argument, consider the following objection. "You seem to be assuming that because empirical science doesn't ascribe any *causal* role to mathematical objects, it doesn't ascribe any role to them at all. But this is wrong: in giving its picture of the physical world, part of what empirical science tells us is that certain physical systems are related in certain *non-causal* ways to certain mathematical objects. Consider, for example, the sentence

(A) The physical system S is forty degrees Celsius.

You are quite right that in making this claim, we do not mean to assign any causal role to the number 40—that we do not mean to suggest that the number 40 is *responsible* in any way for the fact that S has the temperature it has. But nonetheless, we *are* saying something that *involves* the number 40: we are saying that S stands in a certain non-causal relation—namely, the Celsius relation—to that number. Thus, it seems that our empirical theories do not simply express some nominalistic facts and some platonistic facts; rather, they express *mixed facts*. And so it seems that (NC) is false: empirical science does not have a nominalistic content that captures its complete picture of the physical world."

The person who objects in this way fails to appreciate the full significance of the causal inertness of mathematical objects. It is no doubt true that (A) says that S stands in the Celsius relation to the number 40. But since 40 isn't causally relevant to S's temperature, it follows that if (A) is true, it is true in virtue of facts about S and 40 that are entirely independent of one another, that is, that hold or don't hold independently of one another. In other words, if we grant that the number 40 isn't causally related to S—and this is beyond doubt—then we are forced to say that while (A) does express a mixed fact, it does *not* express a *bottom-level* mixed fact; that is, the mixed fact that (A) expresses supervenes on more basic facts that are *not* mixed.[6] In particular, it supervenes on a purely physical fact about S and a purely platonistic fact about the number 40.[7] But this suggests that (A) has a nominalistic content that captures its complete picture of S: that content is just that S holds up *its end* of the "(A) bargain", that is, S does *its part* in making (A) true.[8] (We might also try to say that the nominalistic content of (A) is that the purely physical fact behind (A)—that is, the purely physical fact about S just mentioned—obtains. But we have to be careful here. The purely physical fact behind (A) is a *particular* fact, presumably having something to do with kinetic energy. But the nominalistic content of (A) is not that this particular fact holds—it couldn't be, because (A) doesn't describe any such fact; for instance, it doesn't even broach the topic of kinetic energy. Thus, all we can say here is that the nominalistic content of (A) is that *some* purely physical fact that involves S holding up its end of the "(A) bargain" obtains.)

It should be clear that this argument can be applied to all of empirical science. For since *no* abstract objects are causally relevant to the physical world, it follows that *none* of our mixed sentences expresses a bottom-level mixed fact and, hence, that the mixed sentences of empirical science don't express bottom-level mixed facts. Thus, if empirical science is true, then its truth supervenes upon two entirely independent sets of facts, namely, a set of purely physical facts (or more precisely, nominalistic facts) and a set of purely platonistic facts. But since these two sets of facts are *independent* of one another—that is, hold or don't hold independently of one another[9]—it could very easily be that (a) there does obtain a set of purely physical facts of the sort required here, that is, the sort needed to make empirical science true, but (b) there are no such things as abstract objects, and so there *doesn't* obtain a set of purely platonistic facts of the sort required for the truth of empirical science. But this suggests that empirical science does have a purely nominalistic content that captures its complete picture of the physical world; that content just says that facts of the first sort obtain, that is, that the physical world holds up *its end* of the "empirical-science bargain". That this really captures the *complete* picture that empirical science paints of the physical world should be obvious. For if there obtained a set of purely physical facts of the sort in question here, then even if there were no such things as mathematical objects and, hence, our empirical theories were (strictly speaking) not true, the physical world would nevertheless be just the way empirical science makes it out to be. Now, of course, the actual mixed sentences of empirical science would not be true, but the point is that in moving from empirical science to its nominalistic content—that is, to the claim that the physical world holds up its end of the "empirical-science bargain"—we do not lose any important part of our picture of the physical world.

I conclude, then, that (NC) is true: empirical science does have a purely nominalistic content that captures its complete picture of the physical world. Moreover, since PCI is true, this nominalistic content could very easily be true, even if there were no such things as abstract objects, and so I conclude that (COH) is also true: it is coherent and sensible to maintain that the nominalistic content of empirical science is true and the platonistic content of empirical science is fictional.[10]

As I pointed out above, this is all I need to argue in order to show that nominalistic scientific realism is coherent and tenable, and in order to defend fictionalism against the Quine–Putnam indispensability argument. Nevertheless, I am going to argue in sub-section 3.3 that fictionalism and nominalistic scientific realism are not just coherent and tenable, but actually quite *plausible*. Before I do this, however, I want to address two different worries that people might have about the argument of this section.

First, one might be worried that a scientific anti-realist could use my argument strategy to motivate a view that endorsed the "macro-level content" of empirical science but rejected its "micro-level content". The worry, of course, is that this view is so implausible that it undermines my argument strategy. The fact of the matter, though, is that my argument strategy cannot be used to motivate this view.

The reason is that micro-level entities are *causally related* to macro-level entities. Indeed, if all the micro-level entities in the world suddenly disappeared, all the macro-level entities would disappear along with them. Moreover, empirical science predicts this, because part of its picture of the macro-level of the world is that it is composed of micro-level entities. Thus, empirical science just doesn't *have* a purely macro-level content that captures its complete picture of the macro-level of the world. Thus, there is no viable view that endorses the macro-level content of empirical science but not its micro-level content.

Second, one might be worried that the claim that empirical science has a nominalistic content that captures its complete picture of the physical world is essentially equivalent to the claim that empirical science can be *nominalized*. (There are two reasons why this would be worrisome, if it were true: in the first place, the claim that empirical science can be nominalized is highly controversial, and in the second place, I am assuming in this chapter that empirical science *cannot* be nominalized.) But this worry is just misguided: the claim that empirical science has a nominalistic content that captures its complete picture of the physical world is different from (and much *weaker* than) the claim that empirical science can be nominalized. The easiest way to appreciate this is to notice that empirical theories wear their nominalistic contents on their sleeves. The nominalistic content of a theory T is just that the physical world holds up its end of the "T bargain", that is, does its part in making T true. Thus, while the claim that empirical science can be nominalized is highly controversial, the claim that it has a nominalistic content that captures its complete picture of the physical world is entirely trivial. Indeed, it is no more controversial than the claim that abstract objects (if there are such things) are causally inert.

These remarks suggest that empirical science could have a nominalistic content that captured its complete picture of the physical world even if it couldn't be nominalized. But they don't tell us *why* this is so. The reason is this: even if empirical science could not be nominalized—indeed, even if mathematics were *absolutely* indispensable to empirical science—mathematical objects (if there are such things) would still be causally inert, and so the truth of empirical science (assuming that it *is* true) would still supervene upon two independent sets of facts, namely, a set of purely physical (or more accurately, nominalistic) facts and a set of purely platonistic facts. Now, of course, it would follow from the (assumed) absolute indispensability of mathematics to empirical science that we could never describe all of these purely physical facts in an attractive nominalistic theory. But there would still *be* such facts (assuming there are no mistakes in empirical science) and it would still be true that such facts could obtain even if there were no such things as mathematical objects. Thus, empirical science would still have a nominalistic content that captured its complete picture of the physical world— that content would just say that purely physical facts of this sort obtain, that is, that the physical world holds up its end of the "empirical-science bargain"—and what's more, it would still be coherent and sensible to endorse this nominalistic content while maintaining that the platonistic content of empirical science is fictional. That is, it would still be rational to endorse nominalistic scientific realism. In short, the point here is that it doesn't matter whether our *theories* can be separated into the purely nominalistic and the purely platonistic, because it already follows from the truth of PCI that the bottom-level *facts* are separated in this way.

These considerations suggest that the notion of indispensability is considerably less important than some people have supposed. For we have seen that even if empirical science could not be nominalized, it would still be reasonable to believe only its nominalistic content and to treat its platonistic content as pure fiction. This, I think, is the main reason (although not the only reason[11]) for preferring my response to the Quine–Putnam argument over Field's. On my view, fictionalists do not have to *replace* our current scientific theories with nominalistic theories. They can accept our platonistically formulated empirical theories *as they stand*. The only thing they need to point out is that when they "accept" these theories, they only commit to the truth of their nominalistic contents.[12]

Now, I suppose that one might complain about this, that one might think that we need there to be a true theory of the physical world, or a true and attractive theory of the physical world. But there are a number of rejoinders that fictionalists can make to this complaint. First, they might try to argue that the nominalistic content of empirical science — the claim that the physical world holds up its end of the "empirical-science bargain" — is more or less true and attractive. Second, even if this colloquial claim cannot be considered a true and attractive theory of the physical world, fictionalists can point out that their view does not commit us to the claim that there is no such true and attractive theory, because it does not commit us to the thesis of indispensability. In other words, even if fictionalists allow that we do not currently possess a true and attractive theory of the physical world, they can maintain that we might someday be able to construct one (although they might add here that there is no real motivation to *try* to construct such a theory, that there is nothing wrong with resting content with theories that have true nominalistic contents and fictional platonistic contents). Third, fictionalists can point out that there is no guarantee that there *is* a true and attractive theory of the physical world. If (a) mathematics is absolutely indispensable to empirical science and (b) there are no such things as mathematical objects, then there is no true and attractive theory of the physical world. (This, by the way, provides further motivation for something that we have already seen, namely, that absolute indispensability doesn't establish platonism. It only establishes the disjunction of platonism and the claim that there is no true and attractive theory of the physical world.)

3.3 The Plausibility of Nominalistic Scientific Realism

The first thing I want to do in arguing for the plausibility of fictionalism and nominalistic scientific realism is point out that the idea behind the Quine–Putnam argument is actually very counterintuitive. The idea here is that in order to believe that the physical world has the nature that empirical science ascribes to it, I have to believe that there are causally inert mathematical objects, existing outside of spacetime. It seems to me that this is extremely counterintuitive. From a sheerly intuitive standpoint, it seems much more plausible to suppose that the existence of causally inert mathematical objects is irrelevant to whether the physical world has the nature that empirical science ascribes to it. But this suggests that fiction-alism and nominalistic scientific realism are just as plausible as platonism and ordinary scientific realism.

But I want to back up this appeal to intuition with a more substantial argu-ment. In particular, I will argue for the plausibility of fictionalism and nominalistic scientific realism by (a) presenting (and motivating) a picture of the role that mathematics actually plays in empirical science, and (b) showing that this picture fits perfectly with fictionalism and nominalistic scientific realism — or more pre-cisely, that it fits just as well with these views as it does with platonism and standard scientific realism.

We have seen that our empirical theories do not take mathematical objects to be causally relevant to the operation or state of the physical world. Why, then, do they speak of mathematical objects at all? The answer is this:

> (TA) Empirical theories use mathematical-object talk only in order to construct *theoretical apparatuses* (or *descriptive frameworks*) in which to make assertions about the physical world.

In other words, empirical theories do not make claims of the form 'Physical (or biological, or psychological, or whatever) phenomenon x occurs *because* the math-ematical realm has nature y'. Rather, we can take them as saying things like this: 'The behavior (or state) of physical (or biological, or psychological, or whatever) system S can be *understood* in terms of the mathematical structure M as follows: . . .'. In short, mathematics appears in our empirical theories as a mere descriptive aid: by speaking in terms of the real number line, or a Hilbert space, or some other mathematical structure, we simply make it easier to say what we want to say about the physical world.

I need to argue that (TA) is true and that, because of this, fictionalism and nominalistic scientific realism are plausible. Before I do this, however, I want to make two points about (TA). The first point is that while it is true that mathematics appears in our empirical *theories* only as a descriptive aid, it would be an over-simplification to claim that this is the only role it plays in empirical *science*. The reason is that there is more to science than the conjunction of its theories, and one of the things that scientists do, in addition to stating theories, is make certain kinds of *inferences*, and when they do this, they often use mathematics. But we can ignore this complication here, because the points that I will make about the descriptive role of mathematics apply equally well to its inferential role.[13] Thus, for the sake of brevity, I am going to ignore the inferential role of mathematics and write as if mathematics played a merely descriptive role in empirical science. (The reason I have decided to concentrate on the descriptive role that mathematics plays in the formulation of our empirical theories, rather than the inferential role of mathematics, is simply that I think the former is more important and more interesting.)

The second point I want to make about (TA) is that it is very much in the spirit of what I called the *representational account of applicability* in chapter 5, section 6. The only real difference is that (TA) is more *general*. Both views main-tain that the reason mathematics is relevant to empirical science is that it provides a way of *expressing*, or *representing*, empirical phenomena. But the representational account goes on to take a stand on *how this works*. In particular, the representational account maintains that we use mathematics to represent empirical phenomena by exploiting the fact that certain empirical structures can be homomorphically mapped into certain mathematical structures. The problem with this, as I pointed out in chapter 5, is that whenever mathematics is used in this way, it can be eliminated from the empirical theory in question along Fieldian lines; thus, the representational account commits to the thesis that all of our empirical theories can be nominalized. (TA) avoids this problem by simply not making any claims about the *manner* in which mathematics makes it easier for us to say what we want to say about the physical world. Advocates of (TA) can go along with the representational account in connection with *some* applications of mathematics, for instance, those having to do with temperature and length, but they do not commit to the claim that all applications of mathematics can be handled in this way. And as we will see, it is *acceptable* for me to maintain a neutral stance here on the manner in which mathematics makes it easier for us to say what we want to say about the physical world, because all I *need* here, in order to lay bare the plausibility of fictionalism and nominalistic scientific realism, is the very *general* claim that (TA) makes.

But let me begin by motivating (TA). This, I think, can be rather easily done, because it seems to me that (TA) is fairly obvious. I have two arguments here. First, there is simply no plausible alternative to (TA). The only way to deny (TA) is to maintain that the reason we refer to mathematical objects in empirical science is that they are *important components*, in some sense, of the facts that empirical science is ultimately concerned with. In other words, the view here is that the facts that empirical science is ultimately concerned with are not purely physical facts, but rather *mathematico-physical* facts. But we've already seen (chapter 5, section 6) that this view is untenable.

The second argument for (TA) is just that it seems to accurately depict what goes on in actual applications of mathematics. Consider, for instance, the sentence I was discussing above:

(A) The physical system S is forty degrees Celsius.

Isn't it just obvious that the only reason we refer in (A) to the number 40 is that this provides us with a convenient way of saying what S's temperature state is? What the Celsius scale *does* is correlate different temperature states with different numbers, so that numerals can serve as *names* of temperature states. The reason it is convenient to use numerals here, rather than ordinary names like 'Bill' and 'Ted', is that the various temperature states are related to one another in a way that is analogous to the way in which the real numbers are related to one another. More precisely, and in the more common lingo, the empirical structure of temperature states can be represented by the mathematical structure of the real number line, because the one structure is homomorphic to the other.

One might object as follows. "Look, this is just what the representational account says. What you need to do is show that (TA) applies to the applications of mathematics that the representational account *doesn't* apply to — in particular, applications that are indispensable to empirical science."

This objection can be answered very easily. For the fact of the matter is that (TA) is just as obvious in connection with applications of mathematics that seem as though they might be indispensable as it is in connection with the above use of mathematics in temperature ascriptions. Indeed, the question of whether a given application of mathematics is dispensable or indispensable is wholly *irrelevant* to the question of whether (TA) applies to it. Consider, for instance, the use of mathematics in quantum mechanics (QM). One *might* think that this use of mathematics is indispensable, but regardless of what we end up saying about this, it seems entirely obvious that (TA) applies to QM, that is, the reason we refer in QM to things like vectors and subspaces and real numbers is that this provides us with a convenient way of describing quantum phenomena. (Indeed, what else could we say here? We certainly wouldn't want to claim that we refer to these objects in QM because we simply want to state facts about them, or because we think they are partly responsible for the operation or state of the quantum level of the physical world. It just seems obvious that the reason we refer to these objects is that this provides us with an easy way of saying what we want to say about quantum phenomena.)

But we can really drive this point home — that is, the point that (TA) accurately depicts the use of mathematics in QM — by noting that the Hilbert-space talk appearing in QM is a *representational device*. For instance, we use vectors in Hilbert spaces to represent quantum states; we use Hermitian operators defined on the vectors of Hilbert spaces to represent observable quantities of quantum systems; and we use closed subspaces of Hilbert spaces to represent quantum events (or quantum propositions).[14] Now, this does not mean that what I have been calling the representational account is true of QM, because it does not follow from any of this that we can construct appropriate nominalistic structures that are homomorphic to the platonistic structures at work here. But despite this, it is still true that the Hilbert-space talk appearing in QM is a representational device, and so it seems clear that (TA) accurately depicts this use of mathematics. The question of whether this Hilbert-space talk can be *eliminated* from QM is simply irrelevant to this point.

Now, despite these considerations, one might still wonder how a mere descriptive aid, or descriptive framework, could be indispensable to an empirical theory. I admit that it seems counterintuitive to suppose that a descriptive framework could be *absolutely* indispensable to empirical science; but it is not at all counterintuitive to suppose that a descriptive framework could be *relatively* indispensable, that is, indispensable to some particular theory. To appreciate this, consider again the example of QM, and assume that Hilbert-space talk is a mere descriptive aid to that theory. Regardless of whether it is possible to construct a theory of quantum phenomena that doesn't make use of Hilbert-space talk (or something essentially equivalent), it might very well *not* be possible to construct a theory of this sort that *has the "look and feel" of* QM. Now, of course, in chapter 6, I provided some motivation for the claim that this *is* possible, but that is not relevant here. The important point here is this: the mere fact that Hilbert-space talk appears in QM as a descriptive aid provides no reason whatsoever for concluding that Hilbert-space talk is not indispensable to QM.

Now, again, it may be that (TA) is intuitively at odds with the thesis that mathematics is *absolutely* indispensable to empirical science, but I have already pointed out that there is simply no reason to believe that this thesis is true. Indeed, we have seen that there are fairly good reasons to believe that it's *not* true. Moreover, it is far from clear that the intuition that (TA) runs counter to absolute indispensability can be backed up by an *argument*. I admit to *having* this intuition, but my conviction that (TA) is true is considerably stronger. That is, if I became convinced somehow that mathematics was absolutely indispensable to empirical science, I would sooner give up this intuition than (TA).

In any event, it should now be clear that the whole topic of indispensability is irrelevant to the question of whether (TA) is true. This is clear not just from the fact that (TA) is clearly compatible with the existence of relatively indispensable applications of mathematics, but also from the fact that the arguments for (TA) don't rely upon any assumptions of dispensability. In short, (TA) seems *independently* plausible, and it seems to apply to *all* of our empirical theories, regardless of whether they make indispensable use of mathematics.

Let us move on now. Assuming that (TA) is well motivated, I still need to argue that this conclusion lends plausibility to fictionalism and nominalistic scientific realism. My argument here is very simple. The reason (TA) dovetails with fictionalism and nominalistic scientific realism is that (a) if (TA) is true, then our mathematical theories appear in empirical science as mere descriptive aids — or as aids to our descriptions and our understanding of the physical world — and (b) any use of our mathematical theories along these lines is perfectly compatible with the thesis that these theories are fictional, because descriptive aids — or aids to our descriptions and our understanding — don't need to be true, or genuinely referential, in order to be successful.

That fictions can succeed at aiding our descriptions and our understanding of the physical world — and, indeed, that they can do this as well as truths can — is true in *general*. The challenge to fictionalism is often presented as follows: if fictionalism were correct, then we wouldn't expect mathematics to be any more applicable to empirical science than, say, the novel *Oliver Twist* is. My response is that, in principle, it's *not*! Novels *can* provide frameworks, or theoretical apparatuses, for describing and understanding parts of physical reality. A historical description of the years surrounding the Russian Revolution, for instance, could very easily use talk of the novel *Animal Farm* as a theoretical apparatus, or descriptive aid. We can say something roughly true about Stalin by uttering the sentence 'Stalin was like the pig Napoleon', even though this sentence is, strictly speaking, false. In other words, it seems that the *historical content* of this sentence is roughly true, despite the fact that there was never any such pig as Napoleon and, hence, that the *Animal Farm content* of this sentence is fictional.[15]

My claim here is that it is very plausible to suppose that the situation in empirical science is the same, that the nominalistic content of empirical science is roughly true while its platonistic content is fictional. Indeed, I want to claim that this stance is just as plausible as the standard realist stance. The reason is that the role that mathematics actually plays in empirical science fits just as well with the thesis that our mathematical theories are fictional as with the thesis that these theories are true. To give a bit more detail: we use mathematical-object talk in empirical science to help us accurately depict the nature of the physical world; but we could do this even if there were no such things as mathematical objects; indeed, the question of whether there exist any mathematical objects is wholly irrelevant to the question of whether we could use mathematical-object talk in this way; therefore, the fact that we do use mathematical-object talk in this way does not provide any reason whatsoever to think that this talk is true, or genuinely referential.[16]

To put my point here as starkly as possible, it is this: the reason nominalistic scientific realism is a sensible philosophy of science is that the nominalistic content of empirical science is all empirical science is really "trying to say" about the world. Its platonistic content is something it "says incidentally" in its effort to say what it really "wants to say". Or to use a different metaphor, the nominalistic content of empirical science is its picture of the physical world, whereas its platonistic content is the canvas (or part of the canvas) on which this picture is painted. (And note that if we understand the term 'canvas' very broadly here, so that it applies to any sort of surface that could be covered with paint, for instance, a wall, then canvases are apparently *indispensable* to portrait painting. But despite this, they are still just devices to hold portraits together; they are not *parts* of portraits.)

The conclusion of all this is that empirical science's picture of the physical world could be accurate, even if there are no such things as mathematical objects. Now, we have all sorts of reasons for thinking that this picture *is* accurate, that is, for endorsing the nominalistic content of empirical science, but what the above considerations show is that none of these reasons brings with it a reason to endorse the *platonistic* content of empirical science. And this is why I think that fictionalism and nominalistic scientific realism are plausible views, why I think they are just as plausible as platonism and ordinary scientific realism.

The last point I want to make in this connection is that all of this fits very well with the attitudes of empirical scientists. Imagine a physics professor, Emily, describing various quantum phenomena to a student, Drew, by speaking of Hilbert spaces. And imagine that at the end of Emily's tutoring, Drew says, "Well, I understand all of this perfectly well, but there's one problem: I don't believe in Hilbert spaces; indeed, I don't believe in any abstract objects at all." Now, if Emily is like most physicists, she will find this remark rather bizarre, and she will almost certainly think that Drew has misunderstood the role that Hilbert spaces play in the theory, because she will consider the question of whether there actually exist any abstract Hilbert spaces to be entirely irrelevant. But what I want to claim here is that insofar as Emily is concerned with *physics* — as opposed to, say, *metaphysics* — this reaction is *appropriate*. In other words, it is entirely acceptable for her to respond as follows: "It doesn't matter whether there actually exist any Hilbert spaces. Quantum systems behave in the above manner *anyway*. That is, the nominalistic content of the above story is true." And, again, the *reason* it doesn't matter whether Hilbert spaces exist is that PCI and (TA) are true. In other words, QM's picture of the physical world doesn't depend upon the existence of Hilbert spaces, because those things play a merely non-causal role in the theory, and because the talk in QM of things like vectors and closed subspaces of Hilbert spaces is a mere descriptive aid.

One might object to the argument of this section as follows. "You have given a pretty satisfying view of what goes on in applications. In particular, you've shown pretty clearly that what we do here is use mathematical theories to provide descriptive frameworks for empirical science. Moreover, in doing this, you have shown pretty clearly that the problem of accounting for the applicability of mathematics is not made any more difficult by endorsing mathematical fictionalism. But you haven't yet given an account of applicability, because you haven't explained *why* mathematics is applicable to empirical science. That is, you haven't said why mathematical theories — regardless of whether they're true or fictional — can be used to provide descriptive frameworks for empirical science." I will address this objection in sub-section 4.1.

4. Problems with Platonism Revisited

The above remarks are supposed to provide a complete fictionalist response to the Quine–Putnam argument. Now, in chapter 5 (section 3) I argued that the Quine–Putnam argument is the only really important argument against fictionalism. Therefore, if this is true, then the above remarks constitute a complete defense of fictionalism (assuming that in subsection 4.1 I can adequately respond to the objection I just mentioned in the previous paragraph).

Now, I have said that this book contains a complete defense not just of fictionalism but also of FBP. Moreover, in chapter 8, I am going to assume that both of these views can be defended and discuss the philosophical ramifications of this. But at the end of part I, I noted that there were still two problems that FBP-ists needed to solve, namely, the applicability-indispensability problem and an Ockham's-razor-based problem. I said there that it would be easier to solve these two problems after the arguments of part II had been given. Thus, I now want to return to this topic and explain how platonists (in particular, FBP-ists) can solve these two problems.

4.1 *Platonism and the Problem of Applicability*

If the above discussion succeeds in solving the fictionalist's problem of applicability, then PCI-platonists can solve their problem of applicability in an analogous manner. Indeed, it will be *easier* for PCI-platonists to solve their problem, because they can claim that our empirical theories are true. All PCI-platonists need to establish in order to solve their problem of applicability is that in applying mathematical theories to empirical theories, we do not claim that the mathematical objects in question are causally relevant to the physical world. Thus, if anything even remotely *like* the (TA) view of applicability is correct, then the problem with PCI-platonism evaporates.

But PCI-platonists do encounter a problem here that doesn't seem to arise for fictionalists. Even if (TA) is correct and mathematics is useful only for providing descriptive frameworks in which to make claims about the physical world, one might find it surprising that it can be put to even *this* use. In other words, it's not obvious why theories about a causally inaccessible realm should be useful in providing descriptive frameworks for empirical science; thus, the fact that they *can* be put to such a use needs to be explained.

PCI-platonists can solve this problem by merely adopting FBP. The only reason it might *seem* surprising that mathematics can be used to set up a descriptive framework, or theoretical apparatus, in which to do empirical science is that this seems to suggest that there is an inexplicable *correlation* between the mathematical realm and the physical world. But within FBP, this illusion evaporates: the mathematical realm is so robust that it provides an apparatus for *all* situations. That is, no matter *how* the physical world worked, there would be a mathematical theory that truly described part of the mathematical realm and that could be used to help us do empirical science.[17]

We might try to generate a similar problem for fictionalists, but they can solve it in the same sort of way. The upshot of the platonist's appeal to FBP, in the present context, is that for any physical setup, there is a way to use mathematics to do empirical science. What enables FBP-ists to make this claim is that on their view, any consistent purely mathematical theory is, from a purely ontological point of view, as good as any other. But fictionalists are already committed to this last claim, because they think that all consistent purely mathematical theories are fictions. Therefore, fictionalists can solve the above problem just as FBP-ists do.

Now, one might try to press the above objection (i.e., the objection stated three paragraphs back) in the following way. "Even if we grant that (TA) is correct, and even if we grant that fictionalists and FBP-ists have access to *all* consistent purely mathematical theories, there is still a problem. For what accounts for the fact that *any* of these theories are applicable to empirical science? In other words, what accounts for the fact that any mathematical theory can be used to provide a descriptive framework in which to make assertions about the physical world?"

The main point that needs to be made here is that this is a problem for *every* philosophy of mathematics. More precisely, there's no reason to think that by adopting FBP or fictionalism, we make this problem worse. Indeed, the whole point of this chapter has been to establish that this problem is *not* made worse by the adoption of FBP or fictionalism, because mathematics could be used in the way that we use it, even if it were fictional or about a causally isolated mathematical realm. In fact, it seems to me that fictionalism and FBP are *better off* with respect to this general problem of applicability than various other philosophies of mathematics are, because they save the intuition that mathematics would be applicable to empirical science even if the physical world were utterly different.

These considerations suggest that whatever we end up saying about this problem—that is, the general problem of explaining why mathematical theories can be used to provide descriptive frameworks in which to make assertions about the physical world—we should not think of it as an objection to FBP or fictionalism; indeed, we should not think that it is at all relevant to the problem that I am concerned with here, that is, the problem of whether platonism is true, (i.e., the problem of whether there exist any abstract mathematical objects). Therefore, there is no reason to discuss this general problem of applicability here.

As an aside, though, I would like to say that I do not think it would be very difficult to solve this general problem of applicability. Now, many people—for instance, Wigner and Steiner[18]—have thought that this problem *is* difficult to solve, but it seems to me that for many cases of applicability, the required explanation has *already* been given. For instance, Krantz, Luce, Suppes, and Tversky have shown that the real number line is relevant to length ascriptions, because physical objects are ordered with respect to 'longer than' just as the real numbers are ordered with respect to 'greater than'.

4.2 *Fictionalism, Platonism, and Ockham's Razor*

I am trying to establish the result that fictionalism and FBP are both defensible and that they are equally well motivated. But one might think that such a stance cannot be maintained, because one might think that if both of these views are really defensible, then by Ockham's razor, fictionalism is superior to FBP because it is more parsimonious, that is, it doesn't commit to the existence of mathematical objects. To give a bit more detail here, one might think that Ockham's razor dictates that if *any* version of mathematical anti-platonism is defensible, then it is superior to platonism, regardless of whether the latter view is defensible or not. That is, one might think that in order to motivate their view, platonists need to, so to speak, "take on all comers", that is, refute every different version of anti-platonism.

This, I think, is confused. If *realistic* anti-platonists (e.g., Millians) could make their view work, then they could probably employ Ockham's razor against platonism. But we've already seen (chapter 5, section 5) that realistic anti-platonism is untenable. The only tenable version of anti-platonism is *anti-realistic* anti-platonism. But advocates of this view, for instance, fictionalists, cannot employ Ockham's razor against platonism, because they simply throw away the facts that platonists claim to be explaining. Let me develop this point in some detail.

One might formulate Ockham's razor in a number of different ways, but the basic idea behind this principle is the following: if

(1) theory A explains everything that theory B explains, and
(2) A is more ontologically parsimonious than B, and
(3) A is just as simple as B in all non-ontological respects,

then A is superior to B. Now, it is clear that fictionalism is more parsimonious than FBP, so condition (2) is satisfied here. But despite this, we cannot use Ockham's razor to argue that fictionalism is superior to FBP, because neither of the other two conditions is satisfied here.

With regard to condition (1), FBP-ists will be quick to point out that fictionalism does not account for everything that FBP accounts for. In particular, it doesn't account for facts such as that 3 is prime, that $2 + 2 = 4$, and that our mathematical theories are true in a face-value, non-factually-empty way. Now, of course, fictionalists will deny that these so-called "facts" really are facts. Moreover, if my response to the Quine–Putnam argument is acceptable, and if I am right that the Quine–Putnam argument is the only initially promising argument for the (face-value, non-factually-empty) truth of mathematics, then it follows that FBP-ists have no *argument* for the claim that their so-called "facts" really are facts. But unless fictionalists have an argument for the claim that these so-called "facts" really aren't facts — and more specifically, for the claim that our mathematical theories aren't true (in a face-value, non-factually-empty way) — we will be in a stalemate. And given the results that we've obtained so far, it's pretty clear that fictionalists *don't* have any argument here. To see this, note first that they don't have any non-Ockham's-razor-based argument here. For (a) any non-Ockham's-razor-based argument for the claim that mathematics isn't true would be a non-Ockham's-razor-based argument against FBP; but (b) we already know that fictionalists don't have any (good) non-Ockham's-razor-based argument against FBP, because we've seen that aside from the Ockham's-razor-based argument that we're presently considering, FBP-ists can block every initially promising argument against their view. Thus, the only question here is whether fictionalists have some *Ockham's-razor-based* argument for the claim that mathematics isn't true, or more generally, for the claim that the platonist's so-called "facts" here really aren't facts. But it should be clear that fictionalists don't have any (good) argument of this sort, because Ockham's razor cannot be used to settle disputes over the question of what the facts that require explanation *are*. That principle comes into play only after it has been agreed what these facts are. More specifically, it comes into play only in adjudicating between two explanations of an agreed-upon collection of facts.

Fictionalists might try to respond here by claiming that the platonist's appeal to the so-called "fact" of mathematical truth, or the so-called "fact" that $2 + 2 = 4$, is just a disguised assertion that platonism is true. For since these "facts" obviously entail platonism, to assert that they obtain is just to assert that there are abstract mathematical objects. But platonists can simply turn this argument around on fictionalists: if it is question begging for platonists simply to assert that mathematics is true, then it is question-begging for fictionalists simply to assert that it's *not* true. Indeed, it seems to me that the situation here actually favors the platonists, for it is the fictionalists who are trying to mount a positive argument here and the platonists who are merely trying to defend their view. In other words, if fictionalists want to argue that Ockham's razor dictates that their view is superior to platonism, then they have to provide positive argument for the claim that they can account for everything that needs to be accounted for in this connection. Therefore, if they simply assert that we don't need to explain much of what platonists think we do need to explain, and they don't back this assertion up with any argumentation, then their argument is unacceptable.

Another ploy that fictionalists might attempt here is to claim that what we need to consider, in deciding whether Ockham's razor favors fictionalism over FBP, is not whether fictionalism accounts for all the *facts* that FBP accounts for, but whether fictionalism accounts for all the *sensory experiences*, or all the *empirical phenomena*, that FBP accounts for. In other words, fictionalists might claim that we should replace condition (1) with

(1') theory A accounts for all of the sensory experiences that theory B accounts for.

The problem with this is that platonists will surely just reject the (1')–(2)–(3) version of Ockham's razor. Thus, fictionalists will have to *argue* that this is the proper way to understand Ockham's razor, or to put the point more directly, they'll have to argue that this version of Ockham's razor is a good principle of theory selection. But I don't see how they could possibly argue this point. Indeed, it's not just that fictionalists have no argument in *favor* of the (1')–(2)–(3) version of Ockham's razor; it seems to me — although I don't need this stronger result here — that there are actually good arguments *against* this version of Ockham's razor, that is, good arguments for thinking that this version of the razor is *not* a good principle of theory selection. One such argument is this: even if A accounts for all the sensory experiences that B accounts for, is more parsimonious than B, and is just as simple as B in all non-ontological respects, it may very well be that A is *not* superior to B, because it may be that B accounts for more *facts* than A does and that, because of this, B is superior to A, or just as good as A, despite its lack of parsimony. And a second argument is this: the (1')–(2)–(3) version of Ockham's razor could not be a good principle of theory selection, because it can be used to motivate clearly false theories; for instance, it can be used to motivate solipsism, or external-world anti-realism, over common-sense realism.

(This second argument shows not just that (1')–(2)–(3) is not a good principle of theory selection, but also that it is not Ockham's razor. For while we can use (1')–(2)–(3) to argue that solipsism is superior to common-sense realism, it is surely *not* legitimate to use Ockham's razor — that is, the *real* Ockham's razor — to argue this point. Seen in this light, (1')–(2)–(3) seems more like a *machete* than a razor; for whereas the purpose of Ockham's razor is merely to trim away unsightly blemishes in our theories, (1')–(2)–(3) can be used (by the maniacal solipsist) to hack our worldview to pieces. Less metaphorically, the purpose of Ockham's razor is simply to adjudicate between two explanations of a given set of facts. It cannot be used to adjudicate between realism and anti-realism, because there is no agreed-upon set of facts here, and in any event, the issue between realists and anti-realists is not which explanations we should accept, but whether we should suppose that the explanations we eventually settle upon, using criteria such as Ockham's razor, are really *true*, that is, provide us with accurate descriptions of the world.)

Given that fictionalists cannot motivate the move from (1) to (1'), then, we are back in our stalemate: platonists maintain that it is a fact that $2 + 2 = 4$ and that facts like this require explanation, and fictionalists deny this, but neither group of philosophers has any argument.

Before we move on, it is worth noting that there is also a historical point to be made here. The claim that there are certain facts that fictionalism cannot account for is not an ad hoc device, invented for the sole purpose of staving off the appeal to Ockham's razor. Since the time of Frege, the motivation for platonism has always been to account for mathematical truth. This, recall, is precisely how I formulated the argument for platonism (or against anti-platonism) in chapter 5. And for similar reasons, I do not think that platonists can be accused here of obstinacy; they are not just digging in their heels and refusing to give up on the (face-value, non-factually-empty) truth of our mathematical theories and facts such as that $2 + 2 = 4$. These things have always been central to their view. Platonists are no more obstinate in this connection than fictionalists are, because *neither* camp has any argument establishing the supremacy of its view.

I now move on to condition (3) of Ockham's razor. In order to show that this condition isn't satisfied in the present case, I need to show that there are certain non-ontological respects in which FBP is simpler than fictionalism. My argument here is this: unlike fictionalism, FBP enables us to say that our scientific theories are true (or largely true), and it provides a uniform picture of these theories. As we have seen, fictionalists have to tell a slightly longer story here; in addition to claiming that our mathematical theories are fictional, they have to maintain that our empirical theories are, so to speak, *half*-truths — in particular, that their nominalistic contents are true (or largely true) and their platonistic contents are fictional. Moreover, FBP is, in this respect, more *commonsensical* than fictionalism, because it enables us to maintain that sentences like '$2 + 2 = 4$' and 'the number of planets is 9' are true.

Now, I do not think that the difference in simplicity here between FBP and fictionalism is very substantial. But on the other hand, I do not think that the ontological parsimony of fictionalism creates a very substantial difference in simplicity between the two views either. The reason that we strive for ontological parsimony in theory construction is that by decreasing the ontology of a theory, we tend to decrease the number of "loops and cogs" in the theory, and so we are led in this way to theories that are more elegant and attractive. But in the particular case of FBP, this just doesn't seem to be the case. The immense ontology of FBP doesn't add any complexity — in the sense of "loops and cogs" — to our worldview. Indeed, given the remarks of the last paragraph, the added ontology seems to *decrease* the complexity of our worldview. Moreover, the introduction of abstract objects is extremely uniform and non-arbitrary within FBP: we get *all* the abstract objects that there could possibly be. But, of course, despite these considerations, the fact remains that FBP does add a category to our ontology. Thus, it is less parsimonious than fictionalism, and so, in this respect, it is not as simple as fictionalism. Moreover, since the notion of an abstract object is not a commonsensical one, we can say that, in this respect, fictionalism is more commonsensical than FBP.

It seems, then, that FBP is simpler and more commonsensical than fictionalism in some ways but that fictionalism is simpler and more commonsensical in other ways. Thus, the obvious question here is whether one of these views is simpler *overall*. Or more precisely, the question is this: If two worldviews are equivalent except that one embraces FBP and ordinary scientific realism while the other embraces fictionalism and nominalistic scientific realism, which worldview is simpler overall? It seems to me that the main consideration here, once again, is that there are no good *arguments* on either side of the dispute. What we have here is a matter of *brute intuition*: platonists are drawn to the idea of being able to say that our mathematical and empirical theories are straightforwardly true, whereas fictionalists are willing to give this up for the sake of ontological parsimony, but neither group has any *arguments* here. Thus, on the assumption that there are acceptable responses to all of the arguments against platonism and fictionalism that we know about, for instance, the Benacerrafian arguments and the Quine–Putnam argument, the dispute between FBP-ists and fictionalists seems to come down to a head-butt of intuitions. For my own part, I have *both* sets of intuitions, and overall, the two views seem *equally* simple to me.

PART III

CONCLUSIONS

There's no fact of the matter about these sorts of things, Dorothy.

—Auntie Em

The Unsolvability of the Problem and a Kinder, Gentler Positivism

1. Introduction

We have considered the best arguments — or what I have claimed are the best arguments — against platonism and anti-platonism, and we have found that none of them are cogent. More specifically, we have found that (a) there are no good arguments against FBP (although Benacerrafian arguments succeed in refuting all *other* versions of platonism); and (b) there are no good arguments against fiction-alism (although Fregean arguments succeed in refuting all other versions of anti-platonism).[1,2] Thus, we are left with exactly one viable version of platonism, namely, FBP, and exactly one viable version of anti-platonism, namely, fictional-ism, but we don't have any good reason for favoring one of these views over the other. (It might seem that this very situation — that is, the fact that there seems to be a standoff here — motivates an Ockham's-razor-style argument for anti-platonism. But we just saw at the end of chapter 7 that this argument doesn't work, that fictionalists cannot legitimately use Ockham's razor against FBP.) The first conclusion of the book, then, is that we do not have any good reason for choosing between mathematical platonism and anti-platonism. In other words, the conclusion is this:

> *Weak epistemic conclusion*: we do not have any good arguments for or against the existence of abstract mathematical objects.

What I want to do in this chapter is motivate two stronger conclusions. Both of these conclusions can be seen as suggesting that the metaphysical question of whether there exist any abstract mathematical objects is *empty*, but the two con-clusions cash this out in different ways. The two conclusions can be formulated as follows.

> *Strong epistemic conclusion*: it's not just that we *currently* lack a cogent argument that settles the dispute over mathematical objects — it's that we could *never* have such an argument.

Metaphysical conclusion: it's not just that *we* could never settle the dispute between platonists and anti-platonists — it's that there is *no fact of the matter* as to whether platonism or anti-platonism is true, that is, whether there exist any abstract objects.

I will argue for the strong epistemic conclusion in section 2 and for the metaphysical conclusion in section 3.

(There is an important difference between the metaphysical conclusion and the two epistemic conclusions: the former is about the dispute over the existence of abstract objects in *general*, whereas the latter are only about *mathematical* objects. The reason I formulate the conclusions in this way is not that I think the generalized versions of the epistemic conclusions are false. In fact, I think they are true. My reason for proceeding in this way is simply that the arguments given in this book only support local versions of the epistemic conclusions, whereas my argument for the metaphysical conclusion is, in its essence, an argument about abstract objects in general. I will say a bit more about this in sub-section 3.4.3.)

2. The Strong Epistemic Conclusion

Since FBP is the only viable version of mathematical platonism and fictionalism is the only viable version of mathematical anti-platonism, the dispute over the existence of mathematical objects comes down to the dispute between FBP and fictionalism. The argument for the strong epistemic conclusion that I want to develop in this section is based upon the observation that FBP and fictionalism are, surprisingly, very *similar* philosophies of mathematics. Now, of course, there is a sense in which these two views are polar opposites; after all, FBP holds that *all logically possible* mathematical objects exist, whereas fictionalism holds that *no* mathematical objects exist. But despite this obvious difference, the two views are actually very similar. Indeed, they have much more in common with one another than FBP has with other versions of platonism (e.g., Maddian naturalized platonism) or fictionalism has with other versions of anti-platonism (e.g., Millian empiricism). The easiest way to bring this fact out is simply to list the points on which FBP-ists and fictionalists agree. (And note that these are all points on which platonists and anti-platonists of various other sorts do *not* agree.)

1. Probably the most important point of agreement, and one that I have mentioned on a number of occasions in this book, is that according to both FBP and fictionalism, all consistent purely mathematical theories are, from a metaphysical or ontological point of view, equally "good". According to FBP-ists, all theories of this sort truly describe some part of the mathematical realm, and according to fictionalists, *none* of them do — they are all just fictions. Thus, according to both views, the only way that one consistent purely mathematical theory can be "better" than another is by being aesthetically or pragmatically superior, or by fitting better with our intentions, intuitions, concepts, and so on.[3]

2. As a result of point number 1, FBP-ists and fictionalists offer the same account of undecidable propositions, such as the continuum hypothesis (CH). First of all, in accordance with point number 1, FBP-ists and fictionalists both maintain that *from a metaphysical point of view*, ZF+CH and ZF+~CH are equally "good" theories; neither is "better" than the other; they simply characterize different sorts of hierarchies. (Of course, FBP-ists believe that there actually exist hierarchies of both sorts, whereas fictionalists maintain that there do not exist hierarchies of either sort, but in the present context, this is irrelevant.) Second, FBP-ists and fictionalists agree that the question of whether ZF+CH or ZF+~CH is correct comes down to the question of which is true in the standard model (or models) of set theory (or for fictionalists, the standard *story* of set theory) and that this, in turn, comes down to the question of whether CH or ~CH is inherent in *our notion of set*. Third, both schools of thought allow that it *may* be that neither CH *nor* ~CH is inherent in our notion of set and, hence, that there is no objectively correct answer to this open question. Fourth, they both allow that even if there isn't a correct answer to the CH question in *this* sense, there could still be good pragmatic or aesthetic reasons for favoring one answer to the question over the other (that is, for "modifying our notion of set" in a certain way). Finally, FBP-ists and fictionalists both maintain that questions of the form 'Does open question Q (about undecidable proposition p) have a correct answer, and if so, what is it?' are questions for *mathematicians* to decide. Each different question of this form should be settled on its own merits, in the above manner; they shouldn't all be decided in *advance*, by some metaphysical principle, such as platonism or anti-platonism. (See chapter 3, section 4, and chapter 5, section 3, for a bit more on this.)[4]

3. Both FBP-ists and fictionalists take mathematical theory at face value, that is, adopt a realistic semantics for mathematese. Therefore, they both think that our mathematical theories are straightforwardly *about* abstract mathematical objects, although neither group thinks that they are about such objects in a metaphysically *thick* sense of the term 'about'. The reason FBP-ists deny that our mathematical theories are "thickly about" mathematical objects is that they deny that there are *unique* collections of objects that correspond to the totality of intentions that we have in connection with our mathematical theories; that is, they maintain that certain collections of objects just happen to satisfy these intentions and, indeed, that *numerous* collections of objects satisfy them. On the other hand, the reason that *fictionalists* deny that our mathematical theories are "thickly about" mathematical objects is entirely obvious: it is because they deny that there are any such things as mathematical objects. (See chapters 3 and 4.)

4. Both FBP-ists and fictionalists think that mathematical knowledge arises directly out of logical knowledge (in particular, knowledge of consistencies and consequences) but that mathematical truth is not

reducible to logical truth (because the existence claims of mathematics are not logically true). (See chapter 3, section 5.) A closely related point is that from an epistemological point of view, FBP and fictionalism are on all fours with one another. This, of course, flies in the face of the traditional view that anti-platonism has an epistemic advantage over platonism. (See chapter 3.)[5]

5. Both FBP-ists and fictionalists accept PCI, that is, the thesis that there are no causally efficacious mathematical objects and, hence, no causal relations between mathematical and physical objects. (See chapter 5, section 6.)

6. Both FBP-ists and fictionalists have available to them the same accounts of the applicability of mathematics. In particular, both have the option of either adopting the attitude of chapter 6 (i.e., claiming that mathematics is not indispensable to empirical science) or adopting the attitude of chapter 7 (i.e., granting, for the sake of argument, that there *are* indispensable applications of mathematics to empirical science and simply accounting for these applications[6]). (In addition to chapters 6 and 7, see chapter 5, section 6.)

7. Both FBP-ists and fictionalists are in exactly the same situation with respect to the dispute about whether our mathematical theories are contingent or necessary. Both have pretty good reasons to deny that they are logically or conceptually necessary, because the existence claims of mathematics—for instance, 'There exists a number between 5 and 7', and the null set axiom, which just says that there exists a set without any members—are neither logically nor conceptually true. Moreover, they both seem to be in the same situation with respect to *metaphysical* necessity. In particular, neither can say right now whether mathematics is metaphysically necessary, because we don't have any well-motivated account of what metaphysical necessity is supposed to *consist* in. Now, it might seem that regardless of how we end up defining metaphysical necessity, fictionalists cannot allow that our mathematical theories are metaphysically necessary, because they think these theories are *false*. But it seems to me that this is wrong, that we might settle upon a definition of metaphysical necessity that allows falsehoods to be metaphysically necessary. Consider, for instance, the sentence 'Santa Claus is Saint Nick'. The only important difference between this sentence and 'Muhammad Ali is Cassius Clay'—which is supposed to be metaphysically necessary—is that the latter is true in the *actual* world, whereas the former is not. But since the actual world is no more metaphysically special than the various worlds in which Santa Claus exists but Ali doesn't, it seems that if 'Ali is Clay' is metaphysically necessary, then 'Santa Claus is Saint Nick' ois too. And so one might be inclined to say that 'Santa Claus is Saint Nick' is metaphysically necessary, even though it is false.

Now, of course, anyone who took this line would want to say the same thing about *mathematical* identity sentences like '$2 + 2 = 4$', and perhaps even mathematical relation sentences like '7 > 5'.[7] But none of this is at all helpful with respect to the *existence* claims of mathematics, for instance, the null set axiom. The bottom line here is this: I don't know what to say—from either an FBP-ist or a fictionalist point of view—about the claim that sentences like the null set axiom are metaphysically necessary, because I just don't have any clue what this claim might *mean*.[8] (See chapter 2, sub-section 6.4.)

8. Finally, an imprecise point about the intuitive feel of FBP and fictionalism: both offer a neutral sort of view on the question of whether mathematical theory construction is primarily a process of *invention* or *discovery*. Now, prima facie, it seems that FBP entails a discovery view whereas fictionalism entails an invention view. But a closer look reveals that this is wrong. FBP-ists admit that mathematicians discover objective facts, but they maintain that we can discover objective facts about the mathematical realm by merely inventing consistent mathematical stories. Is it best, then, to claim that FBP-ists and fictionalists both maintain an invention view? No. For mathematicians do discover objective facts. For instance, if a mathematician settles an open question of arithmetic by proving a theorem from the Peano axioms, then we have discovered something about the natural numbers. And notice that *fictionalists* will maintain that there has been a discovery here as well, although, of course, they will not maintain that we have discovered something *about the natural numbers*. Rather, they will maintain that we have discovered something about our *concept* of the natural numbers, or perhaps our *story* of the natural numbers.

I could go on listing similarities between FBP and fictionalism, but the point that I want to bring out should already be clear: FBP-ists and fictionalists agree on almost everything. Indeed, I want to claim—and I will say a few words by way of justification for this below—that they disagree on only *one* point: FBP-ists think that mathematical objects exist and, hence, that our mathematical theories are true, whereas fictionalists think that there are no such things as mathematical objects and, hence, that our mathematical theories are fictional.

This deep similarity between FBP and fictionalism can be used to motivate the strong epistemic conclusion. For if the *only* thing FBP-ists and fictionalists disagree on is the existence of mathematical objects, then it doesn't seem that we could ever settle the dispute, because we have no way of finding out whether such objects exist. Why can't we find this out? For the very reason that Benacerraf thought that platonism is epistemologically unacceptable—because we have no epistemic *access* to the alleged mathematical realm. In other words, the point is this: if there are mathematical objects, then they exist outside of spacetime; therefore, since we have access only to objects that exist within spacetime, we cannot know whether there are any mathematical objects.[9]

Now, on the ordinary way of looking at things, this is *not* a reason to believe the strong epistemic conclusion. For despite our inability to *directly* determine whether there exist any mathematical objects, we might be able to settle the question *indirectly*, by constructing a reductio of platonism or anti-platonism. More specifically, we might be able to derive a false consequence from either FBP or fictionalism. And, of course, historically, this is just what philosophers of mathematics have tried to do. For instance, anti-platonists have tried to argue that platonistic views like FBP could not be right, because they seem to imply an obvious falsehood, namely, that human beings could not have mathematical knowledge; and conversely, platonists have tried to argue that anti-platonistic views like fictionalism could not be right, because they seem to imply an obvious falsehood, namely, that our mathematical theories could not be useful to empirical scientists. But I have already shown that these arguments don't work — that FBP is compatible with our having mathematical knowledge and fictionalism is compatible with mathematics being applicable to empirical science. More generally, we are presently assuming that FBP-ists and fictionalists are capable of blocking *all* such attacks.

Now, by themselves, these considerations don't provide any motivation for the strong epistemic conclusion, because they only show that we haven't *yet succeeded* in finding a cogent reductio-style argument against fictionalism or FBP. What I need to show is that we could *never* find such an argument against fictionalism or FBP. My argument for this claim is based upon the (as-yet-unjustified) assertion that FBP and fictionalism disagree on only *one* important point, namely, the bare claim of the existence of mathematical objects (and the truth of mathematical theories). If this assertion is correct, then it would seem to follow that we could *never* find a cogent reductio-style argument against fictionalism or FBP. For (a) such an argument would proceed by deriving a consequence from either FBP or fictionalism that *isn't shared by the other of these two views* and then arguing that this consequence is false; but (b) if FBP and fictionalism agree on all points except the basic ontological one, then there simply won't be any consequences of FBP or fictionalism to work with here. The only divergence between the two views will be that FBP says that mathematical objects exist (and our mathematical theories are true), whereas fictionalism denies this. But we've already seen (two paragraphs back) that we cannot settle the dispute between FBP-ists and fictionalists by considering only this bottom-level disagreement, because we have no epistemic access to the alleged mathematical realm.[10]

In a nutshell, then, my argument for the strong epistemic conclusion is based upon the following two sub-arguments:

> (I) We could never settle the dispute between FBP-ists and fictionalists in a *direct* way, that is, by looking *only* at the bottom-level disagreement about the existence of mathematical objects, because we have no epistemic access to the alleged mathematical realm;

and

> (II) We could never settle this dispute in an *indirect* way, that is, by looking at the *consequences* of the two views, because they don't differ in their consequences in any important way.

But there is still an unjustified premise here, for I have not yet argued that the *only* significant point on which FBP and fictionalism disagree is the question of whether there exist any mathematical objects. I do not have any really knock-down argument here; I just want to say a few words to show that this premise is very plausible. In particular, I want to motivate the premise by arguing that fictionalism and FBP share the same "vision" of mathematical practice. This point was already apparent, I think, in the above discussion of the similarities between FBP and fictionalism. I considered a wide variety of issues in the philosophy of mathematics there, and we kept finding, in connection with each of these issues, that FBP-ists and fictionalists have available to them the same stances and the same reasons for and against adopting these stances. But what I would like to do now is further motivate the claim that FBP and fictionalism entail the same vision of mathematical practice by providing a metaphysically based *explanation* of this fact.

The explanation, in a nutshell, is this: FBP and fictionalism provide the same vision of mathematical practice, despite the fact that they provide such radically different pictures of the metaphysics of mathematics, because the only features of the two pictures of the metaphysics of mathematics that have any bearing at all on the vision of mathematical practice are features that the two views have in common. More specifically, it seems to me that the vision of mathematical practice that is common to FBP and fictionalism is just about entirely generated by two metaphysical principles that are endorsed by both FBP-ists and fictionalists. The two principles are just the ones mentioned in points 1 and 5 above: fictionalists and FBP-ists both maintain that from a metaphysico-ontological point of view, all consistent purely mathematical theories are equally "good"; and they both maintain that PCI is true, that is, that there are no causally efficacious mathematical objects. It is these two points that generate the common view of undecidable propositions like CH, the common view of mathematical knowledge, the common view of applications, and so on. Moreover, PCI serves to guarantee that the bottom-level point on which FBP-ists and fictionalists *don't* agree will have no bearing on their views of mathematical practice. For if mathematical objects are causally inert, then whether or not there really *exist* any mathematical objects has no bearing on the physical world and, hence, no bearing on what goes on in the mathematical community and the heads of mathematicians.

Now, I do not want to claim that these remarks provide a knockdown argument for the only-relevant-disagreement thesis. It is possible that I am simply over-looking some relevant disagreement between FBP and fictionalism that could lead to a cogent reductio-style argument against one or the other of these two views. Thus, I do not have a knockdown argument for the strong epistemic conclusion. Nonetheless, I do think that the above remarks lend a good deal of plausibility to that conclusion.

I should also point out here that for those of us who know something about the history of philosophy, the strong epistemic conclusion ought to have some independent intuitive appeal. For even if there were some significant disagreement, between FBP and fictionalism (beyond the bottom-level ontological disagreement) it is hard to believe that this disagreement could really lead to a cogent reductio-style argument against one of these two views. Or more precisely: *if* I am right that FBP and fictionalism are the best versions of platonism and anti-platonism, respectively, then it's hard to believe that either of these views could be refuted. The reason is simple: it's hard to believe, at this point in history, after twenty-four centuries of debate, that either platonism or anti-platonism could be refuted. On the contrary, it seems very plausible to suppose that perennial metaphysical views like platonism and anti-platonism can neither be established nor refuted, that the totality of evidence available to us is simply not sufficient to settle disputes of this sort.

Before going on, it is worth noting, as an aside, that if my arguments are correct, then I have motivated a certain "view of mathematical practice". For if FBP and fictionalism are the only two viable philosophies of mathematics, and if they share the same view of mathematical practice, then we have reason to believe that that view is correct. But I certainly don't mean to suggest that we should accept the FBP-fictionalist view of mathematics solely because there are good arguments against all other philosophies of mathematics. It seems to me that the FBP-fictionalist stance on things like undecidable propositions, mathematical knowledge, and applications is *independently* plausible.

3. The Metaphysical Conclusion

The strong epistemic conclusion is strong enough to entail the claim with which I began this book, that is, the claim that what I called the metaphysical project—the project of using considerations about mathematical theory and practice to solve the metaphysical problem of abstract objects—does not work. Thus, I *could* simply end the book right now. But before I do that, I want to explore the possibility of establishing the metaphysical conclusion, that is, the much stronger result that there is no fact of the matter as to whether there exist any abstract objects. Now, I want to emphasize in advance that just as my argument for the strong epistemic conclusion fell short of being knockdown, so my argument for the metaphysical conclusion isn't going to be knockdown either. All I want to do here is take a *first shot* at an argument for this conclusion. And it seems to me that this sort of discussion ought surely to be welcome at this point in time. The metaphysical conclusion is an extremely radical claim, one that is, to say the least, very difficult to justify. But at the same time, I think there are a lot of philosophers who accept the underlying intuition here, that is, the intuition that certain metaphysical disputes, such as the dispute over the existence of abstract objects, are in some sense *factually empty*. But while many of us share an intuition of this general flavor, almost no one knows how to *argue* for it. And it is for this reason that we ought to welcome discussions that yield "first shots" at arguments for the metaphysical conclusion. The present section (in particular, sub-section 3.3) contains a very detailed discussion of this sort.

3.1 Some Introductory Remarks

The metaphysical conclusion is similar in spirit to some of the central tenets of logical positivism. But the view I am going to advance here is rather different in detail. First of all, it is "kinder" than positivism in that I do not wish to attack *all* of metaphysics; I am only going to concern myself with the problem of abstract objects.[11] And second, my view is "gentler" than positivism in that I do not want to claim that the dispute over the existence of abstract objects is *meaningless* (and more generally, I do not want to commit to verificationism). All I want to claim is that the dispute over abstract objects is *factually empty*, by which I mean, very simply, that the metaphysical conclusion is true, that is, there is no fact of the matter as to whether or not there exist any abstract objects. Now, I am going to motivate the metaphysical conclusion by arguing that the sentence

(∗) There exist abstract objects; that is, there are objects that exist outside of spacetime (or more precisely, that do *not* exist *in* spacetime)

does not have any truth conditions. Thus, while I do not claim that sentences like (∗)—that is, sentences that assert the existence or non-existence of abstract objects—are meaningless, I am nonetheless in agreement with the positivists about this much: that the factual emptiness of the dispute over abstract objects is rooted in *semantic* problems with sentences like (∗). The idea here is that sentences can have two different kinds of semantic values—namely, *meanings* and *truth conditions*—and that while (∗) may well have meaning, it is nevertheless semantically ill-behaved, because it does not have truth conditions.

In sub-section 3.2, I will say a bit more about how a sentence could have meaning but no truth conditions and about why I'm not committed to verificationism. But before I do this, I need to clarify what I have in mind when I say that (∗) has no truth conditions, because there is one kind of truth condition that it clearly *does* have. In particular, it is trivial that (∗) has *disquotational* truth conditions, that is, that it is true if and only if there are objects that exist outside of spacetime. But this is irrelevant here, because it doesn't follow from this that there is a fact of the matter as to whether (∗) is true, because it may be that there is no fact of the matter as to whether (∗)'s disquotational truth condition *obtains*, that is, whether there *are* objects that exist outside of spacetime. At any rate, what I have in mind when I say that (∗) has no truth conditions is that it has no *possible-world-style* truth conditions, where the possible-world-style truth conditions of a sentence are identified with the set of possible worlds in which the sentence is true. Now, in saying this, I do not mean to enter into any debate on the nature of truth conditions. I am not saying that possible-world-style truth conditions are "real truth conditions", whereas disquotational truth conditions are not, or anything of the sort. All I am saying is this: regardless of whether possible-world-style truth conditions are "real truth conditions", (∗) does not have them.

Now, it might seem that if (∗) has disquotational truth conditions, then it must *also* have possible-world-style truth conditions—or more specifically, that if (∗) is true if and only if there are objects that exist outside of spacetime, then it is true in just those worlds in which there are objects that exist outside of spacetime. But this worry can be blocked by merely pointing out that it may be — and I will argue that this *is* the case — that there is no fact of the matter as to which possible worlds *count* as worlds in which there are objects that exist outside of spacetime. In other words, I am going to argue that there is no fact of the matter as to which possible worlds count as worlds in which (∗) is true. And from this, it follows immediately that (∗) doesn't have any possible-world-style truth conditions.

One might reply here as follows: "If possible worlds are maximally consistent sets of sentences or propositions, as some philosophers have taken them to be, then it is entirely obvious which worlds count as worlds in which (∗) is true, namely, those that contain (∗), or some essentially equivalent sentence, as a member." My response is that I'm simply *not* taking possible worlds to be maximally consistent sets of sentences or propositions here. I'm thinking of them more along the lines in which David Lewis and Robert Stalnaker have thought of them.[12] More specifically, I'm thinking of them as *ways things could be*, as opposed to descriptions of ways things could be. Now, again, I do not mean to be entering any debate here on the "real nature" of possible worlds; I am not saying that this conception of possible worlds is somehow "better" than the maximally-consistent-set conception. Moreover, I am not saying that the term 'possible' is best understood in terms of *ways things could be*, or anything like that. (Thus, what I'm saying here doesn't undermine anything I said in previous chapters — most notably, chapter 3, section 5 — about there being a primitive anti-platonist notion of possibility.) All I am saying is this: regardless of whether 'possible' should be understood in terms of *ways things could be*, and regardless of whether *ways things could be* are "real possible worlds", it is not the case that (∗) has a well-defined set of *ways things could be* associated with it. I will express this by saying that (∗) doesn't have any possible-world-style truth conditions.

Now, despite these disclaimers, it might still seem illegitimate to base my argument upon an appeal to possible worlds. For (a) I am trying to argue that there is no fact of the matter as to whether there exist any abstract objects, and (b) possible worlds are *themselves* abstract objects. Now, I suppose that one might try to respond to this objection by following Lewis and claiming that possible worlds are *concrete* objects, because they are of the same kind as the actual world. But this response would not be very satisfying, because it is extremely hard to believe that there are really any such things as full-blown Lewisian possible worlds. It is much better to think of possible worlds, that is, ways things could be, as abstract objects of some sort — for instance, as *world properties*, or something like that. But given this, how can I rely upon the *existence* of such things in an argument for the thesis that there is no fact of the matter as to whether there exist any abstract objects? I obviously can't. But I will argue in sub-section 3.4.3 that, contrary to first appearances, my argument *doesn't* depend upon the existence of possible worlds. Thus, all my argument requires is that the notion of a possible world, that is, a way things could be, is *coherent*. But this, I think, is beyond doubt.

We have just seen that my argument for the claim that (∗) has no possible-world-style truth conditions does not commit me to any claims about the "real nature" of possible worlds or truth conditions, and we will see in sub-section 3.4.3

that it doesn't even commit me to the *existence* of possible worlds. But the main point to note here is a more positive one, namely, that my argument for the claim that (∗) lacks possible-world-style truth conditions *does* commit us to the meta-physical conclusion, that is, the thesis that there is no fact of the matter as to whether there exist any abstract objects. Now, I am not suggesting here that the mere fact that a sentence lacks possible-world-style truth conditions already entails that there is no fact of the matter as to whether it is true. This is a very strong claim, and it may well have counterexamples. Consider, for instance, the sentence 'Wilt Chamberlain is tall'. One might think that this sentence lacks possible-world-style truth conditions — that since 'tall' is a vague term, there is no determinate set of possible worlds in which the sentence is true — but despite this, no one could doubt that there is a fact of the matter as to whether this sentence is true, because Chamberlain is over seven feet tall, and so the sentence is clearly true. But as we will see, nothing like this is going on in connection with (∗). I am going to argue for the claim that (∗) lacks possible-world-style truth conditions by arguing that there is no fact of the matter as to which possible worlds count as worlds in which (∗) is true. Moreover, my argument will not turn upon any claims about any *particular* possible worlds. Therefore, it will follow from my argument that there is no fact of the matter as to whether the *actual* world counts as a world in which (∗) is true, and from this, the metaphysical conclusion follows trivially.

I will argue for the metaphysical conclusion and the claim that (∗) has no possible-world-style truth conditions in sub-section 3.3. Then in sub-section 3.4, I will consider some objections to my argument. Before I do any of this, however, I want to explain why the stance I am adopting here does not commit me to verificationism or to the claim that (∗) is meaningless.

3.2 *Meaningfulness Without Possible-World-Style Truth Conditions*

I want to argue that in claiming that (∗) has no possible-world-style truth conditions, I do not thereby commit myself to the thesis that (∗) is meaningless. But before I do this, there is a more important point that needs to be made: even if the claim that (∗) lacks possible-world-style truth conditions does commit me to the thesis that (∗) is meaningless, this does *not* commit me to logical positivism or verificationism. This point can be appreciated very easily. Verificationists are committed to something like the following principle:

(VER) Among indicative sentences, meaningfulness entails in-principle verifiability; that is, a lack of in-principle verifiability entails a lack of meaningfulness.

Now, almost nobody believes (VER) anymore, but despite this, a lot of people do endorse

(METC) Among indicative sentences, meaningfulness entails a posses-sion of possible-world-style truth conditions; that is, a lack of possible-world-style truth conditions entails a lack of meaningfulness.

The idea behind (METC) goes back at least to Frege's suggestion that the sense of a word or sentence is that which determines its extension. This suggestion has been developed by numerous philosophers, including Carnap, Montague, Scott, Lewis, and Kaplan.[13] Let us take Kaplan's view as an example. He takes the meaning of a sentence to be associated with a *character*, or what we might call a *character-function*, that is, a function from contexts to contents, where a content is associated with an *intension-function*, that is, a function from possible worlds to truth values. Thus, for the present purposes, we can think of a character-function as a function from contexts to sets of possible worlds, so that the character-function of a sentence σ assigns to each context c the possible-world-style truth conditions of σ in c.

Now, if you believe that every meaningful indicative sentence is associated with a character-function, then of course, you will believe that (METC) is true. And, indeed, there is something very plausible about this: the idea is that a meaningful indicative sentence (embedded in a context) determines a state of affairs. But by endorsing this sort of view, we do *not* commit to verificationism, or to (VER). For even if every meaningful indicative sentence (embedded in a context) determines a state of affairs, it does not follow that every such sentence determines an *in-principle verifiable* state of affairs. Thus, even if I were to allow that (METC) is true and, hence, that (∗)'s lack of possible-world-style truth conditions entails that it is meaningless, my view would still be "gentler" than logical positivism, because I would *not* be making the claim that (∗) is meaningless because it is not in-principle verifiable. And more generally, I would not be making the claim that (VER) is true, that is, that a lack of in-principle verifiability entails meaninglessness.

This shows that it would be *acceptable* for me to claim that (∗) is meaningless, because it shows that I could do this without committing to verificationism or old-style logical positivism. But for whatever it's worth, it seems to me that (∗) is meaningful. Indeed, this point seems rather obvious to me. If (∗) *weren't* meaningful, we would have no way to account for the fact that so many brilliant people have spent so much time and energy arguing whether or not it is true. Moreover, we *understand* (∗); it says that there are existents that don't exist in the spatiotemporal way that physical objects exist; but if we understand (∗), then surely, it must be meaningful.

Now, if this is right, and if I am right that (∗) has no possible-world-style truth conditions, then it follows that (METC) is false. But this doesn't engender any *problem*, because as far as I can tell, there's no good reason to believe that (METC) is true. The semantic program developed by people like Carnap, Lewis, and Kaplan doesn't provide any argument for (METC), because (to the best of my knowledge) none of these philosophers has ever given an argument for the thesis that their framework applies to *all* meaningful indicative sentences. That is, no one has ever argued that *all* meaningful indicative sentences are associated with character-functions (or more precisely, *non-trivial* character-functions, that is, character-functions that aren't undefined for all contexts). Thus, my attitude is simply this: I think that (METC) is false, because (a) I don't know of any reason to think that it is universally true, and (b) it seems to me that (∗) is a counterexample to it. (But again, if someone produced a good argument for (METC), I would not have to abandon the metaphysical conclusion or the claim that (∗) lacks possible-world-style truth conditions, because I could admit that (∗) is meaningless without collapsing into verificationism or logical positivism.)

I should note here that even if I am right about (METC), it does not mean that the semantic program developed by people like Carnap, Lewis, and Kaplan is wrongheaded, or anything approaching this. It could still be that this program captures the best way of thinking about truth conditions and, indeed, that it captures deep and important facts about meaning. The only thing that follows from the falsity of (METC) about this semantic program is that it doesn't tell us *everything there is to know* about meaning. More specifically, it follows that universal claims like 'Meanings *are* character-functions' are false. But I don't think very many people would want to endorse strong claims of this sort anyway.[14]

One might respond as follows. "If the semantic program developed by people like Carnap, Lewis, and Kaplan doesn't tell us everything there is to know about meaning, what *is* the right story about meaning? And more specifically, if meanings aren't sets of possible worlds, or structured characters (see note 14 for a definition of this term), or anything of this sort, what are they (if indeed there are any *entities* that are meanings at all)?"

I don't need to commit to any particular view here. For one thing, I don't *have* to deny the thesis that meanings are structured characters, or something of this sort; if I wanted to, I could endorse this sort of meaning theory, because, as we've seen, I could admit that (∗) is meaningless without collapsing into verificationism. Now, I do think that (∗) is meaningful, and so I don't think that meanings are structured characters (or anything of this sort). But I don't need to *commit* to this stance here, and so I don't need to say what I think the meaningfulness of (∗) consists in. That is, I don't need to commit to any particular theory of meaning. I should say, though, that I don't see that there's any real problem in this connection anyway, because as far as I can see, the claim that (∗) has meaning but no possible-world-style truth conditions is compatible with just about *all* of the standard theories of meaning (except, of course, theories that take meanings to be things like sets of possible worlds or structured characters). The only thing we need to demand of a theory of meaning in this connection is that it leave room for sentences to be meaningful without determining any *state of affairs* and, hence, without having any possible-world-style truth conditions. But it seems to me that a theory could do this by merely allowing the meaning of a sentence to be "loose" or "imprecise" in a certain sort of way—or better, by merely *avoiding* the claim that meanings are very precise sorts of things that *always* determine well-defined sets of possible worlds to serve as truth conditions. Again, it seems to me that most of the standard views do allow for the possibility of a sentence that has meaning but no possible-world-style truth conditions. Even the view that a sentence is meaningful just in case it expresses a proposition allows for this possibility, because there could be propositions that are "loose" or "imprecise".

(It might seem that the metaphysical conclusion is incompatible with theories that take meanings to be *abstract objects*, for instance, propositions. But we'll see in sub-section 3.4.3 that it's not. For we'll see there that we can "endorse" a theory of this sort without committing to the *existence* of meanings.)

I end this subsection by pointing out that (∗) is not the only sentence that has meaning but no possible-world-style truth conditions. For example, the sentence

(H) My head is asleep[15]

also seems to be in this category. We understand what (H) says, namely, that my head feels similar to the way my arm feels when it is asleep, but we do not know what my head actually has to feel like in order to *count* as feeling similar to the way my arm does when it is asleep. To quote Malcolm, "We do not perceive a clash of meanings [in (H)]. But we do not know what . . . circumstances go with the sentence." Now, Malcolm's point here is the Wittgensteinian point that meaning is determined by use; but if we adopt a *compositional* theory of how meaning is determined, then we can take Malcolm's claim as suggesting that (H) is meaningful (because it contains no clash of meanings) but that it does not have possible-world-style truth conditions (because no circumstances, that is, possible worlds, go with the sentence).

Another example of a sentence that has meaning but no possible-world-style truth conditions is

(G) The world is good.

I think I understand this sentence — in a *loose* way, anyway — but I certainly don't think there's any clear fact of the matter as to what the world would have to be like in order to count as a good world; indeed, I don't think there's any fact of the matter as to whether the world actually *is* good, because I don't think there's any fact of the matter as to what the criteria for this are.

Finally, a more everyday example is

(F) Albert is fat.

This sentence is clearly meaningful, but there is no well-defined set of possible worlds in which it is true, and so it does not have possible-world-style truth conditions. Now, once again, the problem here is that the idea expressed by (F) is, in some sense, *loose*, although the *reason* for the looseness is rather transparent here — it is obviously because 'fat' is vague — and the problem generated by the looseness isn't as *bad* with (F) as it is with (∗), because there are some possible worlds that clearly make (F) true and others that clearly make it false. The problem with (F) is merely that there are *some* worlds that are such that there is no fact of the matter as to whether or not they make (F) true.[16]

3.3 *The Argument for the Metaphysical Conclusion*

In this section, I will argue that there is no fact of the matter as to which possible worlds count as worlds in which (∗) is true. This is all I need to argue, because the claim that (∗) has no possible-world-style truth conditions follows trivially from this, and as we saw in sub-section 3.1, the metaphysical conclusion — the claim that there is no fact of the matter as to whether abstract objects exist, that is, whether (∗) is true — also follows trivially. My argument proceeds as follows.

(i) We don't have any idea what a possible world would have to be *like* in order to count as a world in which there are objects that exist outside of spacetime.

(ii) If (i) is true, then there is no fact of the matter as to which possible worlds count as worlds in which there are objects that exist outside of spacetime, that is, worlds in which (∗) is true.

Therefore,

(iii) There is no fact of the matter as to which possible worlds count as worlds in which (∗) is true.

I take it that (ii) is the more controversial premise here, since it has an epistemic antecedent and a metaphysical consequent. But before I argue for (ii), I want to argue for (i).

My argument for (i) is based upon the observation that we don't know—or indeed, have any idea—what it would be like for an object to exist outside of spacetime. Now, this is *not* to say that we don't know what *abstract objects* are like. That, I think, would be wrong. Of the number 3, for instance, we know that it is odd, that it is the cube root of 27, and so on. Thus, there is a sense in which we know what it is like. What I am saying is that we cannot imagine what *existence outside of spacetime* would be like. Now, it may be that someday, somebody will clarify what such existence might be like; but what I think is correct is that no one has done this *yet*. There have been many philosophers who have advocated platonistic views, but I do not know of any who have said anything to clarify what non-spatiotemporal existence would really *amount* to. All we are ever given is a *negative* characterization of the existence of abstract objects. We are told that such objects do *not* exist in spacetime, or that they do *not* exist in the ways that physical and mental objects exist. In other words, we are only told what this sort of existence *isn't* like; we're never told what it *is* like.[17]

The reason platonists have nothing to say here is that our whole conception of what existence *amounts* to seems to be bound up with extension and spatiotemporality. When you take these things away from an object, we are left wondering what its existence could *consist* in. For instance, when we say that Oliver North exists and Oliver Twist does not, what we *mean* is that the former resides at some particular spatiotemporal location (or "spacetime worm"), whereas there is nothing in spacetime that is the latter.[18] But there is nothing analogous to this in connection with abstract objects. Contemporary platonists do not think that the existence of 3 consists in there being something more encompassing than spacetime where 3 *resides*. My charge is simply that platonists have nothing substantive to say here, that is, nothing substantive to say about what the existence of 3 consists in.

The standard contemporary platonist would respond to this charge, I think, by claiming that existence outside of spacetime is just like existence *inside* spacetime—that is, that there is only *one* kind of existence. But this doesn't solve the problem; it just relocates it. I can grant that "there is only one kind of existence" and simply change my objection to this: we only know what certain *instances* of this kind are like. In particular, we know what the existence of concrete objects amounts to, but we do not know what the existence of abstract objects amounts to. The existence of concrete objects comes down to extension and spatiotemporality, but we have nothing comparable to say about the existence of abstract objects. In other words, we don't have anything more *general* to say about what existence amounts to than what we have to say about the existence of concrete objects. But this is just to say that we don't know what non-spatiotemporal existence amounts to, or what it might *consist* in, or what it might be *like*.

Abstract objects are even more mysterious in this respect than gods and ghosts are. When we conceive of gods and ghosts, we ordinarily conceive of them as having, if not extension, then at least some sort of *energy*, or something along these lines. In other words, gods and ghosts are ordinarily thought to be capable of causally affecting the physical world and, indeed, of doing so at particular spatiotemporal locations. But if they are so capable, then they are *physical* in a way that abstract objects like numbers are not. It is the fact that abstract objects are supposed to be *wholly* non-physical, non-mental, non-causal, and non-spatiotemporal that leaves us at a loss for a conception of what their existence could really amount to.

I take it that if what I have been arguing here is correct, then (i) is true. If we don't have any idea what existence outside of spacetime could be like, then surely, we don't have any idea what a possible world would have to be like in order to count as a world that involves existence outside of spacetime, that is, a world in which there are objects that exist outside of spacetime.

One might object as follows: "We might not know *in advance* what non-spatiotemporal existence would be like, but we know what existence is and we know what spatiotemporality is, and so if we were 'presented' with a situation that involved non-spatiotemporal existence, we would 'recognize' it." But the point of the above argument is precisely that we *wouldn't* recognize it. We can put the point this way: (a) corresponding to every way that the physical world could be set up, there are two different possible worlds, one containing abstract objects and the other not;[19] and (b) if we were "presented" with a possible world, we wouldn't know whether it was a world containing abstract objects or a physically identical world without abstract objects, and what's more, we wouldn't have the foggiest idea what we could do in order to figure this out. The reason for this, if I am right, is that for any such pair of physically identical worlds, we don't know what the *difference* between them really amounts to.

Another objection that one might raise against my argument for (i) can be put as follows. "Platonists might claim that the whole discussion of whether we could know what a possible world would have to be like in order to count as a world in which there exist non-spatiotemporal objects is misguided, because *all* possible worlds count as such worlds. In other words, platonists might claim that (∗) is necessarily true, that is, true in all possible worlds." My response to this is that I simply doubt that platonists have any good *argument* for the claim that (∗) is true in all possible worlds. Indeed, from an intuitive standpoint, it seems that (∗) *isn't* true in all possible worlds; for since (∗) is clearly not a logical or conceptual truth, it would seem that there are some logically and conceptually possible worlds in which it isn't true. Now, of course, platonists might grant this point but maintain that there are no *metaphysically* possible worlds in which (∗) isn't true. But we have already seen (section 2 of this chapter and sub-section 6.4 of chapter 2) that there are no good arguments for this claim. The reason, in a nutshell, is that we don't even have a well-motivated account of what metaphysical necessity is supposed to *consist* in. More specifically, it is totally unclear what platonists could *mean* when they say that the existence of abstract objects is metaphysically necessary. Moreover, it is hard to believe that platonists could solve this problem, that they could come up with a definition of 'metaphysically necessary' that served their needs here, for as I pointed out in chapter 2, there just doesn't seem to be any interesting sense in which existence claims involving abstract objects (e.g., 'there exists an empty set') are necessary but existence claims involving concrete objects (e.g., 'there exists a purple hula hoop') are not.

I have the impression that most people who think that mathematics is metaphysically necessary think that this is simply a *given*. In other words, they think that in trying to construct a definition of 'metaphysically necessary', it is simply a desideratum that our mathematical theories are metaphysically necessary. Now, on this view, *whatever* we end up saying about metaphysical necessity, (∗) will be true in all metaphysically possible worlds. But anyone who takes this line sees the metaphysical necessity of (∗) as a matter of sheer stipulation, or perhaps, intuition. Either way, there is no *argument* here.

Now, of course, if platonists did have a sound argument for the claim that the existence of abstract objects is metaphysically necessary (and if the notion of metaphysical necessity employed in that argument entailed truth[20]), then the metaphysical conclusion could not be correct. But, of course, the central viewpoint that I am trying to motivate in this book is that we don't have any sound arguments for or against platonism, let *alone* the necessity or impossibility of that view. And note that platonists cannot help their cause here by arguing that *if* abstract objects exist, *then* they exist of metaphysical necessity. For even if this were right, it wouldn't yield the desired result. It would tell us (presumably) that either all metaphysically possible worlds contain abstract objects or else none do, but it wouldn't tell us *which* of these alternatives obtained and, presumably, it wouldn't tell us what these worlds would have to be *like* in order to count as worlds in which there exist abstract objects.

These last remarks bring out the fact that there is also an *anti-platonist* version of the objection that I've been considering here. More specifically, anti-platonists might object to (i) on the grounds that the existence of abstract objects is metaphysically *impossible*. But my response to this version of the objection would be essentially equivalent to my response to the platonist version of the objection: there is no good reason to believe that there couldn't exist any non-spatiotemporal objects, and indeed, from an intuitive standpoint, it seems that there *could* exist such objects. What I have been trying to bring out, though, is that while it seems to us that it *could* be that there exist objects outside of spacetime, we don't have any idea *how* this could be so, or what this would be *like*.

I do not want to pretend that the above remarks constitute an airtight argument for (i). My aim has merely been to make this claim seem fairly plausible. In any event, I now proceed to argue for (ii), that is, for the claim that if we don't have any idea what a possible world would have to be like in order to count as a world in which there are objects that exist outside of spacetime, then there is no fact of the matter as to which possible worlds count as worlds in which there are objects that exist outside of spacetime, that is, worlds in which (∗) is true.

At first blush, (ii) might seem rather implausible, since it has an epistemic antecedent and a metaphysical consequent. But the reason the metaphysical consequent follows is that the ignorance mentioned in the epistemic antecedent is an ignorance of truth *conditions* rather than truth *value*. If we don't know whether some sentence is true or false, that gives us absolutely no reason to doubt that there is a definite fact of the matter as to whether it really *is* true or false. But when we don't know what the truth *conditions* of a sentence are, that is a very different matter. Let me explain why.

The main point that needs to be made here is that English is, in some relevant sense, *our* language, and (∗) is *our* sentence. More specifically, the point is that *the truth conditions of English sentences supervene on our usage*. It follows from this that if our usage doesn't determine what the possible-world-style truth conditions of (∗) are, then it simply doesn't *have* any such truth conditions. In other words,

> (iia) If our usage doesn't determine which possible worlds count as worlds in which (∗) is true, then there is no fact of the matter as to which possible worlds count as such worlds.

Again, the argument for (iia) is simply that (∗) is *our* sentence and, hence, could obtain truth conditions only from our usage.[21]

Now, given (iia), all we need in order to establish (ii), by hypothetical syllogism, is

> (iib) If we don't have any idea what a possible world would have to be like in order to count as a world in which there are objects that exist outside of spacetime, then our usage doesn't determine which possible worlds count as worlds in which (∗) is true.

But (iib) seems fairly trivial. My argument for this, in a nutshell, is that if the consequent of (iib) were false, then its antecedent couldn't be true. In a bit more detail, the argument proceeds as follows. If our usage *did* determine which possible worlds count as worlds in which (∗) is true—that is, if it determined possible-world-style truth conditions for (∗)—then it would also determine which possible worlds count as worlds in which there are objects that exist outside of spacetime. (This is trivial, because (∗) just *says* that there are objects that exist outside of spacetime.) But it seems pretty clear that if our usage determined which possible worlds count as worlds in which there are objects that exist outside of spacetime, then we would have at least *some idea* what a possible world would have to be like in order to count as a world in which there are objects that exist outside of spacetime. For (a) it seems that if we have *no idea* what a possible world would have to be like in order to count as a world in which there are objects that exist outside of spacetime, then the only way our usage could determine which possible worlds count as such worlds would be if we lucked into such usage; but (b) it's simply not plausible to suppose that we have lucked into such usage in this way.

One might try to object to the reasoning that I have employed here by trying to find a sentence S that is such that

(A) we don't have any idea what a possible world would have to be like in order to count as a world that satisfies S's disquotational truth conditions,

but

(B) there is clearly a fact of the matter as to whether or not S is true.

Now, by merely finding such a sentence, we would not necessarily have uncovered a problem with my argument, because I have not claimed that *every* sentence that satisfies (A) fails to satisfy (B). In other words, my argument here is concerned solely with (∗), and not with any other sentences. Thus, I can allow that there is a sentence S that satisfies (A) and (B), so long as I can show that there is some relevant disanalogy between S and (∗) that explains why the above reasoning is acceptable in connection with (∗) even if the same sort of reasoning would not be acceptable in connection with S.

It seems to me that there *are* sentences that satisfy (A) and (B). For instance, there are surely some billion-word sentences for which our usage (compositionally) determines perfectly clear possible-world-style truth conditions and which, because of this, have perfectly clear truth values; but for any such sentence, we couldn't know what a possible world would have to be like in order to make the given sentence true, because we can't *process* such sentences. It should be clear, however, that there is an important disanalogy between sentences of this sort and (∗); in particular, (∗) has a very short and simple syntactic structure, and for this reason, we can "process" it. Because of this, it seems to me that considerations about billion-word sentences don't do anything to undermine the above argument about (∗). For while it's easy to see how our usage could determine possible-world-style truth conditions for billion-word sentences without our having any idea what these truth conditions are, it's very *hard* to see how this could be the case with (∗). Thus, it seems to me that whatever we end up saying about billion-word sentences, the above argument still gives us reason to believe (iib), and so it still gives us reason to believe (ii).

Are there any *other* kinds of sentences that satisfy (A) and (B)? Or more specifically, are there any sentences of this sort that are relatively short and syntactically simple, so that the reason (A) is satisfied has nothing to do with an inability on our part to process the given sentences? Well, it might seem that Twin-Earth considerations could generate cases of this sort. Thus, for instance, suppose that somewhere in the universe (but not on Earth) there is a substance — call it XYZ — that is just like H_2O in appearance, taste, feel, and so on, but different in chemical structure. Now, in light of this, consider the sentence

(W) There is water in the Thames

and the English-speaking community of 1650. On the assumption that 1650 utterances of 'water' did not refer to XYZ — that is, that H_2O was the only substance in the 1650 extension of 'water' — it follows that while 1650 utterances of (W) were clearly true, no one alive in 1650 knew what a possible world would have to be like in order to count as a world in which such utterances were true, because none of these people had the ability to distinguish H_2O from XYZ.

First of all, I don't think there is any good argument for the claim that XYZ was not in the 1650 extension of 'water', and so I do not think there is any good reason to suppose that (A) is really satisfied here.[22] But a more important point, I think, is that *whatever* we end up saying about the 1650 extension of 'water', sentences like (W) are not analogous to (*). For (a) we don't have *any idea* what a possible world would have to be like in order to count as a world in which (*) is true; but (b) the members of the English-speaking community of 1650 knew *quite a lot* about what a world would have to be like in order to count as a world in which their utterances of (W) were true. Thus, the ignorance that we possess with respect to (*) is radically more profound than the ignorance that people had in 1650 about sentences like (W). Moreover, given the profound sort of ignorance that we possess here, it is extremely hard to believe that our usage determines possible-world-style truth conditions for (*). It's hard to believe that our usage could determine possible-world-style truth conditions for this sentence when we know virtually *nothing* about what needs to obtain in order for the sentence to be true. Therefore, it seems plausible to suppose that regardless of what we say about sentences like (W), (iib) is true. And so it also seems plausible that (ii) is true.

So it is important to my argument that we don't have *any* non-trivial knowledge about what it would be like for there to exist non-spatiotemporal objects. For in general, if we have *partial* knowledge about what it would be like for there to exist Xs, then it is possible for us to know whether or not there really do exist Xs. For example, if we let a *quermaid* be a mermaid who is *querklempt*, and if we suppose that we don't know anything about the property of being querklempt, then despite the fact that we don't know what a possible world would have to be like in order to count as a world in which there exist quermaids, we do know that there aren't any such things as quermaids (in the actual world), because one of the necessary conditions for the existence of quermaids (namely, that there exist mermaids) is not satisfied. But, again, this case is not relevant to our case, because we don't know *anything* about what a possible world would have to be like in order to count as a world in which there are objects that exist outside of spacetime. That is, we don't know any necessary or sufficient conditions for the existence of non-spatiotemporal objects (aside from trivial ones that wouldn't be of any help here[23]).

Now, I suppose that we could think of the various arguments that have been offered for anti-platonism as attempts to locate necessary conditions for the existence of abstract objects that aren't satisfied; and likewise, we could think of the various arguments for platonism as attempts to locate *sufficient* conditions that *are* satisfied. In other words, we can think of these arguments as attempts to fill in the blanks in the following argument form: "We don't know what it would be like for an object to exist outside of spacetime, but *whatever* it would be like, we know that there are (are not) things that exist in this way, because (a) _____ obtains (doesn't obtain) and (b) if _____ obtains, then there are abstract objects (if there are abstract objects, then _____ obtains)." My response to this is that while we probably can think of the various traditional arguments for platonism and anti-platonism in this way, it doesn't matter, because none of these arguments are sound. Now, of course, this is a sweeping claim that requires quite a bit of motivation. In particular, what I would need to do is respond to every argument for platonism or anti-platonism in the literature. Now, I have already done a good deal of the work here, for I have responded to the most important platonist and anti-platonist arguments from the philosophy of mathematics. But since the metaphysical conclusion is about abstract objects in general, rather than just mathematical objects, what I would really need to do here is respond to *all* platonist and anti-platonist arguments, not just those from the philosophy of mathematics. In other words, I would need to establish a general version of the weak epistemic conclusion, that is, a version that applied to all abstract objects, as opposed to just mathematical objects. In sub-section 3.4.3, I will say a few words about how my responses to the arguments from the philosophy of mathematics can be generalized,[24] but I obviously can't provide a thorough argument here for the claim that all arguments for or against platonism in the history of philosophy fail, because it would take far too much space. (It is worth noting, however, that from a purely intuitive standpoint, the claim that we have no good arguments for or against the existence of abstract objects ought to seem rather plausible. For we usually think of the problem of abstract objects as something like an "unsolved mystery of metaphysics", and this suggests that there are no conclusive arguments on either side of the debate.)

Another worry that one might have about my argument can be expressed as follows. "It could be that we don't know what a possible world would have to be like in order to count as a world in which there are objects that exist outside of spacetime, because we can't 'imagine' or 'wrap our minds around' any state of affairs involving existence outside of spacetime. But even if this is right, (*) could still be true, because it may be that there *does obtain* a state of affairs — which we can't imagine or wrap our minds around — that clearly qualifies as involving existence outside of spacetime."

But in what sense could the state of affairs in question clearly qualify as involving existence outside of spacetime? In order for this to be the case, there would have to be facts of the matter as to the sorts of states of affairs that count as involving existence outside of spacetime. And as we've seen, such facts would have to derive from *our* usage; for in order to be at all relevant in the present context, the state of affairs in question would have to clearly involve what *we* mean by existence outside of spacetime. But I have already argued that, given (i), it is unlikely that our usage determines such facts. Moreover, the question of whether our usage determines such facts is precisely what is at issue here. Thus, in assuming that there *are* facts of the matter here, the above objection begs the question.

This concludes my argument for (iii), which as we've seen, entails the metaphysical conclusion. To summarize, my argument proceeds as follows. We don't know what existence outside of spacetime would be *like*, and so we don't know what the possible-world-style truth conditions of (∗) are, and therefore our usage doesn't determine what these truth conditions are. But since (∗) is *our* sentence, it could obtain possible-world-style truth conditions only from our usage, and so it follows that (∗) simply doesn't *have* any such truth conditions. Now, just because a sentence lacks possible-world-style truth conditions, it doesn't necessarily mean that there is no fact of the matter as to whether it is true or false; but as we've seen, in the case of (∗), this does follow. Therefore, the arguments of this section show that there is no fact of the matter as to whether there exist any abstract objects.[25]

3.4 *Objections*

I have already said that I do not think that my argument for the metaphysical conclusion is anything like a knockdown argument. There are, I think, all sorts of ways in which one might try to object to it. What I would like to do in this sub-section is say a few words about how I would respond to four of the more obvious objections that one might be inclined to mount. The first two of these objections are attempts to turn traditional objections to logical positivism into objections to my kinder, gentler positivism. The last two are objections to my argument in particular.

3.4.1 *Is My Kinder, Gentler Version of Positivism Self-Refuting?*   One of the most famous objections to logical positivism is that it is self-refuting: the verificationist criterion of meaning is not subject to empirical verification, and so, by its own standards, it is meaningless. It seems that a similar sort of objection can be raised against my argument, for it seems that if there is no fact of the matter as to whether (∗) is true or false, then there is no fact of the matter as to whether the meta-physical conclusion is true or false. The reason is that the metaphysical conclusion speaks of the existence of abstract objects, and so if the argument of sub-section 3.3 is sound, then the metaphysical conclusion does not have any possible-world-style truth conditions.

Perhaps this objection can be answered by pointing out that the metaphysical conclusion can be formulated so that it doesn't refer to abstract objects. If we formulate it as the claim that there is no fact of the matter as to whether (∗) is true or false (and hence, no fact of the matter as to whether platonism is true or false), then it will contain the term " 'abstract object' " but will *not* contain the term 'abstract object'. In other words, the metaphysical conclusion, so formulated, will not be about abstract objects; it will be about the *term* 'abstract object' and *sentences* like (∗).

Now, in this case, one might doubt that the conclusion is really a *metaphysical* conclusion at all. One might think it more of a *semantic* conclusion. Perhaps it would be best to simply admit this and leave it at that. But I think that a story could be told about how the semantic-assent version of the metaphysical conclu-sion—that is, the one about 'abstract object', as opposed to abstract objects— "reveals" to us, in some sense, that there is no fact of the matter as to whether there exist any abstract objects. For consider the attempt to deny this. One would wind up saying something like this: "Well, you've shown that there's no fact of the matter as to whether the sentence 'There exist abstract objects' is true, but there still might be a fact of the matter as to whether there exist abstract objects." But this is clearly incoherent.

One might also attempt to say something like this: "Even if you are right about (∗), it could still be that there obtains a state of affairs such that if it were somehow 'revealed' to us, we would decide to say that it vindicates platonism or anti-platonism." Now, I actually doubt that there are any possible states of affairs — aside from the obvious ones that wouldn't be allowed here, such as the state of affairs of there existing (or not existing) abstract objects, or the state of affairs of 3 being prime — that would lead platonists and anti-platonists to an agreement here. But the more important point is that even if we did come to an agreement here, if I am right about (∗), then the agreed-upon conclusion would not have been *forced on us* in any sense, because our current usage doesn't determine that (∗) is true in the worlds in which the given state of affairs obtains. Thus, it seems that in order to refute my argument using a strategy along these general lines, one would need to show that I am, in fact, *wrong* about (∗). In other words, one would have to show that there are (or perhaps could be) states of affairs that *really do* vindicate platonism or anti-platonism. But in order for this to be the case, there would have to be facts of the matter as to what states of affairs count as vindicating platonism or anti-platonism, and as we've seen, these facts would have to be determined by our usage. But I have already argued that it is unlikely that our usage does determine such facts.

3.4.2 Laws of Nature and Superpositions Another well-known objection to logical positivism is that it throws out the baby — indeed, several babies — with the bathwater. More specifically, it is claimed that the machine-gun fire intended to dispense with metaphysical sentences dispenses with other sentences as well, sentences that we would like to salvage. Probably the most important sentences that traditional logical positivism threatens to deem meaningless are *laws of nature*. Sentences such as

(E) All satellites follow elliptical orbits,

especially when they are taken as supporting their counterfactuals, are not verifiable. Thus, according to verificationism, such sentences are meaningless. But they are clearly *not* meaningless, and so verificationism must be false.

It should be clear that my view would not obliterate all of science, as traditional logical positivism threatens to, because my argument does not apply to ordinary laws of nature like (E). The problem with (∗) arose because we don't know what it would be *like* for (∗) to be true, that is, because we don't know what its possible-world-style truth conditions are. But we know exactly what it would be like for (E) to be true, and so there is no problem with this sentence. More generally, we can say this: as long as we have a reasonably clear grasp of the possible-world-style truth conditions of a sentence, my argument doesn't pose any threat to it at all — even if we are cut off, *in principle*, from the possibility of obtaining any evidence whatsoever for its truth or falsity.

As a case in point, consider the sentence

(M) Electron e is spin-up in the x direction and spin-down in the orthogonal direction y.

It has been suggested by some that if we know e's value of spin in the x direction, then we cannot know its value of spin in the y direction and, indeed, cannot obtain any evidence here whatsoever (without altering the system and, hence, giving up our knowledge of e's value of spin in the x direction). Now, I actually think that this is confused: I think we have good reason to believe that if e is spin-up in the x direction, then it simply doesn't *have* any determinate value of spin in the y direction. But let us pretend, for the sake of argument, that we hold a theory that entails that electrons have determinate values of spin for every direction in space at the same time and, moreover, that given that we know an electron's value of spin in the x direction, we are cut off—in principle—from any evidence concerning its value of spin in the orthogonal direction y. Even if this were all true, my argument still wouldn't suggest that there is no fact of the matter about (M). The reason is that we would only have an ignorance of truth *value* in connection with (M), as opposed to an ignorance of truth *conditions*. The fact that it would be an *in-principle* ignorance of truth value is simply irrelevant. For even if we could never know whether (M) was true or false, it is nonetheless the case that our usage determines a well-defined set of possible worlds to serve as (M)'s truth conditions, because there are no constructions in (M), analogous to 'existence outside of spacetime', that leave us at a loss for a conception of what the corresponding state of affairs could be *like*. We know exactly what it would be like for (M) to be true, and so my argument doesn't pose any threat to that sentence.

This discussion of spin brings to mind another problematic case, not a hypothetical one but a real one. Consider the sentence

(S) Electron e is spin-up in the x direction, and it is in a superposition of spin-up and spin-down in the orthogonal direction y.

What is being said here? In particular, what are superposition states *like*? We know a lot about how electrons in such states behave; for instance, if we take an ensemble of electrons prepared in the manner of e and measure them for spin in the y direction, we know that half of them will be spin-up and half will be spin-down. But this doesn't tell us anything about what the internal state responsible for this behavior—the superposition *itself*—is really like. *That* we simply don't know; 'superposition' is just a tag that we hang on something we don't understand. (To be more precise, we can say that a system is in a superposition with respect to a given observable quantity if and only if it does not currently have any of the possible values for that observable; but the problem is that we don't know what it would be like for *this* to be the case; for instance, we don't know what it would be like for an electron to have no determinate position, or momentum, or value of spin in some direction.[26]) So while there may be a disanalogy between (*) on the one hand and sentences like (E) and (M) on the other, there doesn't seem to be any disanalogy between (*) and (S). Thus, by parity of reasoning, I seem forced to claim that there is no fact of the matter as to whether (S) is true.

A Kinder, Gentler Positivism 175

I think there *is* a disanalogy between (∗) and (S), and I would like to motivate
this by likening (S) to the quermaid example discussed in sub-section 3.3. I pointed
out there that we know that there are no quermaids, despite the fact that we don't
know what it would be like for quermaids to exist, because we know that one of
the necessary conditions for the existence of quermaids (namely, that there exist
mermaids) is not satisfied. I also pointed out that one might *try* to motivate platonism (or anti-platonism) in the same way, that is, by locating a sufficient condition for the existence of abstract objects that we know is satisfied (or a necessary
condition that we know is *not* satisfied). But I claimed in sub-section 3.3 (and
partially backed the claim up in chapters 3–6) that no one has ever succeeded in
locating such a condition, or what comes to the same thing, that none of the
traditional arguments for platonism or anti-platonism are cogent. Thus, I con-
cluded that the abstract-object case is different from the quermaid case on this
score. What I would like to point out now is that the superposition case is more
like the quermaid case than the abstract-object case. Actually, it is the mirror image
of the quermaid case: we have good reason to believe in the existence of superpositions, because we know of certain sufficient conditions for their existence that
are satisfied.

The sufficient conditions that I have in mind here are inherent in the arguments against hidden-variables interpretations of quantum mechanics. (There is
no need to say very much about hidden-variables interpretations here; all that
matters is that according to them, quantum systems do not have genuine superposition states; that is, according to them, such systems always have determinate
values for every observable quantity.) The best of these arguments is due to Kochen
and Specker.[27] This argument is a geometrical argument that shows that no spin-1
particle could have a determinate value of spin for every direction in space at the
same time. What I am suggesting here is that the various facts that Kochen and
Specker allude to in their premises combine to form a sufficient condition for the
existence of superposition states. Since these facts entail that spin-1 particles do
not have determinate values of spin for every direction in space at the same time,
they entail that such particles have superposition states and, hence, they provide
a sufficient condition for the existence of superpositions. Thus, since we know
that these facts obtain, we can conclude that there *are* superposition states.

So while it's true that we don't know what superposition states are really *like*,
it's also true that we have good reason to believe that there *are* such states. But as
we saw in sub-section 3.3, this sort of reasoning cannot be employed in the abstract-
object case.

A final worry that one might have about my argument posing a threat to
empirical science can be stated as follows: "If there's no fact of the matter as to
whether there exist any abstract objects, then there's no fact of the matter as
to whether sentences like '3 is prime' and 'The number of planets is 9' are true,
and so there's no fact of the matter as to whether our mathematical and empirical
theories are true." But given what I've argued in this book, I don't see why this
should be considered a problem. I argued in chapter 7 that it is coherent, sensible,
and indeed, plausible to maintain that our mathematical and empirical theories
are *false* — or more specifically, that our mathematical theories are purely fictional

and our empirical theories have true nominalistic contents and fictional platonistic contents. But if this is right, then it's surely acceptable to say (in the particular way that I'm saying it here) that there's no fact of the matter as to whether our mathematical theories are true and that while the nominalistic contents of our empirical theories are true, there's no fact of the matter as to whether their platonistic contents are true. Or to put the point that I'm making here a bit differently, it's not a *criticism* of our mathematical and empirical theories to say (in the way I'm saying it here) that there's no fact of the matter as to whether these theories are true.[28]

3.4.3 *Possible Worlds and Propositions*   The third objection to my argument can be stated as follows. "Throughout your argument, you have spoken of *possible worlds* (and you hinted in sub-section 3.2, although you didn't *commit* to it, that you might also want to appeal to *propositions*). But these are abstract objects. Thus, your argument is unacceptable, because one cannot appeal to abstract objects in arguing that there is no fact of the matter as to whether there exist any abstract objects."

In order to clarify my strategy of response to this objection, I must first digress for a moment. I believe it is possible to do for semantics what I have done in this book for mathematics. What I have shown is that (a) there is exactly one viable version of platonism about mathematical theory, namely, FBP; (b) there is exactly one viable version of anti-platonism about mathematical theory, namely, fictionalism; and (c) we do not, and could not, have any good argument that would settle the dispute between these two views. Likewise, I think it can be shown that (a') there is exactly one viable version of platonism about semantic theory, in particular, an analog of FBP that holds that all possible semantical objects (e.g., propositions and possible worlds) exist; (b') there is exactly one viable version of anti-platonism about semantic theory, in particular, an analog of fictionalism that holds that no semantical objects exist; and (c') we do not, and could not, have any good argument that would settle the dispute between these two views.

For the present purposes, I want to concentrate on (b'). The argument I would provide for this claim would be very similar to the argument I have given in this book for (b). I would begin by arguing that the only way to save all the semantic phenomena that need to be saved is to give very *rich* — indeed, *mathematical* — semantic theories for natural languages. For instance, one thing that an adequate semantic theory for English would have to do is entail, for each English sentence σ, a theorem of the form 'σ means that p'. The next thing I would do is argue that these semantic theories could not be true of any collection of concrete objects. For instance, I would argue that the 'σ-means-that-p' theorems of our semantic theories could only be interpreted as being about abstract objects, in particular, sentence types and propositions. Finally, given all of this, I would argue that the only way to maintain an anti-platonistic view of semantics is to adopt *semantic fictionalism*, the view that semantic theories of natural languages like English are, strictly speaking, not true.

Now, the main problem with semantic fictionalism is analogous to the main problem with mathematical fictionalism; in other words, it is the problem of applicability. More specifically, semantic fictionalism seems incompatible with the fact that we need to refer to semantical objects in order to do empirical science, that is, in order to provide an adequate picture of the physical world. Consider, for instance, the attempt to provide a theory of human belief, or a theory of the semantics of actual physical tokens. In order to construct such theories, we would need to account for the truth of sentences like 'John believes that pigs fly' and 'The sentence token tattooed on Alfred's forehead means that snow is white'. But on the standard view, we will need to appeal to propositions in order to account for the truth of these sentences, because we will need to maintain that the 'that'-clauses in these sentences refer to propositions. But as I have argued elsewhere,[29] this indispensability argument against semantic fictionalism can be answered in the same way that I have (in this book) answered the corresponding indispensability argument against mathematical fictionalism. In particular, semantic fictionalists can endorse nominalistic scientific realism with respect to the empirical theories in question. That is, they can maintain that these theories can succeed in "painting accurate pictures" of the parts of the physical world they're concerned with (e.g., belief states and concrete tokens), even if there do not actually exist any semantical objects like propositions, because such objects play merely non-causal roles in these empirical theories, and because the talk in these theories of semantical objects like propositions is a mere descriptive aid.[30]

Now, given this picture of things, what I want to say about the above objection, that is, the objection that my argument for the metaphysical conclusion is unacceptable because it refers to possible worlds, is that the use I make of these entities is analogous to the use made of propositions in belief psychology and of mathematical objects in physics. More specifically, my argument could be cogent, even if there are no such things as possible worlds, because these entities play a merely non-causal role in my argument, and because the talk in my argument of possible worlds is a mere descriptive aid. In short, the point is that if it could be established that my use of possible worlds is analogous to the psychologist's use of propositions and the physicist's use of mathematical objects, then the objection to my argument would be avoided, because there is nothing wrong with such references to mathematical and semantical objects. The difficulties that I've been discussing in this chapter arise only with the attempt to *use* such references to establish platonism (or for that matter, with the attempt to establish platonism or anti-platonism in some other way).

Now, these brief remarks obviously don't provide a *complete* response to the third objection. In order to do that, I would need to argue at length for the claim that possible worlds play a merely non-causal, descriptive-aid role in my argument and the claim that, because of this, my argument could be cogent even if there are no such things as possible worlds. I am not going to do this here, because I really have nothing new to say in this connection: the arguments I would use here would be essentially equivalent to the ones I used in chapter 7 (and my paper "Attitudes Without Propositions") to argue that mathematical objects (and propositions) play merely non-causal, descriptive-aid roles in empirical science and that, because of this, the picture that empirical science paints of the physical world could be accurate even if there are no such things as mathematical objects (or propositions). (One might think that there is a disanalogy between the two cases, because my appeal to possible worlds is embedded in an *argument* rather than a *theory*. But there is really no disanalogy here, because empirical science contains arguments as well as theories, and we do appeal in these arguments to mathematical objects. I said a few words about this use of mathematical objects in chapter 7, sub-section 3.3.)

(I should also note here that on my view, points analogous to (a)–(c) and (a')–(c') hold not just for mathematics and semantics, but for every area of inquiry that needs to be taken as being about abstract objects. In other words, I believe that we can defend completely general versions of FBP and fictionalism and that we can motivate general versions of the weak and strong epistemic conclusions, that is, versions that hold not just for mathematical objects but for abstract objects in general. Thus, I believe that we do not, and could not, have any good argument for or against the existence of abstract objects.)

3.4.4 *Support for Anti-Platonism?*   The last objection I want to consider is this: "Insofar as your argument for the metaphysical conclusion shows that we have no conception of what it would be like for an object to exist outside of spacetime, it ought to be taken as motivating anti-platonism."

I think this is just wrong. The conclusion of my argument is that there is no fact of the matter as to whether or not there exist any abstract objects, and on its face, this is just as hostile to anti-platonism as it is to platonism. More important, I do not know how to *change* my argument so that it becomes an argument for anti-platonism. One might, I suppose, attempt to use the Quinean doctrine "No entity without identity"[31] here, but this would be to no avail, because platonists do have identity criteria for the mathematical entities in which they believe. For example, two *sets* are identical just in case they contain the same members. (Anti-platonists might also try to use Ockham's razor to mount an argument here, but I blocked that strategy at the end of chapter 7.)

The real reason why we cannot turn my argument into an anti-platonist argument is that anti-platonists have all the same problems in this connection that platonists have. That is, anti-platonists can no more say what the *falsity* of (∗) amounts to than platonists can say what its *truth* amounts to. Put differently, the point is that if W_1 and W_2 are physically identical possible worlds that differ from one another only in that W_1 contains abstract objects and W_2 does not, then anti-platonists can no more say what the difference between W_1 and W_2 amounts to (in a non-disquotational way) than platonists can. The bottom line here is that platonists and anti-platonists are *both* making claims about the nature of the world; thus, if I am right that there is no fact of the matter as to which of these claims is correct, then it follows that the situation doesn't favor either group of philosophers, that is, the claim that there are no abstract objects is just as bad off as the claim that there *are* abstract objects.

4. My Official View

My official view, then, is distinct from both FBP and fictionalism. I endorse the FBP-fictionalist interpretation, or picture, of mathematical theory and practice, but I do not agree with either of the metaphysical views here. More precisely, I am in agreement with almost everything that FBP-ists and fictionalists say about mathematical theory and practice,[32] but I do not claim with FBP-ists that there exist mathematical objects (or that our mathematical theories are true), and I do not claim with fictionalists that there do not exist mathematical objects (or that our mathematical theories are not true).

Notes

Chapter 1

1. The problem with the first characterization is that *outside* is a spatial notion. For brevity, I will speak of abstract objects "existing outside of spacetime", and by that I will mean that they exist, but not in spacetime. Most philosophers of mathematics seem to think that the notion of non-spatiotemporal existence is reasonably clear, and I will assume, for the bulk of this book, that it is. In chapter 8, however, I will question this assumption and discuss at great length what existence outside of spacetime might really amount to.

2. It should be noted that other philosophers have used these terms in different ways. For instance, whereas I have taken the defining trait of platonism to be a belief in non-spatiotemporal objects, Maddy (1990) has taken it to be a belief in the claim that mathematics is about objectively existing objects, regardless of whether they are aspatial and atemporal; I discuss her view in chapter 2, section 5.

One term that I will occasionally use differently is 'mathematical object'. When I am discussing views that take mathematics to be about spatiotemporal objects, I will sometimes call these objects "mathematical objects". But I will always indicate very clearly that this is what is going on, and at all other times, I will use the term in the way defined here, that is, the way that implies that mathematical objects are, by definition, abstract objects. This, I think, is the more standard usage of the term. (In any event, I argue in chapter 2, section 5, and chapter 5, section 5, that any view that takes mathematical objects to exist in spacetime — such as Maddy's view, or rather, her *early* view, for she no longer endorses it — is untenable.)

3. See Field (1980) and (1989); Hilbert (1925); Maddy (1990) and (1997); and Azzouni (1994).

4. This "picture" is summarized in chapter 8, section 2.

5. When I first introduced this view — see Balaguer (1992) and (1995) — I called it 'full-blooded platonism'. Since then, a number of philosophers have commented on the view, but no one seems to like the *name*. For instance, Maddy (forthcoming) has called it 'plentiful platonism' and Field (forthcoming) has called it 'plenitudinous platonism'. (And even *I* am guilty here: in a paper on another topic (1994), I hinted that we might call the view 'super-platonism'.) I think that Field's term is actually better than the original name I used, for the simple reason that it is more descriptive. But for obvious reasons, I like 'FBP' more

than 'PP'. Thus, since this is how I am actually going to be referring to the view, I am going to stick with 'FBP'. Officially, then, I would like to say that the name of the view is 'plenitudinous platonism', or for short, 'FBP'.

6. I may sometimes use the terms 'possible mathematical object' and 'actual mathematical object', but I do this only for rhetorical reasons, to emphasize different things. I do not mean to imply that these terms pick out different *kinds* of objects. I take both of these terms to be coextensive with 'mathematical object'.

7. See Zalta and Linsky (1995); see also Zalta (1983) and (1988).

8. See Frege (1980), pp. 39–40.

9. Poincaré (1913), p. 454.

10. Resnik (1982), p. 101.

11. See Resnik (1997).

12. Like Hilbert and Resnik, Shapiro never broaches the topic of FBP. Moreover, I don't think he ever even commits to the thesis that I have said brings the FBP-ist picture to mind, that is, the thesis that every consistent purely mathematical theory truly describes a structure. But I do think this thesis is lurking behind certain things Shapiro says. Indeed, in chapter 2, sub-section 6.5, I quote a passage from Shapiro that seems to suggest that he endorses this thesis.

13. A few people have asked why I don't just *define* FBP as the view that

(H) All consistent purely mathematical theories truly describe some collection of abstract mathematical objects.

The answer is this: if (H) is true, then this requires explanation, and as far as I can see, the explanation could only be that the mathematical realm is plenitudinous. (Alternatively, one might try to explain (H) by appealing to the Henkin theorem that all syntactically consistent first-order theories have models, but this won't work; see chapter 3, note 10.) In any event, the point here is that by defining FBP as the view that the mathematical realm is plenitudinous, I am simply zeroing in on something that is, in some sense, prior to (H). Moreover, by proceeding in this way, we also bring out the fact that FBP is, at bottom, an *ontological* thesis.

14. Field (forthcoming) and Maddy (forthcoming) and (1997) also have discussed FBP in some of their recent work, but I haven't included them in the above discussion because neither of them wants to *endorse* the view, and in any event, I think they were both led to discuss FBP by reading my earlier work on the view, in particular, my (1992) and (1995).

15. Some people think that Dedekind (1888) held a view of this general sort. Whether or not this is true, the view has been developed recently by Resnik (1981) and (1997); Shapiro (1989) and (1997); and Steiner (1975). The terms 'pattern' and 'position' are due to Resnik.

16. I do not mean to imply that structuralism *cannot* be combined with anti-platonism. In fact, it can; see, for instance, Benacerraf (1965) and Hellman (1989). I am simply discussing a platonistic version of structuralism here.

17. Indeed, this is precisely what Resnik thinks motivates structuralism; it is with this claim that he opens his important paper on structuralism (1981).

18. I have formulated FBP in object-platonist terms, but it is entirely obvious that it could be reformulated in structuralist terms or in a way that made it neutral between these two views. Likewise, I am going to formulate my solutions to the problems with platonism in object-platonist terms, but it will be obvious that a structuralistic FBP-ist could use the same strategies that I use.

19. See the first sentence of Parsons (1990).

20. Resnik has suggested to me that the difference between structuralists and object-platonists is that the latter often see facts of the matter where the former do not. But I do not think that object-platonists are committed to all of the fact-of-the-matter claims normally associated with their view. This will become apparent in chapter 4, when I argue that object-platonists should abandon many of the *uniqueness* claims associated with traditional platonism and endorse a more pluralistic stance. It will become clearer at that point, I think, that there is no important difference between structuralism and object-platonism.

21. See Mill (1843), book II, chapters 5 and 6. A recent advocate of this sort of view is Philip Kitcher; see his (1984). I will discuss Kitcher's view in chapter 5, section 5.

22. Psychologism seems to have been somewhat popular around the end of the nineteenth century, but very few people have advocated it since then, largely, I think, because of the criticisms that Frege leveled against the psychologistic views that were around back then, for example, the views of Erdmann and the early Husserl; see, for instance, Husserl (1891) and Frege (1894) and (1893–1903), pp. 12–15. (Recently, there has been something of a surge of views that *sound* psychologistic, but it's not clear that many of these views should really be interpreted as versions of psychologism; I will say a few words about this in chapter 5, note 21. Also, intuitionism—advocated most prominently by Brouwer (1913) and (1949), Heyting (1956), and Dummett (1973)—is often thought of as a psychologistic view, but this needn't be the case. I will say a bit more about this in chapter 5, section 5.)

23. See Wittgenstein (1956) and Chihara (1990). In connection with conventionalism, see Ayer (1946, chapter 4); Hempel (1945); and Carnap (1934), (1952), and (1956). In connection with deductivism, see Putnam (1967a) and (1967b) and Hellman (1989). In connection with the metamathematical version of formalism, see Curry (1951). As for game formalism, the only advocates of this view that I know of are those, such as Thomae, whom Frege criticized in the *Grundgesetze* (1893–1903), sections 88–131. Finally, Hilbert sometimes seems to accept a version of formalism—see, for instance, his (1925)—but if he does endorse such a view, it is different from the two versions of formalism described here. In any event, I do not think it is possible to sum up his view in a few words.

24. This is Hartry Field's view; see his (1980) and (1989).

25. I am using 'about' here in a "thin" sense. I will say more concerning this in later chapters, but for now, all that matters is that in this sense of 'about', 'S is about b' does not entail that there is any such thing as b. Thus, for instance, we can say that the novel *Oliver Twist* is about an orphan named 'Oliver' without committing to the existence of such an orphan.

26. It should be noted here that fictionalists allow that *some* mathematical sentences are true, albeit vacuously so. For instance, they think that sentences like 'All natural numbers are integers'—or, for that matter, 'All natural numbers are zebras'—are true. This is simply because, on their view, there are no such things as numbers (and, of course, because all sentences of the form 'All Fs are Gs', where there are no such things as Fs, are true). But we needn't worry about this complication here.

27. See Field (1989), pp. 2–3.

28. One fictionalist strategy for solving the problem of applicability—the one that Field employs—is to take a sort of *piecemeal* approach and explain how each different fact about the physical world can be expressed in purely nominalistic terms. On this approach, all the different special cases of the problem have to be handled separately. But on my view, all the different special cases of the problem are solved in the same way.

29. Benacerraf (1973).

30. See Gödel (1951) and (1964); and Maddy (1990).

31. See Quine (1951), section VI; Steiner (1975), chapter 4; Parsons (1980) and (1994); Hale (1987), chapters 4 and 6; and Wright (1983), section xi.

32. See Resnik (1982) and (1997); Shapiro (1989) and (1997); Katz (1981), chapter 6, and (1995); and Lewis (1986), section 2.4.

33. This problem was also made famous by Benacerraf; see his (1965).

34. In addition to the two Benacerrafian worries, there is also a problem about how we could *refer* to mathematical objects and a closely related problem about how we could have *beliefs* about mathematical objects. My solutions to these problems emerge in chapter 4. There is, of course, also a worry about platonism that is based upon Ockham's razor. I respond to this worry at the end of chapter 7. Finally, there is the worry that platonists might not be able to account for the applicability and/or indispensability of mathematics. (It is often assumed that this is only a problem for *anti*-platonists, but I argue in chapter 5, section 6, that this is confused, that platonists also have a problem here.) In any event, I solve this problem in chapter 7.

35. Although this argument is commonly credited to Quine and Putnam—see, for example, Quine (1948), especially pp. 17–18, and (1951), especially pp. 44–45, and Putnam (1971), especially p. 347, and (1975), especially p. 74—it should be noted that Frege appealed to applicability, if not indispensability, in order to refute an ancestor of fictionalism, namely, formalism. See Frege (1893–1903), section 91.

36. Field (1980).

37. Malament (1982).

Chapter 2

1. Thus, Benacerraf seems to assume that if we adopt a Tarskian semantics for mathematics, we are committed to platonism. For whatever it's worth, this assumption is false: fictionalists endorse a Tarskian semantics for mathematics but reject platonism. This, of course, didn't occur to Benacerraf. He was assuming that sentences like 'There is an integer between -2 and -4' are *true*, and so it seemed to him that if we adopt a Tarskian account of the truth conditions of such sentences, we will be committed to things like -3, which, it would seem, could only be abstract objects.

2. I include the word 'entirely' here in order to guarantee that (1) is incompatible with immaterialism about the mind. Without the 'entirely', immaterialists could agree with (1), claiming that human beings exist in spacetime, because they exist *partially* in spacetime.

3. One might, I suppose, try to attack (5) by arguing that we do not have *absolute certainty* in mathematics. But the problem with this is that (5) isn't about absolute certainty. It's about whatever sort of mathematical knowledge we actually have.

4. See Steiner (1975), chapter 4; Katz (1981), chapter 6, especially pp. 206–208; Burgess (1990); Hale (1987), chapter 4, especially sections IV and V; Wright (1983), section xi; and Brown (1990). Moreover, people concerned solely with epistemology—that is, people unconcerned with the issue of mathematical platonism, such as Nozick (1981, chapter 3)—have also provided arguments against CTK. Indeed, there seems to be something of a consensus that even if we ignore mathematical knowledge altogether, there are counterexamples to CTK that show that it can't even handle all empirical knowledge of physical objects.

5. I don't see how anyone could seriously doubt this. If mathematical objects are totally inaccessible to us, then there is at least a prima facie reason to suspect that we couldn't acquire knowledge of them. Now, it might turn out that this prima facie suspicion is

defeasible—indeed, I think it is—but we cannot pretend that there isn't a worry here at all.

6. I do not need to commit here to the claim that prima facie plausibility is closed under logical implication. It may be that *some* implications don't preserve prima facie plausibility. All I need here is that the argument from (3) to (6) preserves the prima facie plausibility of (3). But this seems beyond doubt.

7. I am not claiming that by eliminating CTK from the epistemological argument, we can eliminate the notion of *causation* from that argument; for it may be that that notion will emerge when we unpack the notion of *accessibility*. My only claim is that the epistemological argument needn't rest on any *strong* claim about causation and knowledge. In particular, it needn't place any necessary causal constraint on knowledge. Indeed, it needn't place any necessary constraint at all on knowledge.

8. Field (1989), pp. 25–30, 230–239.

9. The reason Field avoids the word 'knowledge' is that he wants to emphasize that he is not demanding a simple *justification* of our mathematical beliefs. What he wants platonists to provide is an account of the *mechanisms* that *lead* to our mathematical beliefs. But my version of the epistemological argument can no more be answered by a mere justification of our mathematical beliefs than Field's can. After all, my version of the argument already grants that our mathematical beliefs are justified, because it grants that we have mathematical knowledge. The challenge is to explain how the mathematical knowledge that we do have could be knowledge of non-spatiotemporal objects. Now, to meet this challenge, platonists are going to have to address the worry of accessibility created by (1) and (2), and so they're going to have to explain how creatures like ourselves could *acquire* knowledge of non-spatiotemporal objects. Thus, it is no easier for platonists to respond to my version of the argument than to Field's, and so there is no reason for anti-platonists to avoid the word 'knowledge' here.

10. I suppose that one might try to respond to my version of the argument without providing an epistemology by saying something like this. "Regardless of (1) and (2), we know that (3) is false. For insofar as we do have mathematical knowledge, it must be false. Thus, since we clearly can acquire mathematical knowledge, platonists don't have to say *how* we can." The problem with this response is that it flagrantly begs the question, for it assumes that mathematical knowledge could *only* be knowledge of abstract mathematical objects. (I will say a bit more about this in sub-section 6.1, in connection with the epistemological views of Wright and Hale.)

11. Katz has argued in roughly this way against this sort of mathematical intuition; see his (1981), p. 201.

12. These remarks, by the way, suggest that Plato's theory of recollection would be unhelpful in this connection. (See, e.g., *The Meno* and *The Phaedo*.) Now, I don't know whether Plato's view really involved the idea of an information transfer between souls and mathematical objects, but the remarks in the text show that if it did, then it couldn't be right. Now, of course, the idea that the mathematical realm is a kind of "place", the sort of thing that an immaterial soul could "visit" before birth, is simply incompatible with contemporary platonism. But the point I am making here is that even if immaterial souls could "go" to the mathematical realm, they could not acquire any information there, because information could no more pass from a mathematical object to a visiting soul than from a mathematical object to a spatiotemporal brain.

13. It's actually not *that* puzzling. No matter how brilliant they are, people are capable of believing all manner of nonsense when it comes to religion, and I think that Gödel's views on mathematical intuition were deeply connected to his religious beliefs.

14. Gödel (1964), pp. 483–484.
15. See Frege (1919), pp. 530–533.
16. Gödel (1951), pp. 311, 312.
17. Gödel (1951), p. 310.
18. Gödel (1964), p. 484.
19. Maddy first introduced the view in her (1980) and developed it most thoroughly in her (1990). She abandons the view in her (1997), as well as in some earlier papers, such as her (1992) and (1995). I should say, however, that her reasons for rejecting the view are completely different from the ones I present here.

Of course, Maddy isn't the first philosopher to bring abstract mathematical objects into spacetime. Aside from Aristotle, David Armstrong (1978, chapter 18, section V) attempts this as well. But Maddy's version of the view is—from the point of view of epistemology and the philosophy of mathematics—the best and most sophisticated that I know of.

20. Maddy (1990), p. 48.
21. One might object to Maddy's view on the grounds that it cannot be generalized to cover knowledge of mathematical objects that aren't sets. But I will not pursue this here.
22. Further evidence for this point arises from the consideration that the empirical analog of Benacerraf's challenge can be answered with a mere appeal to sense perception. If platonists responded to Benacerraf by claiming that we have the same problem in connection with empirical knowledge of physical objects, the counter-response would be that we do *not* have the same problem, because we can *see* physical objects. I will discuss this issue at great length in chapter 3, section 3.
23. Maddy (1990), p. 59.
24. The reason is that there is simply no other view that Maddy-qua-anti-platonist could adopt. If you believe that sets of physical objects are ordinary concrete objects and that they share their locations with the physical aggregates that make up their members, then it seems that you have no choice but to admit that sets *are* physical aggregates. What else could you say?
25. Maddy (1990), p. 60. See also Frege (1884), section 23.
26. The only other option would be to claim that sets are somehow *mental* objects, that is, that only physical aggregates exist "out there in the world", and that we then come along and somehow construct all the various different sets in our minds. But, of course, Maddy wouldn't adopt this psychologistic view, because she knows that it is no more plausible than Millianism. (I will briefly discuss the problems with psychologism in chapter 5, section 5.)
27. Maddy (1990), pp. 152–153.
28. We cannot identify the non-spatiotemporal/naturalized distinction with the pure/impure distinction. Naturalized-platonist sets are sets of physical objects, sets of sets of physical objects, and so on. In other words, all of the "ultimate building blocks" of these sets are physical objects. In contrast to this, a set is *impure* just in case at least one of its "ultimate building blocks" is a non-set. Thus, all naturalized-platonist sets are impure, and all pure sets are non-spatiotemporal, but hybrid platonists can allow that there are some non-spatiotemporal sets that are impure. For instance, if hybrid platonists countenance the existence of propositions and sets of propositions, then they presumably will want to say that sets of propositions are impure (because propositions are not sets) and non-spatiotemporal (because propositions are themselves non-spatiotemporal).
29. I will discuss these two points in chapter 5, section 5, in connection with my attack on Mill's anti-platonism. It will be fairly obvious there that my arguments apply to physicalistic platonism as well as to Mill's view.

30. Maddy (1990), p. 65.

31. Chihara has argued against Maddy's view in a similar way. See his (1990), pp. 202–204.

32. See Maddy (1990), pp. 64–65.

33. See Maddy (1990), p. 49.

34. Hale makes essentially this point on p. 81 of his (1987).

35. I will discuss this view in sub-section 6.3.

36. See Maddy (1990), chapter 4.

37. Let me say a word about what, exactly, needs to be explained here. I will write as if platonists need to explain how human beings *could* acquire knowledge of mathematical objects, despite their lack of access to such objects. I formulate the demand in this way to emphasize that platonists do *not* have to explain how human beings *in fact* acquire knowledge of mathematical objects. This would be too strong a demand, for it is a demand that would be difficult to meet in connection with our knowledge of *physical* objects. At the same time, however, I want to acknowledge that it is not *exactly* correct to say that platonists only need to explain how human beings *could* acquire knowledge of mathematical objects. This demand is actually too weak: platonists could satisfy this demand very easily by merely pointing out that it *could* be that there exists a God who has set up a pre-established harmony between the mathematical realm and our mathematical beliefs. What platonists really need to provide here is an explanation of how human beings could acquire knowledge of mathematical objects *for which it's at least plausible that mathematical knowledge actually does arise in the given way*. Nonetheless, I will speak as if platonists merely need to explain how human beings *could* acquire mathematical knowledge, because it would be too cumbersome to keep stating this proviso. (Or perhaps I can just stipulate that the 'could' here is a non-standard modality and that the above proviso is embedded in its meaning.)

38. See Wright (1983), section xi; and Hale (1987), chapters 4 and 6.

39. Wright (1983), p. 90.

40. Hale (1987), pp. 124–125.

41. There are *some* anti-platonists who *cannot* admit that mathematical knowledge is a priori, namely, those who think that mathematics is empirical, such as Mill (1843) and Kitcher (1984). But I do not think that empiricist versions of anti-platonism are tenable; see chapter 5, section 5.

42. See Parsons (1980) and (1994); Steiner (1975), chapter 4; and Katz (1981), chapter 6.

43. See Resnik (1982), (1990), and (1997); and Shapiro (1989) and (1997).

44. Some platonists seem to shy away from the term 'mathematical intuition' because they believe (mistakenly, I think) that it is associated with the contact-based view. Another word that some NCTI-platonists have found objectionable is 'faculty', although it's not clear to me what the objection here is supposed to be. It seems to me that the claim that we have a *faculty* of mathematical intuition is no stronger than the claim that we have a *capacity* for mathematical intuition.

45. Talk of *representations* of abstract objects brings to mind Steiner's (1975, chapter 4, section V) distinction between *intuition-that*, that is, intuitive propositional beliefs about abstract objects, and *intuition-of*, that is, internal representations of abstract objects. I don't think this distinction is very important, because I think that intuitions of the two kinds almost always come together. Steiner writes as if human beings could have intuitions-that without having intuitions-of, but this seems wrong to me. If I have an intuition *that*, say, b is F, then what's to stop me from saying that I have an intuition *of* the object b? I suspect that Steiner thinks that intuition-of goes hand in hand with a contact-based theory of in-

tuition. But this is wrong; as we will see, the construction of representations of numbers no more requires contact with numbers than does the formation of beliefs about numbers.

46. The exception to this is Parsons. He seems wholly unconcerned with the worry about reliability, or at any rate, he seems to think that the worry is somehow trivial: at one point (1994, p. 142) he asserts without argument that "intuition of an object involves intuitive knowledge of that object". There is a sense in which this makes Parsons the purest advocate of the NCTI strategy, because he does not fall back upon any other strategy of responding to the Benacerrafian challenge. But it also makes his view the most puzzling of the NCTI-platonist views, because it is totally unclear how an appeal to NCTI can help if it is not conjoined with an explanation of reliability.

47. It is obvious, I think, that people do use the word 'about' in this thin way. We say, for instance, "The novel *Oliver Twist* is about an orphan who . . .", but in saying this, we certainly don't mean to commit to the existence of such an orphan. Now, I suppose that one might wonder what the *truth conditions* of sentences like

(THIN) The sentence S is thinly about the object n

are, but I don't think there's any real mystery here. I haven't taken the time to think of all the scenarios in which (THIN) would be true, but the most obvious is that S contains a singular term that's coreferential with, or that's "supposed to be" coreferential with, the singular term 'n' that appears in (THIN). (The point of the 'supposed to be' clause here is to allow for cases in which the two singular terms—that is, the one in S and the one in (THIN)—are *vacuous*. Thus, for instance, 'Santa Claus' and 'Kris Kringle' are supposed to be coreferential, but 'Santa Claus' and 'Oliver Twist' are not supposed to be coreferential.)

48. I will explain how platonists can solve the problem of belief in chapter 4.

49. There are two ways in which NCTI could be made stronger and, hence, more controversial. First, if NCTI were understood as the view that we are capable of arriving at no-contact intuitions and beliefs that are *thickly* about mathematical objects, then it would be quite controversial (and indeed, as I'll argue in chapter 4, false). And second, if one were to go beyond the *broad* formulation of NCTI in the text and endorse a specific view of the inner workings of the faculty of no-contact intuition, then the resulting theory might be very controversial.

50. See, e.g., Quine (1951), section 6; Steiner (1975), chapter 4, especially section IV; and Resnik (1997), chapter 7.

51. One might worry here that mathematical theories are often developed *in connection with* their applications and not *before* them. But all my argument requires is that at least *once* in the history of mathematics, people had knowledge of an unapplied mathematical theory. It is this that I am taking to be obvious.

52. All of this accords very well with the practice of mathematics and empirical science. Mathematicians do not think that their theories are confirmed by applications, and empirical scientists do not take themselves to be confirming the mathematical theories that they use. In fact, the opposite is true: when empirical scientists use a mathematical theory, they think that we already know it's true. This, of course, is why they feel entitled to use it.

53. Katz (1981), p. 207. I should note that according to Katz, the appeal to necessity is not the only way in which mathematical claims can be justified. Once our intuitions have been systematized into a theory, we can justify the theory by using all of the standard criteria for theory evaluation; see Katz (1981), pp. 14–16, 212–214. But while Katz may well be right here, this is not relevant to Benacerraf's challenge. The reason is identical to the

reason I cited in connection with the Quine-Steiner-Resnik epistemology: what we have here is an *after-the-fact* justification, whereas what platonists need in order to respond to Benacerraf is an account of how the intuitions that engendered the theory could have been accurate in the first place.

54. Lewis (1986), p. 111.

55. Field (1989), p. 238.

56. I should point out here that in opposition to this, Hale and Wright (1992) have argued that the existence of mathematical objects is conceptually necessary. But Field (1993) has argued convincingly that their argument is flawed. The bottom line here is that it just seems wrongheaded to suggest that existence is built into the very *concept* of a mathematical object. Of course, there is much more to be said in this connection, but there is no need to pursue it here.

57. See Resnik (1997), chapter 11, section 3; and Shapiro (1997), chapter 4, section 7.

58. Resnik (1982, p. 101) says: "a pure [mathematical] theory can be falsified by showing that it fails to characterize any pattern at all, that is, that it is inconsistent." It seems to me that the 'that is' here suggests that he thinks that the *only* purely mathematical theories that *don't* characterize patterns are the inconsistent ones. Shapiro doesn't come as close as Resnik does to explicitly stating the thesis, but it seems to me that the thesis is at least "suggested" by the following passage:

> It is conceivable, barely, that arithmetic is incoherent, in which case *no* structure
> is characterized. . . . But it is nonsense to claim that the theory of arithmetic does
> successfully refer to a single, fixed structure . . . but says hardly anything true about
> it. . . . On our view, the language characterizes or determines a structure . . . if it
> characterizes anything at all.

(This passage comes from Shapiro (1997), p. 131, but I should note that Shapiro says the same thing—almost word for word—on pp. 167–168 of his (1989).)

59. I should say, however, that I do not think that the appeal to pattern recognition is philosophically important anyway. This was the point of sub-section 6.2: nothing philosophically important can be accomplished by providing an account of the psychological mechanisms responsible for the genesis of our no-contact mathematical beliefs and intuitions. We might clear up some *psychological* mystery in this way, but we cannot clear up any *philosophical* mystery concerning the inaccessibility of mathematical objects.

Chapter 3

1. FBP was defined in chapter 1, sub-section 2.1. Roughly, it is the view that all the mathematical objects that logically possibly *could* exist actually *do* exist.

2. Field (1989), pp. 26–27.

3. See Benacerraf (1965).

4. A theory is *categorical* if and only if all of its models are isomorphic to one another.

5. Here's another way to put this point: on my view, human beings do not have *de re* mathematical beliefs or *de re* mathematical knowledge. All mathematical knowledge is knowledge by description, and what's more, it is almost certain that none of our mathematical theories yields a uniquely satisfied description.

6. See Field (1989), p. 26.

7. The difference between impure theories and mixed theories is that the former are *mathematical* theories that refer to physical objects, whereas the latter are *empirical* theories that refer to mathematical objects. Examples of the two sorts of theories are, respectively, impure set theory and quantum mechanics. One might also speak of an *applied mathe-*

matical theory. This is a pure theory together with a claim that the theory in question is satisfied by some group of physical objects. An example here would be Riemannian geometry taken as a theory about *physical* space.

8. This might seem surprising, because such theories can be consistent but false. But all I need to do in order to accommodate such theories in my epistemology is shift from talk of consistent theories to talk of theories that do not imply any falsehoods about the physical world. I thank Hartry Field for pointing this out to me. (Note that this shift is irrelevant in the pure case because, here, the theories that imply no falsehoods about the physical world just *are* the consistent theories. This is because inconsistent pure theories imply everything about the physical world, whereas consistent pure theories imply nothing about the physical world; that is, consistent pure theories are *conservative*, in Field's (1989, p. 58) sense of the term.)

9. Note the scope of the existential quantifier here. I am not merely saying that FBP-ists can account for our knowledge that there exist many consistent purely mathematical theories. Rather, I am saying that there exist many mathematical theories such that FBP-ists can account for the fact that we can know that *these theories* are consistent.

10. It might seem that we could provide additional motivation for (v) by appealing to the Henkin theorem that all syntactically consistent first-order theories have models. But I think this is wrong. For whereas the Henkin theorem provides very *unnatural* models for many of our mathematical theories, FBP entails that all consistent purely mathematical theories truly describe parts of the mathematical realm *that they correspond to in a very natural way*, that is, that they are intuitively and straightforwardly (albeit thinly) *about*. Moreover, it is also worth pointing out here that whereas the Henkin theorem applies only to first-order theories, (v) is concerned with higher-order theories as well as first-order theories. (In connection with this last point, one might wonder what I would say about higher-order theories that are syntactically consistent but not semantically consistent. I will discuss this in section 5 when I describe the notion of consistency at work in (v). As we will see, this notion is distinct from both the syntactic and the semantic notions of consistency, although among first-order theories, it is coextensive with both of them.)

11. A bit less generally, the point is that in constructing an epistemology for a theory T, it is legitimate to assume that T is true.

12. The epistemological argument is a reductio ad absurdum: the claim here is that *if platonism were true*, then mathematical knowledge would be impossible. Thus, the version of the argument that's aimed at FBP holds that *if FBP were true*, then mathematical knowledge would be impossible. Therefore, to respond to this argument, FBP-ists have to show that *if FBP is true*, then mathematical knowledge is *not* impossible. (Moreover, I don't see how anti-platonists could alter the argument so that it no longer assumes platonism. For the whole point of the epistemological argument is to talk about the inaccessibility of mathematical objects. Thus, to talk about mathematical objects in this way, anti-platonists need to assume, for the sake of argument, that there *are* such objects and then discharge this assumption at the end of the argument.)

13. The FBP-ist account of (M1) is simple: we can learn what FBP says and recognize that if FBP is true, then *any* theory like T (i.e., any consistent purely mathematical theory) truly describes part of the mathematical realm.

14. Katz has made a similar point. He says (1981, p. 212) that "Empirical knowledge . . . has no advantage over a priori knowledge in encounters with the skeptic."

15. Actually, even if we were trying to provide an *internalist* account, it still wouldn't matter whether any actual knowers assume (at any level) that FBP is true. For in order to solve the Benacerrafian problem, platonists don't need to explain how human beings *actually* acquire knowledge of the mathematical realm. They only need to explain how

human beings *could* do this (or how they *plausibly* could do this—see chapter 2, note 37).

16. One such method tells us to believe *all* consistent purely mathematical theories. Others demand that a theory satisfy other conditions, in addition to consistency. But if FBP is true, then *all* of these methods will be reliable.

17. This last point is important, because it enables FBP-ists to block the worry that 'C and not-C' truly describes the mathematical realm but isn't satisfiable. If we are working within a formal mathematical theory, 'C' and 'not-C' will contradict one another, and so 'C and not-C' will be false. The only way that 'C and not-C' can be taken as truly describing the mathematical realm is if we are in an informal extra-mathematical setting in which the two occurrences of 'C' are read differently. But in this informal setting, there is nothing wrong with saying that 'C and not-C' is informally satisfiable, that is, that it can be given an informal interpretation on which it comes out true, namely, one that interprets the two occurrences of 'C' in different ways. Since we are only speaking of interpretation and satisfiability only *informally* here, there is nothing wrong with this. After all, the sentence 'Aristotle married Jackie Kennedy and Aristotle didn't marry Jackie Kennedy' can also be given an informal interpretation on which it comes out true.

18. It *may* be that, *strictly speaking*, set theory doesn't have any standard *models*. For (a) it may be that in order for a model to count as a standard model of set theory, it would need to have the set of all sets as its domain, and (b) there is no such thing as the set of all sets. This is not a *problem*, however, because all of the claims that I am going to make here about standard *models* of set theory could be reformulated and turned into claims about intended set-theoretic *hierarchies*, or intended *parts of the mathematical realm*. But for rhetorical reasons, I am not going to do this; I am going to be speaking simultaneously of all the standard models for the various different branches of mathematics, and it would simply be too cumbersome to keep adding parenthetical provisos to allow for the above complication about set theory. Thus, since there isn't any real problem here, I am simply going to ignore this and write in terms of standard models. I should note, however, that I will return to this point in section 5, for it will become important there, albeit very briefly.

19. I should note here that Field (forthcoming) has made a point similar to the one in the text. He claims that while FBP is ontologically similar to traditional platonism, it is more like fictionalism in connection with objectivity and methodology. But Field does not see this as an *objection* to FBP.

20. A related objection that one might raise here is this: "FBP isn't a genuinely platonistic view, because (a) it tells us, more or less, that in connection with pure mathematics, existence and truth amount to nothing more than consistency, and (b) this is a very anti-platonistic thing to say." But this version of the objection can be answered very easily, because FBP simply doesn't say that "existence and truth amount to nothing more than consistency". Rather, it says that all the mathematical objects that logically possibly could exist actually do exist, and then it *follows* from this that all consistent purely mathematical theories truly describe some collection of actually existing mathematical objects. Moreover, as I pointed out in my reply to objection 2, it doesn't follow from this that all consistent purely mathematical theories are *true*.

21. One might try to argue here that FBP-ists are already committed to the thesis that CH has a determinate truth value—and, hence, that they cannot adopt a neutral stance here of the sort that I am suggesting—because (a) we can amalgamate all the universes of sets to form a *single* universe, and (b) FBP-ists ought to understand CH as being about this particular universe. I will respond to this worry below, in connection with objection 5.

22. Putnam (1980).

23. It isn't a *real* sequence, because real sequences don't have holes in them. If it were

a real sequence, then we would simply be using '8' to denote 7, '9' to denote 8, and so on. In the theory I'm imagining, we use '8' to denote 8 — or rather, quasi-8, that is, the analog of 8 in this structure. I say this because sentences like '4 + 4 = 8' are true in this structure. What's weird about this structure — or one of the things that's weird about it — is that its numbers (or rather, quasi-numbers) are not closed under successor or addition or subtraction. Terms like 'the successor of 6' and '4 + 3' and '19 − 12' are undefined.

One might respond as follows: "You do have an ordinary sequence of objects here; you've just got some very odd relations and operations defined on it." I would reply: I admit that I've got a denumerable domain, but the weird relations and operations give me a non-sequential, or quasi-sequential, structure.

24. This is a point that *all* platonists — or at any rate, all platonists who maintain that human beings do not have any information-gathering contact with mathematical objects — would make in response to objection 9. For all such platonists would want to respond to this objection by rejecting all principles that suggest mathematical knowledge requires a counterfactual relationship of the above sort.

25. I argued this point in much more detail in chapter 2 by explaining how the various platonist epistemologies not based upon FBP — for instance, those of Gödel, Maddy, and Quine — fail.

26. One might think that non-full-blooded platonists could object to this argument on the grounds that pragmatic considerations are relevant to empirical theory construction as well as to mathematical theory construction. But I responded to this objection in chapter 2.

27. Cantor (1883, p. 564) wrote that "The very essence of mathematics is its freedom."

28. See Kreisel (1967) and Field (1991). I should note that Kreisel's discussion is actually couched in terms of the notion of logical validity and not consistency; but everything he says applies, mutatis mutandis, to consistency. Moreover, Kreisel was not concerned with the fact that his notion of validity was anti-platonistic; indeed, he used platonistic language (in particular, talk of *structures*) in describing the notion. But as is clear from Field's discussion and my discussion here, the view can be developed without using any platonistic language to describe the notion of consistency (or the notion of validity).

29. That this is really the broadest intuitive notion of possibility can be appreciated by noting that the formal notions of syntactic and semantic consistency to which this primitive notion corresponds cannot be made any broader. Or more precisely, the point is that if we try to broaden these two notions, they will no longer be notions of *consistency*.

30. Of course, there would still be a mystery about how human beings could acquire knowledge of abstract mathematical objects — the epistemology that I am proposing here would, I suppose, have to be abandoned along with anti-platonism — but we would know that that mystery was solvable.

31. Let Σ be the set of all higher-order theories that are syntactically consistent but semantically inconsistent. Then the question of whether the intuitive notion of consistency is coextensive with the semantic notion reduces to the question of whether every theory in Σ is intuitively inconsistent. Now, *some* of the theories in Σ do seem to be intuitively inconsistent. For instance, if P is a standard second-order axiomatic theory of arithmetic and G is the Gödel sentence for P, then it seems natural to suppose that P+∼G is intuitively inconsistent, because it seems natural to suppose that it *couldn't possibly be true*. But there is no reason to think that *all* the members of Σ are intuitively inconsistent. Indeed, as the remarks in the text will show, it is quite possible that there are theories in Σ that are *obviously* consistent in the intuitive sense. These theories are in Σ because of "technical difficulties", because there are certain limitations to our model-theoretic apparatus that

prevent these theories from having models, despite the fact that they are intuitively consistent, that is, despite the fact that, intuitively, they *could be true*.

32. It might seem that this creates a problem for me, for I have been assuming here that set theory has models and, indeed, standard models. But I addressed this worry in note 18.

33. One might complain in this connection that our reasons for believing that, say, ZFC is consistent are not logical reasons. But I didn't mean to suggest that whenever we believe that a mathematical theory is consistent, our *reasons* are always logical; I simply meant that in such cases, the *fact* about which we have knowledge—that is, the fact that the given theory is consistent—is a logical fact. (But in any event, there are *some* mathematical theories that are so simple that we *can* acquire knowledge of their consistency via direct logical intuition and reasoning. And if the arguments of this chapter are cogent, then these theories can give us knowledge of abstract mathematical objects.)

34. One might think that FBP-ists have to account for how people could *know* that all of our consistent purely mathematical theories truly describe mathematical objects. But I responded to this worry in section 3.

35. In particular, Field (1989, essay 3) thinks that we have two different kinds of mathematical knowledge, namely, knowledge that certain axiom systems are *consistent* and knowledge that certain theorems *follow* from certain axiom systems. Thus, my platonist epistemology is very similar to his anti-platonist epistemology.

Chapter 4

1. The thesis that Benacerraf was explicitly attacking was the thesis that arithmetic is about objects. I won't go into this, but the present chapter provides a defense of this thesis, as well as a defense of platonism, because the view defended against Benacerrafian considerations here is a version of object-platonism.

2. See Resnik (1980), p. 231.

3. One might worry that a similar argument could be constructed in an *empirical* context. But such an argument would not go through. For we have *perceptual contact* with physical objects, and this serves to ground our concrete singular terms to *particular* objects in a way that our abstract singular terms are *not* tied to particular objects. Now, I am not suggesting here that a mere appeal to perceptibility eliminates all worries about uniqueness in connection with physical-object talk. To name just one problem here, the appeal to perceptibility won't do anything to block Quine-style inscrutability-of-reference worries. My point is simply that the appeal to perceptibility blocks *the worry in the text* from applying in physical-object cases. To see that this is so, consider an attempt to apply this worry in such a case. One might begin here by, for example, telling us to imagine a Twin-Earth version of Bill Clinton who is just like our Bill Clinton in all ways that we've ever considered but different in some way that we've never thought about. Now, I think it's dubious that such a creature could really be just like our Bill Clinton in *all* ways that we've ever considered, but even if we assume that this is possible, it should be clear that our term 'Bill Clinton' doesn't refer to any such creature, because no such creature is appropriately "connected" to us.

4. I am going to defend a version of platonism that embraces non-uniqueness, and so it might seem as though my response is *not* consistent with the falsity of (2) and (3). But my real point is going to be that platonists can *allow* non-uniqueness, not that they have to *commit* to it.

5. See, e.g., Resnik (1981) and (1997) and Shapiro (1989) and (1997). I discuss platonistic structuralism in chapter 1, sub-section 2.1.

6. Actually, I should say that this is how *I interpret* the standard structuralist view. The reason I add this qualification is simply that, to the best of my knowledge, no structuralist has ever explicitly discussed this point. This, I think, is a bit puzzling, because one of the standard arguments for structuralism is supposed to be that it provides a way of avoiding the non-uniqueness problem. I suppose that structuralists just haven't noticed that there are general versions of the non-uniqueness argument that apply to their view as well as to object-platonism. They seem to think that the non-uniqueness problem just disappears as soon as we adopt structuralism.

7. Recall that (S) is implausible, because we think that structures and positions in structures have properties like *being non-spatiotemporal* and *being non-red*, and these properties are not structural properties, that is, they do not have anything to do with the relations that hold between the positions of the given structure. And (S) leads to a contradiction, because the property of having only structural properties is itself a non-structural property.

8. I should note here that Resnik (1997, chapter 10) explicitly *rejects* the idea that isomorphism is the identity condition for structures. His view here is a bit "slippery", because he doesn't want to commit to the claim that structures are *entities*, but ignoring this point for the moment, he allows that two structures can be isomorphic but distinct. I think that this view is superior to the view that isomorphic structures are identical, but because Resnik takes this line, I don't think he has any response to my argument for (2').

9. This conclusion is also suggested by the argument I gave in chapter 1, sub-section 2.1, for the claim that structuralism is not distinct from object-platonism in any important way. If this is right, then we obviously can't make any progress toward solving a real problem with platonism by merely switching to a structuralistic terminology.

10. Actually, while it's clear that Benacerraf's 1965 paper doesn't address (4), one might maintain that there is something like an argument for (4) implicit in his 1973 argument for the claim that we ought to use the same semantics for mathematese that we use for ordinary English. I will respond to this below.

11. It might seem that the thesis that all mathematically important facts are structural facts could be used to motivate structuralism. But the way I have stated the thesis reveals that it is compatible with object-platonism: the thesis is just that all mathematically important facts concern the relations between mathematical objects.

12. See chapter 2, sub-section 6.2, and chapter 3, section 2, for discussions of the difference between metaphysically thick senses of 'about' and metaphysically thin senses of that term.

13. One might object to the view I've been developing here by claiming that (U) is already built into FCNN and, hence, that if there isn't a unique ω-sequence that satisfies FCNN, then nothing satisfies it. But part of what I'm arguing here is that these claims are *wrong*. Now, I suppose there might be some sense in which (U) is built into certain "untutored" conceptions of the natural numbers, but my claim here is that it's not built into FCNN. That is, it's not built into our "educated" conception of the natural numbers, that is, the theoretically influenced conception that's inherent in contemporary mathematical practice.

14. Implicit in the last two paragraphs are my solutions to the problems of belief and reference, that is, the problem of how we could have beliefs about mathematical objects and the problem of how we could refer to mathematical objects. We can sum the solutions up as follows. The only reason one might be worried about how we could have beliefs about mathematical objects, or how we could refer to such objects, is if one thought that when we do these things, there are particular mathematical objects that we *have in mind* and that we are "*connected to*" in some metaphysically *thick* way. But the fact of the matter is that none of our beliefs about mathematical objects, or references to such objects, involve

any such "thick contact" with any mathematical objects. Our mathematical beliefs are only *thinly* about mathematical objects, and our mathematical singular terms refer to such objects only thinly. Therefore, the problems of belief and reference just disappear.

15. See Putnam (1980).

16. For instance, I responded in this chapter to the problems of belief and reference, and I responded in chapter 3 to several objections that were directed toward FBP in particular.

17. The problem of applicability is usually thought of as a problem for *anti-platonism*, rather than platonism. I agree that it's a problem for anti-platonism — indeed, we'll see in chapter 5 that it's the *central* problem for anti-platonism — but I will argue that it's *also* a problem for platonism. (This objection to platonism has been much less discussed in the literature than either of the Benacerrafian objections, but it has not been *totally* ignored. See, for instance, Shapiro (1983b), pp. 531–532; and Kitcher (1984), pp. 104–105.)

Chapter 5

1. See chapter 1, sub-section 2.2, for a definition of fictionalism.

2. Frege appealed only to *applicability* here; see his (1893–1903), section 91. The appeal to *indispensability* came with Quine and Putnam; see Quine (1948) and (1951); and Putnam (1971) and (1975). As for premise (i), Frege argues against numerous anti-platonist attempts to salvage mathematical truth in his (1884) and (1893–1903). See also Resnik (1980) in this connection.

3. Field (1980).

4. If (NI) can be established, then (AA) can also be established. Field's argument for this is based on the claim that mathematics is *conservative*, which (in his lingo) means that for any purely mathematical theory M and any purely nominalistic theory N, if we add M to N, no new nominalistic consequences are generated that don't already follow from N alone. Now, actually, the conservativeness of mathematics only explains why it is *harmless* to use M + N rather than N. The reason that it is actually *helpful* to use M + N rather than N, according to Field, is that it is easier for us to see what nominalistic conclusions follow from M + N than from N alone. In other words, Field's claim is that mathematics is useful to empirical science because it simplifies inference.

I do not want to pretend that this sort of argument for (AA) is problem-free. Shapiro (1983a) has objected to it, although I should also note that Field (1989, essay 4) has responded to his objection. But I will not discuss any of the objections to (AA) here. I will assume that if Field can motivate (NI), then his program can be made to work.

5. Malament (1982) discusses almost all of these objections, but see also Resnik (1985); Shapiro (1983a); and Chihara (1990), chapter 8, section 5.

6. Motivation for the second and third reasons here will emerge in chapter 7, section 3. I will say a few words about the fourth reason in chapter 8, sub-section 3.4.3, but I provide a much more thorough argument in Balaguer (1998).

7. One point needs to be made here that wasn't made in chapter 3. I claimed there that we acquire information about the extension of the anti-platonist notion of consistency by studying the syntactic and semantic notions of consistency, which are platonistic notions. But one might think that anti-platonists cannot make this claim, because they cannot allow that our knowledge of anti-platonistic consistency is increased via platonistic talk of things like models and derivations. (Shapiro argues a point similar to this in his (1993).) But it seems to me that anti-platonists *can* allow that our knowledge is increased via platonistic talk — not just in this case, but generally — because they can maintain that (a) whenever this happens, the platonistic talk in question is merely part of a theoretical apparatus, or

descriptive framework, that enables us to understand the world in the way we do, and (b) because of this, we aren't committed to recognizing this talk as being genuinely referential. I will argue these points at length in chapter 7.

8. We have seen that, very often, when mathematicians make claims of the form " 'S' is true", what they *mean* is that 'S' is true in the standard model. But this is consistent with what I am saying here; for just as 'true' can be interpreted along platonist or fictionalist lines, so too can 'true in the standard model'.

9. Chihara (1990, pp. 163–173) gives an argument against fictionalism that is basically just a special case of this mathematical-practice argument. His argument is a sort of appeal to *history*: he claims that mathematicians and scientists have always taken mathematics to consist of a body of truths. My response to this version of the argument is the same as my response to the version in the text. Now, part of Chihara's argument is that the fact that mathematical assertions are woven into our scientific theories provides evidence for the claim that people have taken mathematics to be true. My response to this facet of Chihara's argument is built into my chapter-7 response to the Quine–Putnam argument; for it will follow from what I say there that the use of mathematics in empirical science is consistent with a fictionalist reading of the 'true' of mathematical practice.

10. The classical statement of this view is given by Putnam (1967a) and (1967b). More recently, Hellman (1989) has advocated a version of deductivism that he calls *modal structuralism*.

11. Thus, for instance, fictionalists are free to endorse Hellman's (1989, chapter 3) account of applicability. They needn't endorse Hellman's deductivist (i.e., conditional) interpretation of mathematics in order to endorse his conditional interpretation of empirical theory. Now, of course, if one thought that Hellman's account of applications was correct, then one would be more inclined to adopt deductivism (or more specifically, Hellman's modal structuralism) than fictionalism. But this is irrelevant to the point I am making here, and in any event, I do not think that Hellman's account of applicability is a good one, because I think that the various problems with the conditional interpretation of mathematics carry over to the conditional interpretation of empirical theory. I will say a few words about these problems below.

12. See Ayer (1946), chapter 4; Hempel (1945); and Carnap (1934), (1952), and (1956).

13. Well, *most* of them do. But not all of them. Game formalists, for instance, do not claim that our mathematical theories are true, and I suspect that Wittgenstein might balk at this claim as well.

14. (a) is trivial. I have already argued for (b). As for (c), the point is pretty obvious in connection with most versions of anti-realism and only slightly less so with respect to the others. For instance, it is obvious with respect to deductivism and formalism, but I can imagine a conventionalist claiming that *our* mathematical theories stand out from all others because they alone correspond to our conventions. The obvious reply to this claim, however, is that *from a metaphysical point of view*, these theories do *not* stand out, because our conventions are arbitrary.

15. The fact that it provides an implausible interpretation of mathematical theory and mathematical practice is not the only problem with Curry's formalism. Another problem is that it might not even be genuinely anti-platonistic, because metamathematical claims like 'S is a theorem of T' have singular terms referring to sentences and formal systems, and these seem to be abstract objects. Now, one might think that formalists could maintain that such claims are about concrete *tokens*, but this is implausible, because formalists have to account for *all* of mathematics, and to do this, they are going to have to countenance *infinitely many* sentences and formal systems.

16. In connection with deductivism, see Resnik (1980) and (1997). The latter work is

also relevant to Chihara's view, and the former is relevant to formalism. See also Frege (1893–1903), sections 88–131, in connection with formalism. See Quine (1936) for an argument against conventionalism. Dummett (1959) and Stroud (1965) are also relevant to conventionalism, as well as to Wittgenstein's view.

17. See Chihara (1990), especially chapter 5, and Wittgenstein (1956). It is, of course, difficult to say exactly what Wittgenstein's view is, but in the present context, it doesn't matter. For (a) in the present context, we can treat all versions of anti-realism together, and (b) regardless of what we say about the *details* of Wittgenstein's view, we will surely want to say that it is a version of anti-realism, because Wittgenstein clearly rejected the idea that our mathematical theories are descriptions of objectively existing entities.

18. One might reply that the notion of error can be analyzed in terms of non-standardness, but I suspect that this could be cashed out only in terms of *types*. That is, the claim would have to be that a person's theory of arithmetic could be erroneous, or bad, if her concepts of 1, 2, 3, and so on were not of the culturally accepted types. But to talk of types of 1's, 2's, 3's, and so on is to collapse back into platonism.

19. See Frege (1884), section 27. Just about all of the arguments mentioned in this paragraph trace to Frege. His arguments against psychologism can be found not just in section 27 of his (1884), but also in the introduction to that work, as well as the introduction to his (1893–1903). See also his (1919) and (1894) in this connection.

20. See Dummett (1973). One might wonder what I have to say about intuitionism. But I have *nothing* to say about it, or at any rate, I have nothing to say about it in the present context. In another context, I would argue that the view is wrongheaded, but that opinion is totally irrelevant to what I am doing here. This is simply because I am concerned here only with theories of the metaphysics of mathematics, and intuitionism is not such a view and does not commit to any such view. For consider: while it is no doubt true that intuitionists could (if they wanted to) endorse a simple-minded version of psychologism like the one discussed in the last paragraph, it is clear that they don't *have* to. One might, for instance, endorse a *fictionalistic* intuitionism. One might think (for whatever reason) that mathematicians should concern themselves only with "mentally constructed objects" and that non-constructive proofs should not be allowed in mathematics, but one might also think—at the same time—that Frege has shown that our mathematical theories cannot be interpreted as descriptions of mental objects, and in light of this, one might think that these theories should be interpreted along fictionalist lines.

21. Recently, there have been a few people (not philosophers) who have come out in favor of views that *sound* very psychologistic. (See, e.g., Hersh (1997) and Dehaene (1997).) But I do not think many of these people would endorse the view that *I* am calling psychologism, that is, the view that our mathematical singular terms actually *refer* to mental objects (and I should note here that Hersh at least is careful to *distance* himself from this view). This, I think, is a pretty general phenomenon: when people seem to be endorsing psychologistic philosophies of mathematics, they usually do not mean to endorse the view that *philosophers* call psychologism. Indeed, it seems to me that when people come to really understand what this view entails—in particular, when they come to appreciate that the dispute between psychologism and fictionalism is a purely *semantic* dispute (i.e., that it has nothing whatsoever to do with ontology or sociology or neurophysiology or, indeed, psychology or any mathematical intuitions we might have)—they almost invariably come to see that psychologism is inferior to fictionalism.

22. Mill discusses his philosophy of mathematics in his (1843), book II, chapters 5 and 6.

23. Someone like Maddy (or rather the early Maddy)—see chapter 2, section 5, for a sketch of her view—could solve this problem by building an infinity of sets of physical

objects out of a finite number of "bottom-level" physical objects. But since Millians cannot countenance the existence of higher-rank sets, they cannot do this. Consider, for instance, a physical world with only two "bottom-level" physical objects, say, b and c; Millians can legitimately claim that there exists a third object in this world—namely, {b, c}—but that is all. Likewise, in a world with three "bottom-level" physical objects—say, b, c, and d—Millians can legitimately recognize the existence of four more objects—namely, {b, c}, {b, d}, {c, d}, and {b, c, d}—but again, that is all. In general, no matter how many "bottom-level" physical objects there are, as long as there are only finitely many such objects, Millians cannot claim that there are infinitely many sets of such objects. Thus, in order to maintain that PA is true, Millians have to maintain that there are infinitely many "bottom-level" physical objects.

24. Mill doesn't have problems only with big numbers like $\aleph_0$. As Frege points out (1884, section 7) he also has a problem with the smallest natural number, namely, 0, for there are no piles of zero objects lying around in the physical world. He also has problems with negative numbers and irrational numbers. Consider, for instance, the sentence '$-2 + -13 = -15$'. It should be clear that this sentence does not say that whenever we push negative-two objects together with negative-thirteen objects, we will always get negative-fifteen objects. Now, one might respond here by pointing out that negative and real numbers can be defined in terms of natural numbers. But it's not clear that Mill can help himself to these reductions, because they make use of higher-rank sets and infinite sets.

25. See Mill (1843), book II, chapter 5, section 5.

26. See Kitcher (1984), chapter 6.

27. It is not obvious that *all* of the above problems are solved by Kitcher's view. For instance, while Kitcher does not identify sets with aggregates of physical matter, it is not clear that he can handle all of the higher-rank sets that he needs to. In Kitcher's version of set theory, we replace sets with the collecting-operations of an ideal agent. Thus, I think it is pretty clear that Kitcher can account for the existence of higher-rank sets, for an ideal agent can have higher-rank groupings of lower-rank piles of blocks. But can Kitcher go all the way here? For instance, if b and c are blocks, can Kitcher make sense of the difference between {{{{{{{b, c}}}}}}} and {{{{{{{{b, c}}}}}}}}? Has the ideal agent *done* something seven times in the one case and eight times in the other? If so, *what*?

28. Kitcher (1984), p. 117.

29. All of the quoted phrases in the last two sentences come from Kitcher (1984), p. 108.

30. In addition to Frege (1884), see, for example, Hempel (1945); Resnik (1980), chapter 4; and Skorupski (1989), chapter 5.

31. I am not the first to detect a problem for platonism here. See Shapiro (1983b), section II.3, and Kitcher (1984), pp. 104–105.

32. It should not be surprising that fictionalists endorse PCI. Since they don't believe in mathematical objects, they cannot believe in causal relations between mathematical objects and physical objects.

33. Of course, platonism is still relevant here; fictionalists, for instance, accept PCI *because* they reject platonism.

34. That PCI entails this claim can be seen in the following way: insofar as S's temperature plays a causal role in determining its behavior, if the bottom-level fact of S's temperature is a fact partly about the number 40, it would follow that 40 plays a causal role in determining S's behavior, which contradicts PCI. Now, I suppose that one might try to maintain that it could be that both (a) C(S,40) is bottom-level and causally efficacious and (b) 40 is *not* causally efficacious. But this is impossible. For if we assume that C(S,40) is causally efficacious and that 40 is not, then it would seem to follow that there is some

purely physical fact F about S *alone* that is responsible for the causal efficacy in question here. But this is just to say that C(S,40) is *not* bottom-level, that it supervenes on F (and some purely mathematical fact about the number 40). After all, F will be the *complete* fact of S's temperature state, because it will be doing *all* the causal work that the fact of S's temperature state is supposed to do.

35. For example, the temperature states are ordered with respect to 'cooler than' as the real numbers are ordered with respect to 'less than'. Thus, what we want when we define our temperature function Φ is a function that preserves these structural similarities. The Fahrenheit, Kelvin, and Celsius scales are three such functions, but of course, there are infinitely many other functions from physical objects to real numbers that would do just as well.

36. See Field (1980), chapter 7.

Chapter 6

1. Malament (1982).

2. Most of these "other objections" are also discussed by Malament (1982). For instance, one such objection is that Field's nominalization is simply *inadequate*, that is, that his nominalistic theory of gravitation does not do everything that the platonistic version of the theory does. Another objection is that Field's version of gravitation theory isn't genuinely nominalistic, because (a) it contains second-order quantifiers and (b) it commits to the existence of spacetime points. (This last issue is discussed at length by Resnik (1985). See also Shapiro (1983a) and Chihara (1990) for other objections.) I think that all of these objections can be answered, but I will not pursue this here.

3. Field (1980), chapter 7.

4. Krantz, Luce, Suppes, and Tversky (1971).

5. The reason Φ is a homomorphism rather than an isomorphism is that there can be many physical objects of the same length and, hence, many physical objects associated with the same real number.

6. One might worry that this presupposes that matter can be carved up indefinitely. But we can ease this worry by merely shifting from talk of physical objects to talk of *parts* of physical objects (or of course, to talk of points and regions of spacetime).

7. There's no way to avoid this. The representation theorems we're concerned with establish that a certain relationship holds between a platonistic structure and a nominalistic structure. Thus, to prove these theorems, we are going to have to talk about the abstract objects contained in the platonistic structures, and so there is no sense trying to avoid the claim that Φ is an abstract object.

8. Field (1980), chapter 8.

9. Malament (1982), p. 534.

10. For a precise definition of 'orthomodular lattice', see Hughes (1989), section 7.3. It is worth noting that the set of events associated with a *single* observable can be structured into a Boolean algebra; it is only when we "paste" two or more of these together that we get the weird non-distributive structures of QM.

11. One might wonder whether the quantifier 'every quantum system' is nominalistically acceptable. It is, because I am only quantifying over *actual* quantum systems here. This is sufficient because, according to my definition, '$(A,\Delta,r) \leq_P (A',\Delta',r')$' says that it's a *law of nature* that every quantum system has a propensity of the sort described in the text. Now, of course, one might wonder whether nominalists can legitimately make use of the notion of a law of nature. I think they *can*, but I will not try to justify this claim here, because I am only trying to argue that QM doesn't raise any *special* problems for nomi-

nalists, that is, problems they don't already have. After all, if nominalists can't account for there being laws of nature, then it would be rather pointless to try to nominalize QM.

12. Putnam seems to adopt something like (i) in his (1970); Field (1980, p. 55) mentions this as a strategy that one might adopt in trying to nominalize physics, but he doesn't pursue the strategy at all.

Chapter 7

1. Recall from chapter 5 that PCI (the principle of causal isolation) is the claim that there are no causal interactions between mathematical and physical objects. We saw in chapter 5 that, contrary to common belief, it is the acceptance of PCI that really generates the problem of applicability.

2. What does it mean to say that a particular theory T makes indispensable use of mathematics? It means that there is no theory N that is a nominalization of T. Now, to count as a nominalization of T, N has to satisfy three conditions. The first two conditions are obvious: N has to be formulated in purely nominalistic language, and it has to be empirically equivalent to T. But there is also a third condition that needs to be satisfied: intuitively, N has to have the *look and feel of T*. Can we replace this intuitive idea with something a bit more precise? Perhaps this could be done in terms of *representation theorems* holding between the nominalistic structures of N and the platonistic structures of T; but this might not be the *only* way to appropriately capture the "look and feel" of a theory. (We will see in note 3 why it is important to include this look-and-feel condition here.)

One might think that there is also a fourth condition here, namely, that N must be theoretically *attractive*, so that, for instance, the Craigian reaxiomatization of the nominalistic consequences of T would not count as an acceptable nominalization of T. But we can take this condition to be built into the look-and-feel condition. That is, we can just stipulate that whenever T is attractive and N is unattractive, N doesn't have the look and feel of T. (Actually, we could probably take the empirical-equivalence condition to be built into the look-and-feel condition as well.)

3. One might object as follows. "The distinction between relative and absolute indispensability is useless. For if one of our empirical theories, say T, is *true*, and if mathematics is indispensable to T, then mathematics is indispensable to the project of doing empirical science." My response to this objection is already implicit in note 2. Even if T cannot be nominalized, there could still be a nominalistic theory N that saved the same phenomena as T, and was just as attractive as T, but wasn't a nominalization of T, because it didn't have the "look and feel" of T. Or more graphically, it might be that there is a completely alien way of doing empirical science that could lead to a weird-looking (but nonetheless attractive) nominalistic description of the phenomena that T is concerned with.

4. I put 'about' in scare quotes here to indicate that I am using the term in a metaphysically thin sense. According to this usage, the claim that the platonistic content of empirical science is about an abstract mathematical realm does not entail that there *is* a mathematical realm. See chapter 2, sub-section 6.2.

5. Here's another reason for thinking that nominalistic scientific realism is genuinely realistic. One of the central arguments for endorsing scientific realism, rather than instrumentalism, is that by claiming that our empirical theories are true, we *explain* their empirical adequacy. But this is no argument against nominalistic scientific realism, because (a) the truth of the nominalistic content of our empirical theories explains their empirical adequacy as well as full-blown truth does, and (b) full-blown truth doesn't explain truth of nominalistic content, except in a trivial sort of way. (The trivial explanation here would simply be an instance of the rule that 'P & Q' explains 'P'; more specifically, the explanation

here would be that the nominalistic content of empirical science is true, because the nominalistic content of empirical science is true and the platonistic content of empirical science is true.)

6. Strictly speaking, I should say: *if (A) is true*, then the mixed fact that it expresses supervenes on more basic facts. For if (A) *isn't* true, then at least one of the facts in question here won't really exist. I leave this proviso out for the sake of rhetorical elegance, and in what follows, I will do the same thing on a few more occasions.

7. This point seems fairly obvious to me, but I provide an *argument* for it in chapter 5, note 34.

8. One might worry that the sentence 'S holds up its end of the "(A) bargain"' is not purely nominalistic on the grounds that when we unpack the expression '(A) bargain', we will encounter the platonistic lingo of (A), in particular, the term 'forty'. But fictionalists can maintain that in talking about the "(A) bargain", we are really just talking about a token of the sentence (A), and so the expressions in (A)—for instance, 'forty'—are being mentioned here but not used.

9. That the two sets of facts really are independent of one another follows from PCI. For it follows from this principle that (a) whether or not there exist mathematical objects has no bearing on whether there obtains a set of purely physical facts of the sort required for the truth of empirical science, and (b) the state of the physical world has no bearing on whether there obtains a set of purely platonistic facts of the sort required for the truth of empirical science.

10. It is worth noting that the view developed here is somewhat similar to Nancy Cartwright's (1983) view. She is not really concerned with the issue of whether platonism is true or false—she is more concerned with physical objects than with mathematical objects—but she seems to think that an empirical theory gives us reason to believe in entities of a certain kind only if entities of this kind play *causal roles* in the theory.

11. I mention a couple of other reasons in chapter 5, section 2.

12. It is worth pointing out that my response to the Quine–Putnam argument is superior not just to Field's response but also to the response given by Terence Horgan (1984) and Geoffrey Hellman (1989). The main reason for this is that the Hellman–Horgan response also involves the claim that our empirical theories can be replaced with nominalistic surrogates, in particular, by counterfactual surrogates. I think there are pretty good reasons for preferring the standard versions of our empirical theories to these counterfactual surrogates, but a more important point to be made here is that the claim that our empirical theories can be nominalized in a Hellman–Horgan-type way might be just as controversial as the claim that they can be nominalized in a Field-type way. For as Hellman points out, he needs to find a way of specifying (in nominalistic terms) *the way the physical world actually is*. Now, Hellman claims that this is weaker than what Field needs, that is, weaker than a full-blown nominalization, but (a) this seems debatable, and (b) even if Hellman does need to do less than Field needs to do, he hasn't shown that he can do it.

13. In order to take the same line on the inferential role of mathematics that I take on its descriptive role, I do not need it to be the case that there are nominalized versions of our platonistically formulated arguments. But I do need it to be the case that if we have a (sound) argument for C that takes $P_1, \ldots, P_n$ as premises and that's formulated in platonistic terms, so that at least one member of $\{P_1, \ldots, P_n\}$—and perhaps also C—refers to, or quantifies over, mathematical objects, then whenever the nominalistic content of $\{P_1, \ldots, P_n\}$ is true, the nominalistic content of C is also true. But I think it's pretty clear that this *is* the case. For if the given argument is really sound, then whenever $\{P_1, \ldots, P_n\}$ is true, C is also true. Thus, whenever $\{P_1, \ldots, P_n\}$ is true, the nominalistic content of C is true, since it is included in C. But it follows from this that whenever the nominalistic content

of $\{P_1, \ldots, P_n\}$ is true, the nominalistic content of C is true (which, again, is just what I need) because there is nothing in $\{P_1, \ldots, P_n\}$ but not in the nominalistic content of $\{P_1, \ldots, P_n\}$ that's at all relevant to whether the nominalistic content of C is true. This is simply because (a) what's in $\{P_1, \ldots, P_n\}$ but not in the nominalistic content of $\{P_1, \ldots, P_n\}$ is just the *platonistic* content of $\{P_1, \ldots, P_n\}$, and this is solely about the mathematical realm, that is, not about the physical world at all; and (b) the nominalistic content of C is solely about the physical world and not about the mathematical realm at all; and (c) since PCI is true, it follows that if the platonistic content of $\{P_1, \ldots, P_n\}$ is solely about the mathematical realm and the nominalistic content of C is solely about the physical world, then the former is not relevant to the truth value of the latter.

The same conclusion could also be established by appealing to the fact that our mathematical theories are *conservative*, in Field's sense of the term (see chapter 5, note 4, for a definition). But I think it's important to recognize that we only need to rely upon PCI here.

14. More generally, we use lattices of closed subspaces of Hilbert spaces to represent *event spaces*.

15. The reason the sentence 'Stalin was like the pig Napoleon' is analogous to sentences that use mathematical singular terms to describe the physical world, despite the fact that 'Napoleon' is not an *abstract* singular term, is that this sentence doesn't relate Napoleon and Stalin in a causal way. Thus, the sentence 'Stalin kissed the pig Napoleon' is *not* analogous to sentences that use mathematical singular terms to describe the physical world, and the sort of analysis that I have been trying to motivate for the latter could not be used for the former.

16. Prima facie, it might seem that if our empirical theories contained fictional material, then this could "infect" the picture that these theories paint of the physical world. But what we've seen is that as long as the fictitious entities are not taken to be causally efficacious, this cannot happen.

17. Perhaps this is a bit strong. Perhaps there are *some* physical setups for which no mathematics whatever could be helpful. But we don't need anything nearly as strong as the claim about *all* physical setups in order to eliminate the feeling that there is some sort of extraordinary coincidence at work in the applicability of mathematics. All we need is this: for *most* physical setups, there is a mathematical apparatus that could be used to help us do empirical science. Even with just this weaker thesis, it no longer seems marvelous that, in our particular case, we are able to use mathematics to set up a descriptive framework in which to do empirical science. But the acceptance of FBP certainly seems to give us reason to accept this weaker thesis about most physical setups; thus, within FBP, it should not seem miraculous that theories of a causally isolated mathematical realm can be used in the way we use them. (I suppose that one might worry that since there are *infinitely many* possible physical setups, the use of the word 'most' here is a bit problematic. I will not pursue this, because I think it's clear that however the details get worked out, the appeal to FBP does eliminate the feeling that there's a miraculous correlation at work in the use of mathematics to provide descriptive frameworks for our empirical theories.)

18. See Wigner (1960) and Steiner (1989).

Chapter 8

1. Fictionalism and FBP were both defined in chapter 1, section 2.

2. Actually, the situation with respect to non-fictionalistic versions of anti-platonism was a bit more complicated than this remark suggests. I argued that (a) realistic versions of anti-platonism fall to Fregean attack, and (b) all versions of anti-realistic anti-platonism

could, in the present context, be treated together. I then argued very quickly that fiction-alism is the best version of anti-realistic anti-platonism, because all other versions of the view commit to awkward, non-standard interpretations of our mathematical theories that seem to fly in the face of mathematical practice.

3. One might wonder whether there's a difference between FBP and fictionalism in connection with *in*consistent purely mathematical theories. FBP-ists think that while con-sistent purely mathematical theories can be "better" than one another only for aesthetic or pragmatic reasons, or because they fit better with our concepts, all of these theories are "better" than inconsistent theories for a different sort of reason, in particular, because they truly describe parts of the mathematical realm, whereas inconsistent theories do not. But fictionalists think that consistent and inconsistent theories are *both* false. So does this mark an important difference between the two views? I don't think so. For according to fiction-alists, inconsistent theories couldn't possibly be true, whereas consistent theories could, and this already seems to make the latter "better" than the former for what appears to be an objective, non-aesthetic, non-pragmatic reason. Now, of course, fictionalists also think that inconsistent theories are "bad" for aesthetic and pragmatic reasons, and because (if they're syntactically inconsistent) everything follows from them, and so on; but of course, FBP-ists would agree on these points.

4. I am not saying that every advocate of fictionalism holds this view of undecidable propositions. For instance, Field, (1998) seems to think that open questions about undecid-able set-theoretic propositions do not have any objectively correct answers (although he allows that there can be good reasons for choosing a theory that settles an open question, and he seems to think that when we do this, the given answer to the question becomes correct). But in the present context, this is irrelevant, because fictionalists and FBP-ists can *both* take this line. The real point I am making here is that FBP-ists and fictionalists have available to them the same views on undecidable propositions and the same reasons for favoring and rejecting these views. The view outlined in the text is just the view that *I* endorse.

5. That mathematical platonists and anti-platonists are on all fours, epistemologically speaking, is a point that has been argued by Shapiro (1993) and Resnik (1997), chapter 5. But they have argued this point by arguing that anti-platonists face serious epistemological difficulties that are just as problematic as those that platonists face, whereas I have argued the opposite, that is, that *neither* group faces any serious problems here. I do not claim that we can say right now exactly how we acquire the kinds of knowledge we have; I merely claim that there are no good reasons to think that either platonism or anti-platonism is incompatible with the kinds of knowledge that we have or that they claim we have. In other words, I do not think there is any serious epistemological problem with platonism or anti-platonism.

6. The account of indispensable applications that I offered in chapter 7 is not the only account that FBP-ists and fictionalists might offer here. But all the same accounts are available to both. In particular, we have seen that there is no viable account of applicability that's available to FBP-ists but not to fictionalists, because the existence of mathematical objects is irrelevant to the applicability of mathematics, because PCI is true.

7. The reason we might take this line with '7 > 5', even though we wouldn't take it with *empirical* relation sentences like 'Ali hit Foreman', is that there are no possible worlds in which (a) 7 and 5 both exist but (b) '7 > 5' is false.

8. We saw in chapter 2, sub-section 6.4, that it can't be that the null set axiom is metaphysically necessary for anything like the reason that 'Ali is Clay' is metaphysically necessary. The latter sentence is metaphysically necessary because it is true in all worlds in which its names denote, or something to this effect. But if we took this line with the

null set axiom, we would have to allow that *all* existence claims are metaphysically necessary, which of course, is wrong.

9. This is different from the original Benacerrafian argument. That argument is supposed to show that platonism is false by showing that even if we assume that mathematical objects exist, we could not know what they are *like*. This Benacerrafian argument was refuted in chapter 3. The argument I am using here, on the other hand, is not directed against platonism or anti-platonism; it is aimed at showing that we cannot know which of these views is correct, that is, that we cannot know whether there exist any mathematical objects.

10. One might object that the disagreement over the truth values of our mathematical theories is *distinct* from the basic ontological disagreement and, indeed, that this gives us a substantive disagreement that might lead to a reductio-style argument against one of the two views. But the reason I have lumped this disagreement together with the basic ontological disagreement is that the only way to use the disagreement over truth values to generate a reductio-style argument here would be to derive a *further* consequence from one of the two views that was falsifiable. The reason I say this is that it is no easier to "directly ascertain" whether our mathematical theories are true than to "directly ascertain" whether there exist any mathematical objects; indeed, the only way to do the former would be to do the latter first. Therefore, the point in the text applies to the disagreement over truth values as well as to the basic ontological disagreement: we cannot settle the dispute between FBP-ists and fictionalists by considering only these two disagreements, because we have no epistemic access to the alleged mathematical realm.

11. This is not to say that I think this is the only metaphysical problem that is factually empty. In fact, I think this phenomenon is quite general: for any question Q, if Q is genuinely metaphysical (that is, having to do with matters that go *beyond the physical*), then there is no fact of the matter as to its answer. But despite this, I do not think that very many of the questions and problems that we ordinarily call "metaphysical" are empty. I think that the vast majority of these questions and problems (e.g., the question of whether human actions and decisions are determined or free or random, the mind–body problem, and the question of whether God exists) are really *physical* questions and problems and, hence, *not genuinely metaphysical*. Thus, I do not think they are empty; I think there are facts of the matter as to their answers and solutions, and I think these answers and solutions can — in principle — be discovered empirically, or scientifically. For more on this, see Balaguer (1999); I argue there that the problem of free will and determinism is, in fact, an empirical problem.

12. See Lewis (1973) and (1986); and Stalnaker (1984).

13. See Frege (1892); Carnap (1947); Montague (1968); Scott (1970); Lewis (1983); and Kaplan (1989).

14. As things have been set up here, meanings clearly *aren't* character-functions. For there are all sorts of cases in which two sentences have different meanings but the same character-function — for instance, 'The function f is Turing computable' and 'The function f is partial recursive'. Kaplan would respond to this by saying that meanings are just *associated* with character-functions and that different meanings can be associated with the same character-function. Others might try to salvage the claim that meanings *are* characters by switching to talk of *structured characters*, where a structured character might be something like a character-function together with something that specified the syntax of the sentence in question as well as semantic facts about the individual words in the sentence. But in the present context, none of this is relevant. All that matters is that no one has any *argument* for the claim that *every* meaningful indicative sentence is associated with a (non-trivial) character-function.

15. I take this example from Norman Malcolm's essay on Wittgenstein in the *Encyclopedia of Philosophy*. I do not know whether the example is originally Wittgenstein's.

16. We might say something like this about (G) as well. That is, it may be that there are some worlds that are clearly good and others that are clearly bad. But then again, maybe not.

17. One might respond that the negative conditions placed on the existence of abstract objects here are good enough, that platonists don't need to do any more than this. But the arguments of this sub-section will show that they do need to do more; for they'll show that if we don't know what non-spatiotemporal existence could be *like*, then there is no fact of the matter as to whether there are any objects that exist in this way.

18. Of course, there are things like Oliver Twist *pictures* in spacetime, but that is beside the point.

19. Actually, there are infinitely many different possible worlds here, each containing a different set of abstract objects. But we can ignore this complication and suppose that either no abstract objects exist or else all logically possible abstract objects exist.

20. We saw above (section 2) that there is some motivation for the idea that we should define the term 'metaphysically necessary' in a way that allows certain *falsehoods* to be metaphysically necessary.

21. One way to think of a *language* is as a function from sentence types to meanings and/or truth conditions. And the idea here is that *every* such function constitutes a language, so that English is just one abstract language among a huge infinity of such things. But on this view, the truth conditions of English sentences do *not* supervene on our usage, for the simple reason that they don't supervene on *anything* in the physical world. We needn't worry about this here, though, because (a) even on this view, which abstract language is *our* language will supervene on our usage, and (b) I could simply reword my argument in these terms.

22. According to one view, the 1650 extension of 'water' included both H_2O *and* XYZ, because this extension was determined by the 1650 *concept* of water, and there was nothing about chemical structure built into that concept. According to another view, the 1650 extension of 'water' included everything relevantly like the stuff that the people of 1650 actually called 'water'. On this view, the question of whether XYZ was in the 1650 extension of 'water' reduces to the question of whether XYZ is "relevantly like" H_2O. Now, of course, we recognize an important difference between XYZ and H_2O, but it's not clear that this is relevant. After all, we're talking here about the 1650 extension of 'water', and as far as the people of 1650 were concerned, XYZ *was* relevantly like H_2O. So even on this second view of reference, it's hard to see how one could motivate the claim that the 1650 extension of 'water' didn't include XYZ.

23. For instance, we know that it is necessary and sufficient for the existence of non-spatiotemporal objects that there exist non-spatiotemporal objects. But this is trivial and unhelpful.

24. I discuss this in more detail in Balaguer (1998).

25. I note in passing that my position here is somewhat similar to Kripke's (1972, pp. 23–24, 156–158) view that it is *impossible* for unicorns to exist. His point is that (a) there was never enough said about unicorns to pick out a unique species, and therefore (b) no counterfactual situation could properly be described as one in which unicorns exist. My point is that there has not been enough said about what existence outside of spacetime would be like to determine what sorts of possible worlds count as worlds in which things exist outside of spacetime. But, of course, the conclusion that I want to draw is very different from the one that Kripke wants to draw. In particular, I would not claim that it is impossible for abstract objects to exist. Indeed, I wouldn't even claim that they don't *actually* exist. I

consider these claims to be as bad off as the claims that abstract objects do exist and that they must exist.

26. This, of course, is a large part of the reason why we do not know how to interpret quantum mechanics.

27. Kochen and Specker (1967).

28. Given this, one might wonder whether it's a criticism of *platonism* to say (in the way that I'm saying it here) that there's no fact of the matter as to whether it is true. I think it is a criticism, because I think there are important disanalogies between this case and the cases of mathematics and empirical science—disanalogies having to do mainly with the intentions of platonists, mathematicians, and empirical scientists—but there is no need to go into any of this here.

29. See Balaguer (1998).

30. I do not need to discuss (a') here, because it is not relevant to the present objection to my argument. But it is worth noting that the situation there is the same: the problems encountered by the semantic version of FBP are exactly analogous to the problems encountered by the mathematical version of FBP, and the responses that I would give to the former are analogous to the responses that I have given in this book to the latter.

31. Quine (1969), p. 23.

32. That is, I am in agreement here with the kinds of FBP-ists and fictionalists that I've described in this book.

Bibliography

Armstrong, D. M. (1978) *A Theory of Universals*, Cambridge University Press, Cambridge.

Ayer, A.J. (1946) *Language, Truth and Logic*, second edition, Dover Publications, New York.

Azzouni, J. (1994) *Metaphysical Myths, Mathematical Practice*, Cambridge University Press, Cambridge.

Balaguer, M. (1992) "Knowledge of Mathematical Objects," Ph.D. dissertation, CUNY Graduate Center, New York.

——. (1994) "Against (Maddian) Naturalized Platonism," *Philosophia Mathematica*, vol. 2, pp. 97–108.

——. (1995) "A Platonist Epistemology," *Synthese*, vol. 103, pp. 303–325.

——. (1998) "Attitudes Without Propositions," *Philosophy and Phenomenological Research*, vol. 58.

——. (1999) "Libertarianism as a Scientifically Reputable View," *Philosophical Studies*.

Benacerraf, P. (1965) "What Numbers Could Not Be," reprinted in Benacerraf and Putnam (1983), pp. 272–294.

——. (1973) "Mathematical Truth," *Journal of Philosophy*, vol. 70, pp. 661–679.

Benacerraf, P., and Putnam, H., eds. (1983) *Philosophy of Mathematics*, second edition, Cambridge University Press, Cambridge.

Brouwer, L.E.J. (1913) "Intuitionism and Formalism," reprinted in Benacerraf and Putnam (1983), pp. 77–89.

——. (1949) "Consciousness, Philosophy, and Mathematics," reprinted in Benacerraf and Putnam (1983), pp. 90–96.

Brown, J.R. (1990) "Π in the Sky," in Irvine (1990), pp. 95–120.

Burgess, J. (1990) "Epistemology and Nominalism," in Irvine (1990), pp. 1–15.

Cantor, G. (1883) "Über Unendliche, Lineare Punktmannigfaltigkeiten," *Mathematische Annalen*, vol. 21, pp. 545–591.

Carnap, R. (1934) *Logische Syntax der Sprache*, translated by A. Smeaton as *The Logical Syntax of Language*, Harcourt Brace, New York, 1937.

——. (1947) *Meaning and Necessity*, University of Chicago Press, Chicago.

——. (1952) "Meaning Postulates," *Philosophical Studies*, vol. 3, pp. 65–73.

——. (1956) "Empiricism, Semantics, and Ontology," reprinted in Benacerraf and Putnam (1983), pp. 241–257.

Cartwright, N. (1983) *How the Laws of Physics Lie*, Clarendon Press, Oxford.

Chihara, C. (1990) *Constructibility and Mathematical Existence*, Oxford University Press, Oxford.

Curry, H.B. (1951) *Outlines of a Formalist Philosophy of Mathematics*, North-Holland, Amsterdam.

Dales, H.G., and Oliveri, G., eds. (forthcoming) *Truth in Mathematics*, Oxford University Press, Oxford.

Dedekind, R. (1888) *Was sind und was sollen die Zahlen?*, translated by W.W. Beman as "The Nature and Meaning of Numbers," in Dedekind, *Essays on the Theory of Numbers*, Open Court, Chicago, 1901, pp. 31–115.

Dehaene, S. (1997) *The Number Sense*, Oxford University Press, New York.

Dummett, M. (1959) "Wittgenstein's Philosophy of Mathematics," *Philosophical Review*, vol. 68, pp. 324–348.

———. (1973) "The Philosophical Basis of Intuitionistic Logic," reprinted in Benacerraf and Putnam (1983), pp. 97–129.

Field, H. (1980) *Science Without Numbers*, Princeton University Press, Princeton.

———. (1989) *Realism, Mathematics, and Modality*, Basil Blackwell, Oxford.

———. (1991) "Metalogic and Modality," *Philosophical Studies*, vol. 62, pp. 1–22.

———. (1993) "The Conceptual Contingency of Mathematical Objects," *Mind*, vol. 102, pp. 285–299.

———. (1998) "Mathematical Objectivity and Mathematical Objects," in C. MacDonald and S. Laurence (eds.), *Contemporary Readings in the Foundations of Metaphysics*, Basil Blackwell, Oxford, pp. 389–405.

———. (forthcoming) "Which Undecidable Mathematical Sentences Have Determinate Truth Values?," in Dales and Oliveri (forthcoming).

Frege, G. (1884) *Der Grundlagen die Arithmetik*, translated by J.L. Austin as *The Foundations of Arithmetic*, Basil Blackwell, Oxford, 1953.

———. (1892) "Über Sinn und Bedeutung," translated by H. Feigl as "On Sense and Nominatum," in A.P. Martinich (ed.), *The Philosophy of Language*, Oxford University Press, Oxford, 1990.

———. (1893–1903) *Grundgesetze der Arithmetik*, translated (in part) by M. Furth as *The Basic Laws of Arithmetic*, University of California Press, Berkeley, 1964.

———. (1894) Review of Husserl's *Philosophie der Arithmetik*, in *Zeitschrift f̈r Philosophie und philosophische Kritik*, vol. 103, pp. 313–332.

———. (1919) "Der Gedanke," translated by A.M. Quinton and M. Quinton as "The Thought: A Logical Inquiry," in E. Klemke, (ed.), *Essays on Frege*, University of Illinois Press, Urbana, 1968, pp. 507–535.

———. (1980) *Philosophical and Mathematical Correspondence*, University of Chicago Press, Chicago.

Gödel, K. (1951) "Some Basic Theorems on the Foundations of Mathematics and Their Implications," in his *Collected Works*, Volume III, Oxford University Press, Oxford, 1995, pp. 304–323.

———. (1964) "What Is Cantor's Continuum Problem?," reprinted in Benacerraf and Putnam (1983), pp. 470–485.

Hale, R. (1987) *Abstract Objects*, Basil Blackwell, Oxford.

Hale, R., and Wright, C. (1992) "Nominalism and the Contingency of Abstract Objects," *Journal of Philosophy*, Vol. 89, pp. 111–135.

Hellman, G. (1989) *Mathematics Without Numbers*, Clarendon Press, Oxford.

Hempel, C. (1945) "On the Nature of Mathematical Truth," reprinted in Benacerraf and Putnam (1983), pp. 377–393.

Hersh, R. (1997) *What Is Mathematics, Really?*, Oxford University Press, New York.

Heyting, A. (1956) *Intuitionism: An Introduction*, North-Holland, Amsterdam.

Hilbert, D. (1925) "On the Infinite," reprinted in Benacerraf and Putnam (1983), pp. 183–201.

Horgan, T. (1984) "Science Nominalized," *Philosophy of Science*, vol. 51, pp. 529–549.

Hughes, R.I.G. (1989) *The Structure and Interpretation of Quantum Mechanics*, Harvard University Press, Cambridge, MA.

Husserl, E. (1891) *Philosophie der Arithmetik*, reprinted by M. Nijhoff, The Hague, 1970.

Irvine, A., ed. (1990) *Physicalism in Mathematics*, Kluwer Academic Publishers, Norwell, MA.

Kaplan, D. (1989) "Demonstratives," in J. Almog, J. Perry, and H. Wettstein (eds.), *Themes from Kaplan*, Oxford University Press, Oxford, pp. 481–563.

Katz, J. (1981) *Language and Other Abstract Objects*, Rowman and Littlefield, Totowa, NJ.

———. (1995) "What Mathematical Knowledge Could Be," *Mind*, vol. 104, pp. 491–522.

Kitcher, P. (1984) *The Nature of Mathematical Knowledge*, Oxford University Press, Oxford.

Kochen, S., and Specker, E.P. (1967) "The Problem of Hidden Variables in Quantum Mechanics," *Journal of Mathematics and Mechanics*, vol. 17, pp. 59–87.

Krantz, D., Luce, R.D., Suppes, P., and Tversky, A. (1971) *Foundations of Measurement*, Academic Press, New York.

Kreisel, G. (1967) "Informal Rigor and Completeness Proofs," in I. Lakatos (ed.), *Problems in the Philosophy of Mathematics*, North-Holland, Amsterdam.

Kripke, S. (1972) *Naming and Necessity*, Harvard University Press, Cambridge, MA. Second edition, 1980.

Lewis, D. (1973) *Counterfactuals*, Basil Blackwell, Oxford.

———. (1983) "General Semantics," in his *Philosophical Papers*, volume 1, Oxford University Press, New York, pp. 189–232.

———. (1986) *On the Plurality of Worlds*, Basil Blackwell, Oxford.

Maddy, P. (1980) "Perception and Mathematical Intuition," *Philosophical Review*, vol. 89, pp. 163–196.

———. (1990) *Realism in Mathematics*, Oxford University Press, Oxford.

———. (1992) "Indispensability and Practice," *Journal of Philosophy*, vol. 89, pp. 275–289.

———. (1995) "Naturalism and Ontology," *Philosophia Mathematica*, vol. 3, pp. 248–70.

———. (1997) *Naturalism in Mathematics*, Oxford University Press, Oxford.

———. (forthcoming) "How to be a Naturalist About Mathematics," in Dales and Oliveri. (forthcoming).

Malament, D. (1982) Untitled book review of Field's *Science Without Numbers*, *Journal of Philosophy*, vol. 79, pp. 523–534.

Mill, J.S. (1843) *A System of Logic*, Longmans, Green, and Company, London.

Montague, R. (1968) "Pragmatics," in R. Klibansky (ed.), *Contemporary Philosophy—La Philosophie Contemporaine*, Nuova Italia Editrice, Florence.

Nozick, R. (1981) *Philosophical Explanations*, Harvard University Press, Cambridge, MA.

Parsons, C. (1980) "Mathematical Intuition," *Proceedings of the Aristotelian Society*, vol. 80, pp. 145–168.

———. (1990) "The Structuralist View of Mathematical Objects," *Synthese*, vol. 84, pp. 303–346.

———. (1994) "Intuition and Number," in A. George (ed.), *Mathematics and Mind*, Oxford University Press, Oxford, pp. 141–157.

Plato. *The Meno* and *The Phaedo*, both translated by G.M.A. Grube in *Five Dialogues*, Hackett Publishing, Indianapolis, IN, 1981.

Poincaré, H. (1913) *The Foundations of Science*, G.B. Halsted (trans.), The Science Press, Lancaster, PA.

Putnam, H. (1967a) "Mathematics Without Foundations," reprinted in Benacerraf and Putnam (1983), pp. 295–311.

———. (1967b) "The Thesis That Mathematics Is Logic," reprinted in Putnam (1979), pp. 12–42.

———. (1970) "On Properties," reprinted in Putnam (1979), pp. 305–322.

———. (1971) "Philosophy of Logic," reprinted in Putnam (1979), pp. 323–357.

———. (1975) "What Is Mathematical Truth?" reprinted in Putnam (1979), pp. 60–78.

———. (1979) *Mathematics, Matter and Method: Philosophical Papers Volume 1*, second edition, Cambridge University Press, Cambridge.

———. (1980) "Models and Reality," reprinted in Benacerraf and Putnam (1983), pp. 421–444.

Quine, W.V.O. (1936) "Truth by Convention," reprinted in Benacerraf and Putnam (1983), pp. 329–354.

———. (1948) "On What There Is," reprinted in Quine (1961), pp. 1–19.

———. (1951) "Two Dogmas of Empiricism," reprinted in Quine (1961), pp. 20–46.

———. (1961) *From a Logical Point of View*, second edition, Harper and Row, New York. (First edition 1953.)

———. (1969) "Speaking of Objects," in *Ontological Relativity and Other Essays*, Columbia University Press, New York, pp. 1–25.

Resnik, M. (1980) *Frege and the Philosophy of Mathematics*, Cornell University Press, Ithaca, NY.

———. (1981) "Mathematics as a Science of Patterns: Ontology and Reference," *Nous*, vol. 15, pp. 529–550.

———. (1982) "Mathematics as a Science of Patterns: Epistemology," *Nous*, vol. 16, pp. 95–105.

———. (1985) "How Nominalist Is Hartry Field's Nominalism?," *Philosophical Studies*, vol. 47, pp. 163–181.

———. (1990) "Beliefs About Mathematical Objects," in Irvine (1990), pp. 41–71.

———. (1997) *Mathematics as a Science of Patterns*, Oxford University Press, Oxford.

Scott, D. (1970) "Advice on Modal Logic," in K. Lambert (ed.), *Philosophical Problems in Logic: Recent Developments*, Reidel, Dordrecht, pp. 143–173.

Shapiro, S. (1983a) "Conservativeness and Incompleteness," *Journal of Philosophy*, vol. 80, pp. 521–531.

———. (1983b) "Mathematics and Reality," *Philosophy of Science*, vol. 50, pp. 523–548.

———. (1989) "Structure and Ontology," *Philosophical Topics*, vol. 17, pp. 145–171.

———. (1993) "Modality and Ontology," *Mind*, vol. 102, pp. 455–81.

———. (1997) *Philosophy of Mathematics*, Oxford University Press, New York.

Skorupski, J. (1989) *John Stuart Mill*, Routledge, London.

Stalnaker, R. (1984) *Inquiry*, MIT Press, Cambridge, MA.

Steiner, M. (1975) *Mathematical Knowledge*, Cornell University Press, Ithaca, NY.

———. (1989) "The Application of Mathematics to Natural Science," *Journal of Philosophy*, vol. 86, pp. 449–480.

Stroud, B. (1965) "Wittgenstein and Logical Necessity," *Philosophical Review*, vol. 74, pp. 504–518.

Wigner, E. (1960) "The Unreasonable Effectiveness of Mathematics in the Natural Sciences," *Communications on Pure and Applied Mathematics*, vol. 13, pp. 1–14.

Wittgenstein, L. (1956) *Remarks on the Foundations of Mathematics*, translated by G.E.M. Anscombe, Basil Blackwell, Oxford.

Wright, C. (1983) *Frege's Conception of Numbers as Objects*, Aberdeen University Press, Aberdeen, Scotland.

Zalta, E. (1983) *Abstract Objects: An Introduction to Axiomatic Metaphysics*, D. Reidel, Dordrecht.

———. (1988) *Intensional Logic and the Metaphysics of Intentionality*, Bradford/MIT Press, Cambridge, MA.

Zalta, E., and Linsky, B. (1995) "Naturalized Platonism vs. Platonized Naturalism," *Journal of Philosophy*, vol. 92, pp. 525–555.

Index